Professional Resource Development

Joe Kranz

Jan Frauen

Prentice-Hall, Englewood Cliffs, New Jersey 07632

Library of Congress Cataloging-in-Publication Data
Kranz, R. J.
  Professional resource development.

  Includes index.
  1. Success.   I. Frauen, J. K., (date).
II. Title.

BF637.S8K73   1986   158'.1   85–19357
  ISBN 0–13–725771–6

Editorial/production supervision and
   interior design: Fred Dahl
Cover design: Photo Plus Art
Manufacturing buyer: Ed O'Dougherty
Cover photo courtesy Apple Computer, Inc.

Printed in the United States of America

10 9 8 7 6 5 4 3 2 1

ISBN   0-13-725771-6   01

Prentice-Hall International (UK) Limited, *London*
Prentice-Hall of Australia Pty. Limited, *Sydney*
Prentice-Hall Canada Inc., *Toronto*
Prentice-Hall Hispanoamericana, S.A., *Mexico*
Prentice-Hall of India Private Limited, *New Delhi*
Prentice-Hall of Japan, Inc., *Tokyo*
Prentice-Hall of Southeast Asia Pte. Ltd., *Singapore*
Editora Prentice-Hall do Brasil, Ltda., *Rio de Janeiro*
Whitehall Books Limited, *Wellington, New Zealand*

My contribution to this book is dedicated to my father,
who always encouraged my writing efforts.
He praised me when he knew I needed it.
He sometimes teased, goaded, and cajoled—
but he inevitably boosted my morale.
In short, he helped me to believe in myself.
He died about a year before this book became a reality.

Were he still alive he'd probably say, "Aren't you glad you listened to me?"
. . . Yeah, Dad—thanks!

Jan

Contents

Preface

More! Somehow there had to be more to personal development than hygiene, makeup, hair care, posture, exercise, and social graces. Though these aspects of development are necessary, their dominance of personal development texts seemed too limiting.

It became our mission to find a broader, more realistic base of study to expose readers to areas of possible development that would enhance their personal, business, and career lives. Soon the choice of topics went from the extremely limited to the nearly limitless. The potential of people stretches to infinity, and so too does the combination of skills each might choose to become, whatever he or she may select.

In the main, the sections included in this book were selected because of their universal application. A section on communication seemed imperative since this is so often cited as a major problem in business, in personal relationships, and in maintaining world peace.

Health, hygiene, personal appearance, and related topics still hold their place in this treatment of personal development. Goals, planning, and reviewing life and its directions are good business. It does not matter if applications are made at the workplace or in the "business" of life. Everyone has a need to know where he or she is going.

Careers, jobs, money—these items are thrust into each life. Preparation for handling each is going to make the struggle with them a little easier. Behavior, time management, potential, and related topics provide opportunities for readers to look inside themselves for self-help as they stumble, striving all the while for new and better opportunities for themselves.

All in all, the presentation touches many aspects of a person as he or she endeavors to develop self and a self-philosophy.

The book is not a panacea. It is rather a thought-starter for individuals who want to realize that life is for learning.

Its intention is to stimulate your desire to learn more about each subject.

It will inspire you to continue to search for a better *you!* It will point out the importance of strengthening your shortcomings and accentuating and capitalizing on your attributes.

It will emphasize the significance of a sense of humor. Without being able to laugh *at* yourself and *with* others, you may as well "hang it up." A healthy sense of humor can enhance the joy of your successes as well as diminish the frustration of failure.

Your authors found fulfillment and creative satisfaction, coupled with a real learning experience while writing this book. We hope you too will derive similar feelings after reading and studying this text.

Persons develop every day. The direction of that development may either be left to chance or controlled and guided by choice. This is the real lesson and message of *Professional Resource Development.*

Acknowledgments

We wish to express our deep appreciation and gratitude to our families. One patient wife, one indulgent husband, and collectively eleven children, twelve grandchildren, and an assortment of sons and daughters-in-law.

Thanks!

Joe and Jan

CHAPTER 1

The Choice Is Yours

Silver and gold . . . silver and gold. Songs have been written about silver and gold. Songs may even have been written about uranium, platinum, and oil. Of concern here, however, is not the musical impact of these resources, but rather the simple fact that these resources are considered valuable. Each has its own unique properties that give it value. Great quantities of time and money are expended to develop these resources and to make each and every possible use of their potential.

Yet these resources are of no consequence without the one resource with more potential than any other—the resource that every individual has the power to control and shape. This resource is the most dynamic and dramatic of all, the resource that discovers, explores, examines, and controls all others: the human resource—you!

As valuable as this resource is, it is useless unless it is developed. This book is designed to be to personal development what the Whitman's Sampler is to candy. It gives you tastes of the many concepts that influence personal development.

- This first chapter explains the subjects you will be dealing with and why.
- Chapter 2 explores attitudes. More specifically, it emphasizes the influence of a positive attitude on your health and happiness as you move toward your goals.

- Chapter 3 is devoted to goal setting and self-analysis. You can begin to direct your personal life and career and to become what you intend to become—not leave your future to chance.

- Chapters 4 through 10 deal with health, hygiene, physical well-being, appearance, and social graces—the outward signs of you, the person. The section offers hints on using your appearance and wardrobe to put you in a more powerful position with employees, interviewers, and clients.

- Communication is explored in Chapters 11 and 12, with a brief look at body language and other communication methods.

- Transactional analysis (Chapter 13), assertiveness (Chapter 14), and right-brain/left-brain and neuro linguistics (Chapter 15) are touched upon lightly to expose you to the more scientific, interesting, and important parts of your development.

- In Chapter 16, you will how learn to listen, not just hear.

- Chapters 17 through 22 deal with career planning, interviews, career advancement, time management, and realizing your potential.

- The final chapter covers the area of personal finance—the "root" of it all.

These subjects are presented simply to familiarize you with them. Everything you will ever need to know about personal development is *not*—repeat *not*—contained in this book. Neither is it contained in any other one publication. Hundreds of magazines are published week after week, month after month, year after year, all containing articles and illustrations on health and exercise, on fashion and clothing, and on makeup and appearance.

Other books on the subject are usually based on one principle or approach. But one is not enough. Relying on one approach is like a carpenter's carrying one tool. Each person is complex, and so complex are the situations and circumstances in each person's life that the "bag of tools" must be extensive.

You will therefore be exposed to a variety of concepts that influence personal development, including makeup, hair care, hygiene, and clothing. This personal development approach entails more than jumping jacks and deep knee bends, more than social graces and wardrobe planning. It is most certainly these things, but it encompasses a great deal more. It's a combination of character and personality. It's what you are inside and what you display on the outside.

This book is written with the hope that this exposure will compel you to pursue these concepts in depth and lead you to discover still other avenues of interest. The goal is that you never cease to strive for betterment in your pursuit of personal development.

You Are Responsible

Your personality and character have been developing for a long time before you ever decided to open a book on the subject. Every person, place, and thing that comes into contact with you influences you. However, regardless of your history, you are equipped with the power to evaluate all of your experiences and become what you want to become. The questions to ask yourself are: Has your development to this point been by design or by accident? Have you taken the responsibility for your development? Or have you unconsciously just happened to become what you are?

If you are looking for a theme, then, let it be this: From now on, you are going to take the responsibility for the way you look, act, think, and feel. Even if you decide to act contrary to every concept in this text, there will be no problem. The main idea is for you to become what you want to become *on purpose*—to accept the fact that you are responsible for what you are. *You had no part in your creation.* However, you have *every* responsibility for the development of that creation. One thing belongs wholly to you. It is yours to do with as you wish. That is *you!* There is no one else exactly like you.

For this reason, a personal development course should be a prescription course. It should match you and your individual needs. As obvious as this statement is, it becomes equally obvious that no book can specifically address only one individual. A book can, however, start you thinking along many new lines, help you make decisions, and assist you in obtaining the information you need to fully develop yourself. Consider this analogy: This book contains all the roadside signs and other advertisements inviting you to dine at various restaurants. Each sign tells you something about a particular restaurant's location, its atmosphere, and its specialty. Yet *you* have to decide whether you feel like steak or seafood or chicken or a hamburger.

In the same way you will be exposed to many concepts during the next several weeks. Give each your attention. Sample them all, like a giant smorgasbord. Some will have more meaning for you, and some will have less. Follow up on the concepts that intrigue you most. There are people and books and resources galore that address in depth all of the concepts contained here. Like the roadside signs and the advertisements, this course is intended to whet your appetite for personal development, not satisfy it.

Ultimately, only you can write the prescription for your development. Look upon the experience of this course as an exposure to the ailments, symptoms, and possibly cures for your development. Your background and knowledge will tell you which medications you need in order to be a healthier member of society and meet your desires for success.

Are You Tough?

How tough are you? How *really* tough? If you are thin-skinned, you will not get all you can out of this course. If you can take it and you have the kind of instructor who is willing to "tell it to you straight," you can make this the most profitable learning experience of your life.

An instructor of personal development is not always the most popular person on the faculty, because this individual must pick on you personally. It is the person's responsibility—yes, *responsibility*—to tell you, sometimes repeatedly, that you need a bath, that your five-day deodorant pad is on its twenty-first day, or that you have terminal zoo breath. No one likes to hear these things about themselves, and no one likes to say these things. Yet if the instructor won't tell you, who will? Your friends won't because they want to stay your friends, or they will just avoid you because nobody wants to start a personality fight. Nobody is perfect. Consequently, most individuals know that, if they start "picking" on you, even in the spirit of trying to help, you will find an imperfection in them and retaliate. Then the fight is on. The instructor knows that he or she is not perfect, either, but the job must be done if you are to have your best chance for acceptance and success in life.

Most of the questions you will be asked are self-analysis questions. Your answers can only be more or less right or wrong because the answers call for, and reflect, opinions . . . your opinions. What both you and your instructor need are communication and feedback, because how you see yourself can vary tremendously from how others see you.

Compete

To be alive is to be competitive. Unless competition causes too much conflict or produces poor results, it is a good situation. Unless you lack confidence in your ability to perform, you should never fear getting into competitive situations. The fear of competing can be overcome by knowledge and practice in the areas in which you wish to succeed. This book is aimed at instilling confidence in you.

It is also aimed at introducing you to skills that will enable you to meet that challenge. The skills you need to succeed at personal endeavors are the same skills you need to be successful and advance in your career. As you become acquainted with the material covered, remember that this book is trying to help you develop personally so that you will be equipped to cope in the world of employment.

Have Fun

Learning should be fun. Laughter in a classroom doesn't mean that learning is not taking place. So if you find that once in awhile you smile, chuckle, or even laugh out loud, we are for it and encourage it. We believe in taking our subject seriously, but, if we take ourselves too seriously, the fun of writing and learning can be lost.

Make Up Your Mind

Will this writing change you? It won't unless you want it to, and it won't by itself. Unless you have the initiative to pursue the ideas offered, any change you make will be superficial and temporary. To make any real change is to (1) decide to change, (2) never stop learning, and (3) use your knowledge in a positive way and demonstrate your knowledge through behavior. Professionally confident and competent individuals know who they are and where they are headed. The only way to gain such confidence is to acquire knowledge and to exercise your knowledge through practice.

If you want to get more out of a workday than just a payday or more out of a payday than just tired, then you can start now by beginning to think and act as you want. The choice is yours and has always been yours. This book will make you realize that. You will encounter people who will help you; you may succeed in part because of them. You will meet people who will hinder you; you must succeed in spite of them. In any event, *you* are the key to you.

All this book can do is give you ideas; you must capitalize on the ideas. If the ideas in this book were money (and in a metaphoric sense they are), you could spend them and have nothing left. Or you could invest them and watch them continue to grow and add to themselves. Our hope is that you hang on to these ideas and add to them with even more information. We hope they will help you in your personal life as well as in your career—to become what you choose.

CHAPTER 2

Attitude

A Pinch of Personality and Add-a-tude

Exploring attitudes at this early stage is important because you will soon form an attitude about this study—if you haven't already. Inasmuch as initial attitudes about people and things are formed from first impressions, you have certainly formed some opinions from what you have studied to this point.

On the other hand, inasmuch as attitudes sometimes change in time, this chapter will have you examine your attitude about a great many things. Notice how carefully this is worded: Nowhere has it been said that the object is to change your attitude. In response to such a statement, some would certainly have to ask, "What's wrong with my attitude?" There may be absolutely nothing wrong with your attitude. Then again . . . ! Ultimately you must decide whether your attitude needs changing. You must determine: Am I the kind of person I would like to be around?

Self-Control

At the heart of the discussion about attitude is self-control. How good is your rapport with yourself? How much influence do you let others exercise over you and your emotions? A person's state of mind can be changed—easily and rapidly—by words or circumstances. Others can have a tremendous influence over you and your attitude because of your emotions.

Love, a deep and passionate emotion, makes for a good example. Even though no one can define it or really knows how to express it, everyone is an expert on love. If you have ever been in love or thought you were, you know that the person you loved greatly influenced your feelings. Your moods could be changed by a simple word or action. You could be made to feel invulnerable when that person said, "I love you." You could be made to feel lower than a grasshopper's arches if you happen to see that special someone laughing and enjoying the company of someone else.

Unfortunately, the list of people who influence you is nearly endless. It includes, but is not limited to, the one you love, parents, brothers, sisters, peers, bosses, rich uncles, bankers, customers, clergy, friends, acquaintances, even strangers. Then there is *you*, the most important and influential person in your life. Yet you are often the least listened to, because of the interference that you let disrupt the signals you should be giving yourself.

Share Positive Attitudes

Perhaps you are basically a shy person—quiet, unassuming. You think it's impossible for someone like yourself to have a very positive attitude. *Wrong!* What you are looking at, really, is not a handicap at all, but a quality that could prove to be your greatest asset. No one has ever said that, to have a positive attitude, you must be bold or even very forward.

Yet the more you share your positive attitude, the more positive you become. To prove this to yourself, share your smile with everyone you meet, greeting

them with a pleasant response, being cheerful, giving encouragement where needed, and having genuine confident thoughts.

Remember this song, "Make Someone Happy"? You can do this! The first "someone" that you should make happy is yourself. Then you will have the opportunity to make a great many "someones" happy too. The song, of course, refers to a special someone, and in that sense you will be able to make that special someone feel special because *attitudes are contagious!*

Another song tells us, "You Have to Accentuate The Positive—Eliminate The Negative." If your attitude is negative, it is almost guaranteed that you will be eliminated. Negativeness leads eventually to losing out, whether it is not getting a job, not keeping a job, not getting a promotion, not keeping a friend, not getting along at home—the list is endless. Nothing is as annoying as individuals who are negative about themselves, their surroundings, or their abilities. Everyone has been given some ability. Positive attitudes give us the confidence and assertiveness we need to develop our ability. And, since few people are really downright cocksure about themselves, upbeat attitudes can be highly contagious! *Optimism, combined with realism, is a formula for positiveness!*

Absolutely nothing can be substituted for a positive attitude. While some people may find that being positive comes naturally, others—who are not so fortunate—may have had a negative outlook most of their lives. This second group may seem to come on as being balky, resistive, and generally contrary to others, as well as to themselves. If you feel you belong in this category, you may not always be sure you can accomplish your goals. Yet you must always have positive enough attitudes to *try.*

Your disposition and outlook on life are extremely transparent, whether you think so or not. Like wearing your heart on your sleeve, a positive attitude shows—in your eyes and in your smile. You can hear it in your voice and see it in your personality. Your attitude affects and accounts for some of your physical appearance. Your carriage, for instance, is indicative of your attitude. If you have a positive outlook, it is just natural that you will stand straighter, with shoulders back. By contrast, the outward signs of a negative attitude might be standing with your weight on only one foot and slumping your shoulders. Being positive is not accidental; you have to want to make it happen. As in so many things, it's mind over matter; you reflect how you feel.

A positive attitude gives you confidence and assurance, so that you can expect more of yourself. With a positive outlook, you can expect to go as far as you want in life.

Finally, you cannot fake positiveness; it must be sincere and something you want. Your whole being will profit from a genuine, sincere attitude. On the other hand, insincerity will catch up with you sooner or later—and very likely at the most embarrassing of times.

Attitude Checklist

Perhaps this is a good time to take a self-examination of your positive attitudes:

1. Am I aware and confident of my special skills and abilities?
2. Am I capable of handling people?
3. Do I have trouble making and keeping friends?
4. Am I aware of my weaknesses as well as my strengths?
5. Do I ever give encouragement to others?
6. What sets me apart from others and perhaps makes me stand out in a crowd?
7. What are some things I do that make me feel proud?
8. What are some things I do that make me feel happy?
9. Can I make a decision and stick to that decision?
10. Do I, for the most part, control my emotions?
11. Do I usually think something good is going to happen?
12. Do I like me?

Contagious Attitudes

Just like a communicable disease, attitudes are catching. With just a couple of thought-starting examples, you will be able to think of many experiences of your own in which an attitude has been "catching."

First let's take a look at the professional mood manipulators, the people in the entertainment industry. For example, after enjoying a comedy movie and getting your money's worth in laughs, don't you leave the theater retelling your favorite lines from the movie and enjoying a "favorite" laugh? The mood of the movie carries over and the enjoyment continues after the initial experience. Yet what happens when you decide to treat your sentimental side to a "tear jerker"? You leave the theater with a sigh, and you carry some of the sadness with you as you remember how cruel the world can sometimes be. The movie makers are the masters, and they capture you for hours at a time.

Now consider the people who have made a study of grabbing you by the attitude for only 30 seconds at a time. Yet they can still motivate you to react. These are the people who write and produce commercials. Think about it—they do a good job!

With all their polish, study, and finesse, however, they are pikers when it comes to emotional manipulation. We, the people, prey on each other's emotions constantly. For example, think about the last time you felt really good and greeted a friend or fellow employee with a sincere and cheery, "Good Morning!" Did you receive a sarcastic reply, such as, "Is it?" or "What makes you think so?" or a similar grinchy response. You might have recovered, said to yourself, "grouch," and went happily on. Or maybe—just maybe—it took away just a little of your positive feelings.

One thing you must do for sure is to try instilling a positive attitude in that person. Such persons can be approached in many ways; just be certain you use

a great deal of tact. Try calling attention to the way they are dressed or compliment their hair, their shirt or blouse, or a picture they carry. Most of all, show some genuine interest in *something* that perhaps diverts their negativeness and get them to an all-new beginning. Sometimes being positive may seem to be always resting on your shoulders, but in the long run it pays off tenfold. No person can remain negative for any length of time if enough positive things are said to and about them. If compliments seem to fail, offer to help with something—anything. Another good habit to establish early in the day is to leave others with a pleasant word. Eventually they will be doing the same thing to you.

Have you ever given any thought to people who suffer an illness of a serious and perhaps lengthy nature—or a terminal illness? Dealing with such a catastrophe would be next to impossible if you lacked a positive attitude. Perhaps something of this nature would be the greatest test of positiveness; becoming negative would be so easy.

A sense of humor is essential, too, in maintaining a positive attitude. Actually, with a sense of humor, almost anything is possible. For instance, when things turn sour at home or at work, you can laugh at what you might at first think is disaster. Laughter, it has been said, is the best medicine. Like positive attitudes, a sense of humor is contagious; it catches on very quickly.

Smile

A smile is probably your biggest and most valuable asset. You must have it on your face often and always in your voice, but it must be sincere. Nothing is more annoying than coming into contact with phonies, either face-to-face or on the telephone, especially if they are "icky sweet." Sincerity is the name of the game. Some people are difficult to be around or to deal with, but you must constantly put your best foot forward. Every person, no matter how abrasive, has a good feature. Sometimes you have to hunt for it a long time, but, rest assured, it's there—even in the most annoying creatures. When you discover that virtue, play it up to yourself and be thankful for at least one good point. A sense of humor, as mentioned earlier, is essential to making it through many bad days. Be able to laugh at yourself, especially when you err. If you are truly sincere with your humor, it rubs off on even the most antagonistic people.

A positive attitude brings immediate rewards to the person who possesses and displays it. With a positive outlook you tend to feel good about yourself, and others become more comfortable around you and, as a result, happier. Ask yourself this question: "Wouldn't you rather be with the people who can laugh and see the bright side of even a bad situation than to associate with grouches and complainers?" Being positive puts a spring in your step, exhilarates your spirit, and adds a new sparkle to your life—and to the lives of your associates.

For most people, achieving this most desired attitude takes practice and a great deal of determination. It *can* be done! Some people, however, are "experts" at being positive; they make it appear to be second nature. Watching experts in action is inspiring. No matter how many things happen to detract from their positiveness, they move along smoothly and flawlessly. With continued practice and usage of this positive attitude, *anyone* can soon appear to be carrying on effortlessly. Inevitably, with a positive attitude, you will eventually build self-confidence. This aura will shine on fellow workers, family members, friends, bosses, acquaintances, and everyone with whom you come into contact. If you are a person with a positive attitude, you will most likely be optimistic, relaxed, clear, pleasant, kind, wise, and undeniably happy. All these traits go hand in hand. Almost like falling dominos, the chain reaction continues, and the ultimate result is sustained contentment. You must extend yourself at all times.

Ask yourself, how do others view you? How do you create the other person's perception of you? Set a precise goal to remain positive and create positiveness among those about you. Your positive attitude will affect your morale, sensitivity, creativity, and personal growth.

If you are in constant contact with someone who is incredibly negative, you can bring that person around to a more positive way of thinking. Even with people who are unbelievably resistant to change, you will find that, if you are persistent and sincere, your positive demeanor will rub off—if only in a small way. Expecting instant changes in attitude is unrealistic, if the person suffers from "blue funk" most of the time. (Although "blue funk" means different things to different people, we will think of it as a constant state of negativeness and depression.) Think how gratifying it would be to see even the slightest change in these "funky" persons: a smile, when they normally come to work, to school, or to the breakfast table at home with a grumble, no smile, and a monogrammed shirt saying, "I am negative!"

Although everyone at one time or another feels negative about certain situations, pretending that you are instead feeling positive doesn't hurt.

Misery Loves Company

Undoubtedly you have heard the saying, "Misery loves company." It surely is true. Someone who is having a bad day inevitably looks to associate with someone else who is in a similar state of mind. Usually, these persons end up making each other even more miserable.

When you are having a bad day, wouldn't it make more sense to seek out someone having a good one? That someone can help you get back into your own positive way of looking at things, rather than dragging you farther into a negative posture.

Sometimes realizing why an individual is so negative is helpful. But if that is impossible, perhaps you should focus on changing that person's attitude to positive rather than finding the cause of negativeness. For example, consider a student trying to learn from an extremely negative instructor. If you were the student, stop for a minute after class with a remark or two pertaining to the day's lecture and how beneficial it was for you. Or you might mention that you hope to be able to comprehend all the obvious knowledge this teacher has to impart. Coloring the truth to be positive toward some people is not necessary, but stretching a point now and then certainly doesn't hurt.

Never act bored with people or happenings—even if you are! Sometimes it seems next to impossible to build an optimistic, enthusiastic view of the way things are going; often problems seem insurmountable. Yet a positive approach is the only sane approach. You should always try to think of yourself in a positive manner. Here again, you may have doubts or depressions, but you don't have to show them. If you succeed in not letting them show, you will undoubtedly rise above them. Being positive entails enthusiasm and energy. You have to constantly make the effort to appear interested and fully attentive to people. *Never* show boredom, even toward people who you might think are unimportant.

Some people can find a difficulty for every solution, others a solution for each difficulty. Sometimes things go sour no matter what you do to make them right. Sometimes there is very little doubt that you are going to lose, no matter what. You can win even in a losing battle, in a manner of speaking, by having a positive attitude. Be determined to learn something of value from your loss and don't give in to the situation by becoming negative.

You Are Tested Daily

Everyone's potential to think positively is tested and retested each day. The pressures of work, opportunities missed or not recognized until too late, and the lack of money are a few of the most frequently encountered deterrents to a positive attitude. When things go well, when business is good, being positive is easy.

Norman Vincent Peale says it this way in *The Power of Positive Thinking* (Englewood Cliffs, NJ; Prentice Hall, 1952, p. 138): Feelings of confidence depend upon the type of thoughts that habitually occupy your mind. Think defeat and you are bound to feel defeated, but practice thinking positive thoughts, make it a dominating habit, and you will develop such a strong sense of capacity that regardless of what difficulties arise you will be able to overcome them.

Habit and practice keep coming to the foreground whenever you want to develop a skill. These ideas are the keys to becoming a good goal-setter and planner, and they are the heart of the process by which you become a positive thinker. How well you do once again depends on how much you really want to be a positive person.

Have you ever wanted, for example, to learn the words to a popular song? One way is to listen to a recording over and over and over again until you have it memorized. Implanting positive thoughts or training yourself to think positively can be accomplished using the same techniques. If you have a tape recorder, give yourself a pep talk. Then play it back whenever you need a reminder or a boost in your resolution to take command of your attitudes.

Attitude Maintenance

A positive attitude can be fragile. Perhaps you have convinced yourself of the value of being positive, and you've worked to establish this attitude. Then along comes someone or some circumstance that presents an overwhelming temptation for you to become dejected, depressed, and otherwise negative. Be prepared for this to happen, and realize that it will. But be realistic enough to work through these times and bounce back as soon as you can to your positive outlook. Being positive takes determination. The more often you bring yourself back from a negative frame of mind, the easier it will become for you to make a comeback. To maintain or revive your positiveness:

- *Review your successes.* Review past accomplishments. Remind yourself just how good you can be. Save any positive letters, evaluations, comments. Take a look at your old yearbook, in which all your classmates wished you well.

- *Take plenty of time to prepare.* Prepare, prepare, prepare, prepare, prepare, prepare, prepare—and then prepare some more. To repeat the word more than ten times would probably be redundant. However, if you have not grasped the importance of preparation, then reread this paragraph until you do. Preparation builds your confidence and increases your positive expectations. "The better prepared you are, the luckier you seem to become." When you're prepared, you're ready for anything. You will not lose your positive outlook to the element of surprise.

- *Take work, not self, seriously.* Put everything you've got into your work. In this instance, "work" means the activities you've undertaken to accomplish your goals. If you take yourself too seriously, you may become oversensitive to criticism, defensive, and argumentative. You can cost yourself your positive attitude by not keeping your mind open to different ideas. Laughing at yourself is a great attribute. We human beings are pretty funny creatures, you know, and being one of the members of this vast club, you are one of its comedians by birth.

- *Stick with winners.* Losers gobble up winners. Just as misery loves company and negativeness can bombard positive attitudes, losers want to drag winners down. Get your positive reinforcement from successful people. Success and positive thinking follow each other like the steps on a staircase. When losers are given a choice of two calamities, they usually choose both. Winners don't plan on disasters happening in the first place, which is why their positive outlook brands them as winners. With which group would you rather identify?

- *Visualize results.* Visualize the results you plan to achieve and see them clearly. This technique is vitally important, as you will discover in the chapter on developing your potential. Suffice it to say that, when you picture yourself having something, it becomes real to you, and your desire to possess it intensifies. The possibility of its becoming a reality is increased immensely. So keep vivid pictures of what you plan to achieve in your mind.

- *Do whatever you do on purpose.* Evaluate what you are doing, where you are, and where you are going so that you stay on track. Also don't forget that you, and you alone, are ultimately responsible for what you are and what you will become. Whatever you decide, do it, because you intended to.

Failure

By this time it should be safe to talk about failure. The word should no longer be threatening but rather viewed for what it is—an opportunity in disguise. Among your inalienable rights is the right to fail. The only right that perhaps should be denied is the right *not* to try.

Introducing failure in a segment dealing with positive attitudes may seem self-contradictory. Usually such a section deals with accentuating the positive and eliminating negative thinking. Well, the fear of failure is responsible for most negative attitude responses. Eliminate the fear, and you eliminate the negative. Accepting failure for what it is, a learning experience, begins to put failure in a positive perspective.

Whenever people say, "I learned the hard way," they mean they learned through experience and mistakes. There's nothing wrong with making mistakes. There's nothing wrong with failure. There's nothing wrong as long as that mistake or failure is, in fact, used as a learning experience. It is nothing more than a detour that, once analyzed, brings you sharply back on the right track.

Failures are setbacks and they can be expensive—no doubt about it. Take, for example, a person who decides to make a geographical move of a thousand miles to take a job only to find out after a short period of time that the new position, for whatever reason, is not going to work out. The costs of relocation can be extremely expensive in dollars alone, but the cost in time is also highly significant. This money and time could have been spent in becoming established in what could have been a real opportunity.

Is this kind of experience a total loss? Not if you are thinking positively. What can you learn? Perhaps next time you're presented with a similar situation you will give yourself, and the opportunity, a probationary period. Maybe you should make a step-by-step plan for adjusting to a new situation. Maybe, for example, you should not move all your belongings and burn all your bridges behind you. Instead, take only the necessities for, say, a three-month period to adjust to the location, to adjust to the job, and to evaluate the long-term implications.

The danger arises when you do not recognize mistakes and failures as learning experiences. When they go unnoticed, unrecognized, unadmitted, and, worst of all, repeated, you begin to establish the *habit* of failure.

A Positive Challenge

Being positive does not mean being gullible and naive. It does not mean that you do not understand what's happening around you. Neither do you neglect or ignore the ugliness in the world. You are as aware of circumstances as anyone. The difference in you as a positive person is that you choose not to let the circumstances get you down.

Negative people have been heard to say that those who go around happy all the time obviously don't understand the situation. Positive persons understand all right—not only the situation but how they fit into it. These persons seek alternatives, choose their reactions, and live with them. They ask themselves if something can be done and if they can do it, and then they proceed to get it done. If their actions cannot influence a situation, they accept this fact and live with it. A serenity prayer says it best: "Let me change those things I can change, accept those things I cannot change, and have the wisdom to know the difference."

Let's see if you can apply your positive attitude to a typical negative situation:

A secretarial pool can be a melting pot of criss-crossed possibilities for negativism. Everyone's skills naturally vary. One boss dictates more clearly than the next. One is more courteous than another. Each administrator wants one certain secretary to do the bulk of his or her work, but so does another administrator who seems to always get the choice worker first. The choice secretarial worker would rather work with a different administrator altogether.

Jealousies flare on both sides of the desk. The merry-go-round begins. The administrators are angry at the other administrators, the secretaries are angry at the other secretaries, the secretaries are peeved at the administrators and the administrators at the secretaries, the men are upset with the women, the women are upset with the men, and the men at the men, and the women at the women, and these at those, and those at them, and . . . and . . . and—*hold it!*

What is the positive approach to this situation? Working with a co-worker can be difficult. You must put aside jealousies, either professional or personal. Try to overlook things that you *can* overlook and make the best of them. Try to compliment those troublesome people, and show your appreciation when they do something worthwhile. By being positive you may gain their friendship and confidence, and soon things will be going along more smoothly. You must give and take a great deal when you work alongside another person for an eight-hour day. Even under the best of circumstances and relationships, this situation can be trying. Now for a situation or two calling for a positive outlook. Here are the situations with a few positive views. If you can think of any others, please feel free to add them.

Situation 1: You have just painted yourself into a corner. No doors or windows are within reach. You have no choice but to sit in that corner until the paint dries, which will take four hours. *But . . .*

1. At least no one can get to you for four hours to give you another job to do.
2. You've learned how not to paint a floor.
3. You have plenty of time to admire how well you have done the job so far.
4. No one will ruin your job by coming into the room too soon. You are right there to stop them!
5. This will give you a heck of a good story to tell your friends (providing you can laugh at yourself)!

There are many more positive thoughts for this situation. Think of two or three more yourself.

Situation 2: Although you and another employee of seemingly equal qualifications are eligible for the same promotion, the other employee gets the promotion.

1. The person who gets the promotion, knowing you very nearly had the position, respects your abilities and asks your advice. The other administrators already know you are a valuable employee.
2. You don't have the added headaches that go with the position.
3. You are still accepted by your peers, and you may continue the friendship you had without feeling the pressures of new relationships.
4. Keep going if you can—there are more possibilities.

Situation 3: You have just flunked a test.

1. Flunking is proof that you don't know as much as you should to succeed in this world. This is a chance to restudy so that you will be as prepared as you want to be.
2. The test told you how much you do know, as well as how much you don't know. You are not starting all over.

Now that you have run through these examples to give you a feel for their usefulness, here are a couple of open-ended similar situations. Just as physical exercise keeps the body alert, mental practice with positive thinking keeps your attitude in trim.

Situations 4, 5, 6: Here are three more chances for you to get positive!

- You are reading a book. When you get to the last page you find it has been torn out, . . .
- You buy 100 shares of a brand new stock from a stockbroker. The next day the stock goes down $10 a share . . .
- The vase your favorite "rich" aunt gave you is broken the day before she is to visit you for the week . . .

On Your Own

You might make a practice of providing yourself with similar situations to keep in touch with your positive thinking. You probably won't even have to think very hard. Most of the time a situation or situations that occurred earlier in your day will provide you the practice you need. Use these opportunities to apply your strategies and obtain real benefits for yourself.

Last Thoughts

A few last thoughts. Some of them may cause you to smile. More importantly, each should cause you to think.

- If you were to fall from the twentieth floor of a skyscraper, would you say, "So far, so good" at the tenth floor?
- Are you the kind of person who is able to find a little bad in the best of things?

- Do you think of "O" as the last letter in the word "zero" or the first letter in "opportunity"?
- When you wake up each day do you say, "Good morning, Lord" or "Good Lord, it's morning"?
- When you have half a glass of water, do you see it as half full or half empty?
- Are you afraid of making pot roast for fear of ending up with roast pot?
- Disappointment should be taken as a stimulant and never as a failure.
- Don't hate your enemies . . . you made them.
- Some people back their cars into the driveway at night so that they can start their next day by going in the right direction—forward!

CHAPTER **3**

Goals

You Can't Score Without Goals

Success isn't something that happens. It's something you make happen. If being successful is important to you and for you, you must set goals to get the most out of your efforts. Then you have to formulate a plan to achieve those goals. Goal setting is essential to your personal development, particularly as you direct your career and your life.

The process of setting goals and planning to attain those goals is often compared to deciding to take a vacation. First you choose a destination (or set a goal), and then you make a plan to get there and back. For example, let's assume that you are in New York and your destination is Los Angeles, California. With Los Angeles as your goal you plan to reach that goal by car. The plan includes short-range goals including how far you can go before you need to stop for fuel, when and where you will stop to eat, and how far you can travel until you need to rest. Your plan includes gathering maps and marking checkpoints that keep you on the right road. You consider the amount of money you will need, along with the kinds and amount of clothing you want to pack. Time is an important factor when you make this plan; you must allow for unforeseen setbacks, such as detours and/or mechanical breakdowns.

Goals and plans for your life and those for your career development are much the same. You need long-range goals, you need short-range goals, and you need a plan to make sure you are traveling toward your goals. Any road is the

right road—if you don't care where you are going. And if you don't know where you're going, you can't possibly know if or when you get there!

When you have set your goals, both long- and short-range, as well as your plan to achieve these goals, you must schedule frequent evaluations to assist in determining your progress. Through these evaluations you review your actions to see which have been successful and which have failed to produce the desired results. These frequent checks—of where you are in your life, where you have been, where you are going—are as necessary as regular references to a map during a long drive across country.

Goals, both long- and short-range, must be specific. Everything is relative and holds different meanings for individuals. For example, if your goal is to be "wealthy," your idea of wealth may be quite different from that of someone else. To you, "wealthy" may mean $100,000, while to someone else it may mean $1 million or another amount either between these two figures or beyond them. Your goals, then, must be specific in terms of where you are going. The more specifically you state your goals, the more easily you can measure them, and the more simply you can establish checkpoints of progress. Your goals become more real in your mind.

So instead of saying to yourself that your long-range goal is wealth, state your overall goal as $1 million. More specifically, "By the time I am_____years old, I will be at a certain point." Then establish short-range goals as checkpoints along the way, such as, "My five-year goal is_____; within one year, I will have_____; and my six-month goal will be_____."

Be Explicit

Define your goal explicitly, so that later you have no doubt that you actually achieved what you started out to accomplish.

Make commitments to yourself so that you are not tempted to engage in the evasion game. As an example of evasion, you might tell a friend, "We will have to get together for lunch one of these days." Yet if you are willing to make a commitment, you would say something more concrete, such as, "Let's get together Wednesday at 11:30 at the Midtown cafeteria for lunch." To get commitment you must set deadlines for yourself and live by them. Without specifying the time element, you avoid commitment.

While setting goals may, on the surface, seem like a pretty easy task, it can actually be difficult. Goal setting is work. Some goals won't be achieved because unforeseen circumstances come up or because the goal setter didn't think things through. This again only proves that goal setting is a difficult task, not that the time spent on the process is wasted. Like anything you do, you get better at it through practice and experience. Most worthwhile goals are hard to achieve. Yet their being hard to achieve doesn't make them bad goals. After all, if they do not entail some difficulty, they do not present a challenge.

When you commit to a goal, you reject other goals. So look at your options before you choose the best one for you. Once you choose a goal you must begin some kind of activity to reach it. You begin to spend mental and physical energy to attain it. Prepare yourself for the possible pitfall of misdirecting your energy if you have chosen a wrong goal. Should this happen, don't lose heart. It can happen to even the most experienced goal setters.

Perhaps it is more appropriate to say that goals should be realistic. If this goal-setting business is new to you, give yourself a break. Make very sure that some of the first goals you set for yourself are attainable. If you want to be worth $1 million, start with $100. If you want to lose 100 pounds, start with 10. Build in some degree of difficulty, but give yourself an opportunity to be a winner. As you become more confident you will become more bold in your goal-setting practices.

Goals should be realistic and demanding. They should be lofty, yet attainable. While this advice may sound self-contradictory, it actually isn't. If you never challenge yourself, you will never know whether you can reach goals that are presently beyond you. Again, you must set short-term goals that present you with successes on your way to your more lofty goals. Success gives you positive reinforcement and resolve to reach the next plateau on the way to your ultimate goal.

Attaining only what you can reach at this moment is not an achievement. In golf, for example, let's say you can always make a double bogie (that's two over par for you nongolfers) without trying very hard. Striving to make par, then, is going to take extra practice on the driving range and more concentration on the fairways and on the greens. But if you try hard enough and really want it badly enough, you will be able to shoot par golf and maybe eventually subpar golf. This example pertains to everything you want to do with your life. If you set a goal for yourself, and if you are willing to work hard enough and make choices to sacrifice some of the nonessential activities, you will be able to achieve your goal.

Put your goals on paper. When you write your goals down in black and white, you can make up your plan more easily. Formulate a step-by-step plan to reach each of your plateaus as measuring sticks of your progress. As you work toward these plateaus, set up definite measures of success or failure. For example, let's say that your goal is to lose 20 pounds. Progress can be easily measured by planning to step on your bathroom scale at set intervals, say once a week. You should not, however, just state, "I will lose 20 pounds," start dieting, and wait for the 20 pounds to magically disappear on the scale. You must set intermediate goals: five pounds the first two weeks, then one or two pounds a week—whatever is realistic and achievable without being too easy. You must work for improvement, or it will not mean anything to you when you achieve it.

If you are 100 pounds overweight, 20 pounds is not really a challenge for you. Nor will it make much difference in your appearance. Challenge yourself! Which is the master—you or your stomach? What is your ultimate objective? What size do you really want to be able to wear? How much is too much? What is a safe, sensible weight loss? You should plan very carefully and set your objectives step-by-step until you have reached the final goal, your planned weight loss.

With your weight loss plan set up and underway, you may want to continue to improve yourself in other ways to keep up with your new image. Begin to plan for the improvement of your mind, also.

You're in Business

Everyone alive is in business for herself or himself. It makes no difference if you earn your living working for a large multinational company or own your own hotdog stand. You must have goals and plans for your career and business growth.

Eventually you leave the surroundings of the workplace and take on total responsibility for managing your life. As manager of your own destiny, both careerwise and personally—and often the two overlap—you have the same four primary responsibilities as do the managers of any other enterprise. You must exercise:

1. Planning
2. Organizing
3. Directing and coordinating
4. Evaluating and controlling

Every skill needed by the manager of a business, large or small, is needed by each individual to manage the business of life.

Each of these four key functions is continuous and overlaps with the others. While one plan is being organized and carried out, another plan is being formulated. Plans must be continuously evaluated and coordinated. Each plan, as it works out, opens new possibilities. Each of these possibilities must be examined and weighed. If the projections are positive and enhance the long-range goals, they can be incorporated into the general plan. In this way, the long-range plan is expanded and improves continuously. If the new avenue ends in a deadend, you must retrace your steps and adjust the plan accordingly. This process is always a part of any successful, growing business—as well as an essential part of the life plan of anyone who expects to grow and prosper as a person.

To set logical and attainable goals, you must be realistic and practical. Yet you may have high ideals or standards to meet. If you find you have set a goal that is unattainable within a reasonable time, you might consider modifying it. Modification, however, should be administered only after it is apparent that the goal cannot be met. You should not consider modification as a failure as long as you do not make a habit of modifying. Nor should you consider making your goal easier just for the sake of being able to say you accomplished it.

Again, remember the four steps or functions of good management:

1. Planning
2. Organizing
3. Directing and coordinating
4. Evaluating and controlling

You're Started

In your quest for self-improvement, you have decided to take this course in personal development. Because you are reading and studying in this area, you have already taken a major step in self-improvement. You are attempting to increase your knowledge of how to improve yourself. The best approach to this or to any project is a systematic listing of the steps toward that goal. Here is a suggested ten-step approach to self-development:

1. Analyze yourself, where you are, where you want to go.
2. Appraise your current level of knowledge and skill. Write down your goals for achievement.
3. Identify the steps needed to reach your goals.
4. Arrange your goals in order of priority.
5. Separate your goals into the two categories of immediate and long-term accomplishments.
6. Establish a sequence for obtaining the knowledge you want.
7. List obstacles that may slow your progress.
8. List the resources—people, materials, time—that you will need to support you.
9. Put dates beside your goals.
10. Test your goals against the criteria of reasonableness, achievability, measurability, time, and ease of evaluation.

Right now, you might be saying, "This is great stuff. One of these days I'm going to sit right down and do it." Stop a moment and think. This is your life and you aren't going to get a second chance at it. Life is time—time is life. Time is not reversible and you cannot replace time that is gone or wasted. Before you can master your life, you must master your time. You have all the time in the world at your fingertips, but remember that there isn't any more of it. You are forced to spend every minute of it every day. How you spend it today will determine how you will spend tomorrow and every tomorrow of your life. Nothing is more important in your life than your time. Every person has exactly 168 hours a week. Are you using that richness of time to your best advantage—or are you wasting precious time just letting life go on?

Managing your time is not filling every minute with busy work and compulsive movement. It is the wise use of your time, including giving yourself time for just sitting (if you enjoy just sitting). It is planning your time efficiently, not compulsively, so that you can enjoy your work and your leisure time. It is giving yourself time to dream about possible objectives, no matter how far-fetched they may seem. It is taking time to smell the flowers while you spread the compost. It is living your life, not just existing from day to day.

Continuous Task

Managing your time efficiently, and thus your life, is a constant task. You cannot make one plan, decide that it works, and live with it for the next fifty years. You should redefine the more important aspects of the plan and re-evaluate them at frequent intervals. What is right for you at this moment may not work well in two years. By updating and redefining your plans, you put more meaning into them. Look for problems that may have arisen and false projections that did not come true; make corrections when and where necessary. As you rework your plan and refine it, projecting new goals and measuring success and failure becomes easier. Your plan becomes better and better, and so does your life.

Reworking and evaluating your plan has another positive aspect. Careful thinking and planning involve goal setting and decision making. This forces you to identify your goal-setting criteria and to define clearly your priorities. Defining priorities helps settle the conflict you feel between your own needs and the needs of others. As you recognize your own priorities, you are better able to weigh them against the priorities from work, family, and friends. When you have listed these needs, you can then write down your long-range, mid-range, and short-range plans. When you have listed all the priorities you must recognize, you must rearrange the items on it in their order of priority.

Writing this list of needs on a piece of paper helps your decision making and planning. List making is not just an exercise in penmanship; it serves several purposes. It helps you to make a decision when you actually see the problem written down, along with several other needs and priorities. It helps you to take stock of your lifetime, how you are spending that time, where you are now, what you have achieved, and what you hope to achieve. The written list helps motivate you to achieve your long-range goal or goals. It helps you to feel more in control of your life if you are following a plan. It provides an accurate measurement of how far you have come and how far you have yet to go. Last, but not least, it reduces unnecessary conflict with yourself and with others in how you use your time.

In making your life plan, you might find the following or similar guidelines helpful:

1. Identify your values—the why of a situation, the motivation. These values can be concrete or abstract. They call for imagination, creativity, assumptions, integrated decisions, structure modification, and change.

2. Define your objective clearly and quantitatively. Vagueness permits the plan to slide and run off track frequently.

3. Budget your time as well as your assets when planning.

4. Coordinate your objectives and your efforts so that you are not working against yourself in professional and personal planning.

5. Define your objectives in terms of quality, quantity, time, and cost (both monetary and personal).

6. Be realistic in assessing both the immediate and remote consequences.

7. Use systematic forecasting and analysis of all your objectives and plans.

8. The secret ingredient is constancy of purpose.

Use these guidelines in a step-by-step procedure to plan your self-improvement project as well as your life objectives.

- *Step 1:* Identify your values. What do you really want to achieve with your life, both personally and professionally? What is your basic motivation?

- *Step 2:* Set up the exact goal you wish to achieve and determine what opportunities you have or may have to reach that goal. Plan also for setbacks and how you will overcome them.

- *Step 3:* Identify possible alternatives if you reach a solid block in your first attempts. If there are no alternative routes, perhaps your basic planning should be reconsidered.

- *Step 4:* Pinpoint exact objectives on the way to your ultimate goal. Use these objectives as reassessment stops to evaluate your achievements to date and to plan the next move.

- *Step 5:* Identify intermediate objectives on your way to the long-range goal.

- *Step 6:* Determine the cost in time, effort, and sacrifice. Whether your goal is personal or professional, it has a cost. You must determine if the objective is worth the cost. If it is, realistically, go for it.

- *Step 7:* Organize your plan, step by step. Schedule it carefully, giving yourself sufficient time to reach each middle-range goal and to achieve the final goal.

- *Step 8:* Fill in the small print. Plan each detail of your schedule and begin to make that schedule a part of your regular routine so that it becomes habit.

- *Step 9:* Identify your control points. If your plan is sliding off schedule, put a control step into action to snap you back on the track and start your plan running smoothly again.

- *Step 10:* Re-evaluate your plan and your achievements to date against your overall master plan frequently. See again, preferably in black and white, where you started, how far you have come, and whether you are on schedule. Make minor adjustments. If you find that you have drifted far from the original plan, make major adjustments.

A final word on problems. If a problem arises, don't assume that the basic plan is wrong. Before junking the plan and starting over, you must determine the how and why of the problem, along with possible solutions. To handle problems, you must:

1. Define or identify the problem.
2. Determine why the problem arose at this particular time.
3. Examine alternative solutions. Try to find more than one solution and assess the value of each solution.
4. Select the best solution.
5. Act on that solution.
6. Evaluate the result of that action.
7. If the problem seems to be insurmountable, perhaps outside advice from a friend or a professional in the field might help.

Plan Your Life

The most important thing to remember is that your life is not going to "come out all right," unless you do something to help it. You are responsible for the rest of your life. Plan to make that life special for you and for those around you by planning. Achieve at your highest potential as a human being and you cannot help being a success in the eyes of all who know you.

Picture yourself wandering alone in the desert—hungry, thirsty, tired. There is sand to the left of you, sand to your right, sand in front and back with nowhere to go. Where you are going looks like where you have been.

You certainly have a goal—to get out of there. Yet this is a general goal. You can only guess at a direction to take. One direction looks as good as any other, and as long as you don't specifically know where you are going, any direction will do.

Suddenly, you spot an oasis. Your whole being changes. You might even muster a small smile as your heart pounds and your pace quickens. You begin moving in the direction of that oasis. "Direction" is the key word. You take a direction because you have found a definite goal.

The goal is what gives your mind and body direction.

Your self-imposed task is to establish goals for yourself. Only you know which goals and achievements are going to give you satisfaction. You determine

your goals—only you! You and only you determine the amount of effort to put forth. And, again, you derive the satisfaction.

The importance of the accomplishment and the amount of satisfaction forces you to answer another huge question: What are you willing to give up to reach your goal? If a reduction in weight is important, you must give up the taste of delicious, mouth-watering food. If promotions at the job are important, you may have to give up some friends and social events to work later hours. If your goal is indeed important enough, the sacrifice becomes not so important as it may

first seem. If what you have to give up is more important, then perhaps the goal is not as vital as you first thought. If this is true, re-examine what you want and set a new goal. In the example, perhaps you would just reverse your goal and strive for social popularity, sacrificing the career ladder and being happy with your present position. You can't have everything. As a comedian once quipped, "You can't have everything. Where would you put it?"

Know What You Want

Knowing what you really want, you can consciously decide what you have to do to get it. This process makes you happier because you are aware of what you have and what you can't have—and you decided things would be that way.

You need some exact goals right now. You need them, first of all, simply to get the most out of this study. If you continue through this book without goals, you will miss the chance to put into practice what you learn as you go.

Your goals are not really important to anyone but you. Yet you may need some help to make your life and career goals more dominant in your mind. Before going any farther, begin right here. We hope you have some real dreams.

Make a list of ten personal goals you will want to achieve in the next ten years:

1. _____
2. _____
3. _____
4. _____
5. _____
6. _____
7. _____
8. _____
9. _____
10. _____

Make a list of ten career goals you will want to achieve in the next ten years:

1. _____
2. _____
3. _____
4. _____
5. _____
6. _____

7. _____
8. _____
9. _____
10. _____

Now do a couple of exercises that will bring you back closer to earth. On a separate sheet of paper, *make two more lists of what you may have to give up to accomplish the goals for your personal life and your career.*

Finally, what knowledge, preparation, and skills do you need to assist you in the pursuit and realization of these goals?

We sincerely hope that this in-depth self-evaluation is much more than just a class assignment.

If you think your goals and dreams are too foolish to share, that's all right. Use some that you feel are acceptable in the class setting. It's still a good exercise. Then go home and use the same techniques for your real dreams. Be a dreamer, shoot high; nothing is ridiculous. But also be brutally frank and honest with yourself about the hard work and sacrifices that your goals will take.

This is only the beginning. You must control the element of time. To help you to deal with this element, you will be shown (in a later chapter) how to apply time management to your personal endeavors, as well as to your career pursuits.

Setting goals and working toward them is work. You must keep in touch with your progress at all times to be effective. If you ever desired to be your own boss, this is your opportunity. You and only you are in charge of what you do with your life. What you accomplish is what you want to accomplish, whether you planned for it or simply didn't plan for anything else.

If you haven't consciously set goals for yourself—particularly life and career goals up to now—you may very well encounter an emotional experience called anxiety. Don't wait for it to go away. The only way to deal with it is to tackle head-on the task that you would rather avoid.

Get Started

Get started. Allow for some self-directed interruptions—some procrastination, if you will—but, for heaven's sake, don't wait for divine inspiration. You aren't suddenly going to get a vision and a sudden urge to work. If, by some quirk of nature, this were to happen, you would probably be in the shower anyway. You can't wait around for your ship to come in if you haven't sent one out!

Commit yourself to spend some time to sit down and at least think about where you are going and how you are going to get there. You'll soon get some ideas good enough that you won't want to forget them. So you must make a few notes.

Taking Charge

If your career plan provides for climbing the business ladder, then sooner or later you are going to have to take charge of something. If you are going to be boss and not bossy, you must take charge of someone or some activity. In this sense, "taking charge" means seeing what needs to be done and doing it either yourself or through others. Before you can be responsible for expensive equipment or other persons' performance, you need to take responsibility for your own actions.

Start now, with goals and plans for your personal growth and your career direction.

To take charge, you have to face three fears time and time again. But you have a lot of company. All the people who have made the initial decision to actively participate in their own lives deal with these fears everyday. These fears are:

1. Fear of failure.
2. Fear of success.
3. Fear of conflict.

Afraid of failure? Who isn't? For that matter, who hasn't failed at some time? Maybe a softer word is "mistake." Everybody makes mistakes; so simply give yourself permission to make some.

The main thing is to admit that you do err, learn from mistakes, and try hard not to make the same ones over. Also think about the things you've done right. Remember the mistakes for what they really are: learning experiences. However, if you must dwell on something, dwell on your successes to give yourself positive strokes.

Afraid of success? Why not? After all, a success is a new experience and most people are afraid of the unknown. The best thing you can do is prepare for it. If you truly set your goals and actively work to achieve them, you will. So you might just as well think about and prepare yourself for success.

Afraid of conflict? Few people enjoy disagreement or criticism. Once again, however, you must realize that everyone is entitled to an opinion and that you too are entitled to your opinion. If and when there is conflict, be sure to begin with an open mind and listen; you might pick up an idea you like. If not, then disregard what has been said. A difference of opinion can be constructive. In an argument, however, no one wins.

Vague dreams, hopes, or aspirations are not goals. They can become goals when you begin to state them in specific terms and planned-for results. Then you must make a commitment to their achievement.

- Put them in writing.
- Make them specific.
- Be able to measure their achievement.
- Make them realistic and attainable.
- Put a time frame on their achievement.

Plan

Planning is the backbone of your personal development program. It is the explicit step-by-step layout of what is necessary to reach your ultimate goal.

When you plan, you make a series of decisions of how, when, and where to take action.

As you plan, you make a great many assumptions, and you cannot be certain that everything will work out. So you must allow for changes as you go, just as you may very well run into construction projects as you travel the highways on your well-planned vacation. As you establish your plan, therefore, you consider alternative moves.

Two dangers must be avoided. One is spending so much time planning that you never get around to taking any action. This can, of course, become so discouraging that you abandon the whole idea of setting goals and eventually go back to wandering through life. The other danger is the reverse—plunging into activity before taking enough time to plan thoroughly. Expending energy and getting nowhere is highly discouraging.

Remain flexible. Be ready to adjust plans and redirect activity when you see that additional activity in the same direction is going to be counterproductive.

"Plan your work and work your plan." This phrase is commonplace in business. You must plan to accomplish something before you begin to expend energy. If you don't know what you are going to do, why would you do anything?

Managers are encouraged to spend a certain amount of time each day to plan for the next day's activities. When they arrive in the morning, no time is wasted figuring out where to begin.

Planning is crucial to how effective you can be in attaining your goals. It puts you in control. Be organized; prioritize each and every task.

Planning must be handled on a step-by-step basis. Plan long-range, just as you made long-range goals. Plan short-range, so that one small success leads to another seemingly small success. Establishing a pattern of successes encourages you to keep going.

Nothing is particularly difficult if you divide it into small jobs.

You can make planning a habit. Once you make a habit, your habit can make you.

Don't become discouraged. In major league baseball, if batters achieve a .300 batting average, they are heroes. That is the equivalent of being right three out of ten times. If they bat .400—or are right 40% of the time—they are immortalized. Give yourself room to be wrong, but don't settle for that. The great question is not whether you have failures, but whether you settle for failure.

How do you climb a ladder? One step at a time. How do you get from the East Coast to the West Coast? One mile at a time. How do you eat an elephant? One bite at a time. The point is that the only way to accomplish a major goal is to break it down into smaller units or bites.

As you plan, look at the top of your mountain, your major goal. If a long period is involved, consider how far you need to be in a year. Then figure how far you should progress each month. Next consider what you need to be doing each week and, yes, how much should you accomplish each day. When you know what has to be done each day you won't get up in the morning wondering when to begin or what to do. You know, and your plan of action is under way.

Getting organized is your next step. In the business world, "organizing" means setting up rules and a structure to control personnel, equipment, money, and materials to reach the goals of the enterprise. Similarly, you are the sole proprietor of your personal life and development, and you must make yourself primarily responsible to realize your attainment of goals. Remind yourself, at this time, that a clear definition of goals is absolutely necessary to putting together

a good organizational structure. Planning provides performance standards and evaluation methods as you work toward your goals. The key is organizing yourself and your resources, as well as describing the sequence of activities, needed to accomplish those goals.

Resources at your command could be other people who have accomplished goals similar to yours. You may wish to talk to these people for advice. Money might be a consideration. For example, do you need reference material, books on dieting, or equipment? Do you want to go so far as to purchase a rowing machine? Of the many considerations as you get organized, one of the greatest is scheduling and allotting your time.

Controls

"Controlling," in the case of your personal development, is a matter of self-control. In business, it refers to influencing other people to work toward common business goals. In your personal applications, it means how much influence you have over yourself. Can you self-direct? How good is your willpower? Control requires the ability to self-motivate, to do your best, and to resist putting off your plan. Straying from your plan can be the result of such rationalizations as: "I've worked so hard putting all of my goals and plans together that I think I'll wait until next week to get started." Or, "I've been at this for several days (weeks, months, or whatever). I owe myself a vacation."

Don't let such rationalizations put you off track. Of course, you must allow yourself rewards. But be careful that the vacation you owe yourself doesn't become extended indefinitely. Build in rewards and plan for them as well. Get organized! This process is tough; have no doubt about that at the outset. Few people find opportunity because it comes disguised as hard work.

Finally, you must control and evaluate yourself and your progress. You must take a look at yourself to see if your plan is really being carried out and your goals met. If not, use your analytical ability to make new plans. If your original plan doesn't work, be alert to the difference between reasons and excuses.

In the control function, you compare actual results with projected results, using the standards set in the planning stage. Also measure results against the control points or checkpoints set at that time too.

Whatever the result of your evaluation, take action to make corrections and begin again. You may very well be ahead of schedule, in which case you may want to consider accelerating your plan to achieve your goal sooner than anticipated.

If it hasn't become obvious already, it will soon: Planning, organizing, directing, and controlling constitute a continuous cycle, because they keep you moving toward that goal. At this point, you should see the necessity of goal setting, planning, directing, and controlling to get what you want for yourself.

A great many good publications on the subject treat goal setting as the only subject, offering charts and giving you an in-depth process. You can read, reread, and read again the need for setting goals for yourself, but the only way to attain your goals is to get started doing it.

You are in business for yourself, just as certainly as if you owned the corner store. Everyone is in business for himself. So you are responsible for what you do or don't do with your talents, knowledge, and skills. You are also responsible for the *development* of those talents, knowledge, and skills. If your decision is not to do anything, that's okay; however, be sure you know that *you* are responsible for that decision.

- Ever heard of a football field without an end zone?
- Ever heard of a basketball court without baskets?
- Ever heard of a baseball diamond without homeplate?
- Ever heard of golf greens without holes?

Of course not. *You can't score without goals!*

Summary Questions

1. Set a goal—a short-term goal for this coming weekend. Describe your goal, your plan, your map—from setting your goal to its attainment.

2. Why is it important to set specific rather than general goals?

3. Use the ten-step approach to self-development to set a realistic but challenging goal for yourself.

4. You were asked to make lists of: (a) ten personal goals, (b) ten career goals, (c) what you would have to give up, and (d) what knowledge, preparation, and skills you need in the pursuit of the goals. If you did the exercise, you may want to adjust it. If you haven't done it, do it now.

5. Explain fear of failure, fear of success, and fear of conflict.

6. How important is it for you to allow for rewards for yourself in your quest for your goals?

7. "Opportunity is disguised as hard work." Explain this statement.

8. Refer to question 4. Repeat this activity using a five-year period. (Ten years can be too broad a base at the beginning.) Bringing your goals and plans into a five-year range may be more realistic for you.

CHAPTER 4

Hygiene

Clean Up Your Act

If cleanliness is next to godliness, as stated by John Wesley, then dirtiness is next to no one. Few things you can say or do turn people away from you and from your ideas as effectively as poor personal hygiene. The adage that even your best friends won't tell you may be true. Although best friends might not say so, you should get the hint if they offer you an hors d'oeuvre by pointing to it from across the room. If the only way your boss asks for that report is over the telephone, perhaps you had better take a personal hygiene inventory. (Due to the nature of some material in this and the next chapters, such as shaving or makeup, the discussion may be directed specifically to the male or female reader.)

Contrary to what some people must believe, soap and water do not corrode the skin. A good deodorant does not cause underarm cancer. A frequent bath or shower does not shorten your life or cause you to shrink, and cologne is *not* a coverup for body odor! All this may sound ridiculous or absurd since most people today do bathe regularly. Some people, however, always seem to be just a little out of step with reality. You catch a whiff of them occasionally. You have probably seen, at least once, the expensively dressed person with limp, oily hair and a dark line just behind the ears and under the back of the jawline. The elegant suit does not cover up the obvious neglect in that person's hygiene. Or you may have observed an individual modeling a beautiful outfit with enough dirt under the fingernails to start another country! It would have to be a private country because, heaven knows, no one would want to share it!

Part of your regular routine should contain a scheduled time slot for preparing yourself for tomorrow. Remember that everyone you meet is going to see that image in the mirror that *you* see each morning. A checklist of "To Do's" is helpful until the ritual becomes as routine as setting your alarm at night. The following list of seven "To Do's" provides a guideline:

1. If you are used to bathing at night, be sure to do so, rather than putting it off until morning.
2. Lay out your clothing for tomorrow.
3. If you take medications or vitamins, lay them out the night before to save time and to prevent forgetting to take them.
4. Make certain makeup, shampoos, towels, and washcloths are available.
5. Be sure your alarm is set.
6. Be sure that electrical aids, such as the razor, curling iron, or blow dryer, are working.
7. Do anything that will allow breakfast preparation to go smoothly and quickly.

Wardrobe preparation is part of your personal hygiene. Before going to bed, you should:

1. Decide what you are going to wear in the morning.
2. Decide what color or colors you want.
3. Lay out clean undergarments.
4. Choose the necessary accessories to complement your attire.
5. Make coats, overboots, gloves, hats readily available if the weather warrants.

Follow a regular schedule of personal care each and every day. Just as you allot yourself extra time to get to work or school on time, so you should allot a specified period to get ready for work or school. Do not slight yourself. You should allow time to prepare yourself for the day.

The following self-test helps you to analyze your grooming habits. Score yourself on a scale of one to three:

1 = seldom   2 = often   3 = always

_____ 1. Do you take a bath or shower daily?
_____ 2. Do you use a deodorant or antiperspirant daily?
_____ 3. Is your deodorant or antiperspirant effective?
_____ 4. Do you put on clean undergarments daily?
_____ 5. Do you wear fresh hose or socks every day?
_____ 6. Do you push your cuticles back as you dry your hands and feet after bathing?

_____ 7. Do you wash your face thoroughly before bed each night to remove makeup and the day's grime?

_____ 8. Do you check your fingernails daily for chips and jagged edges?

_____ 9. Do you have your hair trimmed or cut regularly?

_____ 10. If you wear your hair long, is it styled, neat, and combed at all times?

_____ 11. Do you wash your hair frequently, using a dandruff treatment if necessary?

_____ 12. Do you brush your teeth at least twice a day?

_____ 13. Do you use a mouthwash?

_____ 14. Do you get enough sleep so that you look and feel refreshed?

_____ 15. Do you shave when necessary, if not daily, so that your face is smooth and clean-shaven at all times?

_____ 16. Do you apply your makeup so that it looks fresh and natural?

_____ 17. Do you take time to freshen up during the day?

_____ 18. Do you use a foot spray or powder daily?

A small cut on clean skin isn't much of a problem, but on dirty skin it can become infected and lead to serious trouble. When you bathe doesn't matter. What's important is that you bathe *every day*. If you are devoted to showers, you may not know that sitting in a tub full of warm water does more than get you clean. It relaxes you and soothes away petty problems as you wash away the day's accumulation of dirt. On the other hand, if you are strictly a tub bather, try an invigorating shower. Standing under running water can pep you up and make you feel ready to face the world again.

First on your schedule should be a good bath or shower: not just a rinse and dry, but a good, solid scrub. Along with the obvious benefit of getting rid

of all the day's grease and grime, a brisk scrubbing tones up the skin and gives it a healthy glow that all the magic potions on Madison Avenue cannot duplicate. It doesn't matter what soap you use. Use whatever you prefer, whether it is deodorant, cosmetic, perfumed, or Grandma's homemade lye soap. The scrubbing is what is important. Lather up and enjoy yourself.

After the bath, a light dusting with a talcum powder is a nice finishing touch. It is cooling and soothing to the skin, and it helps to keep you feeling fresh all day.

Look at your hands. Are the nails bitten off short and ragged? Are the cuticles rough and the nails dull? For the feet and hands a nailbrush is a very good idea. The bristles get all the dirt from under the nails and at the same time loosen the cuticles so that they may be easily pushed back with an orange stick after the bath. An orange stick may also be called an orange wood or a cuticle stick. It can be purchased in any drug or department store for very little. It is a stick about 5 inches long, not quite as thick as a pencil, pointed on one end and wedged on the other. The round end can be used for cleaning under the nails and the wedge end is used with gentle pressure to push back the cuticles.

Never peel nail polish off. Use a remover instead. Peeling nail polish off not only gives an unsightly appearance, but it causes the nails to peel off too.

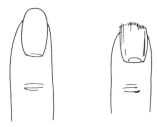

Use only one of the many liquid nail polish removers on the market. Many contain a conditioner that is good for the nails and does not cause the nail to dry out. Some polish removers, however, also remove the natural oil from the nail.

Not the least of sins is nail biting. Nothing looks as disgusting as chewed nails. If you are a nail biter, concentrate on breaking this habit now—if not yesterday! Until you get the nails to grow out, refrain from using polish on them. If you insist on wearing polish, be sure it is only the colorless type. Color only calls attention to them. If your hands are dry, be sure to use a good hand lotion after washing and drying them. Some people's palms perspire a great deal; put a little baby powder on them if you have this problem.

Pampered Feet

Next check those feet. Are the toenails neatly trimmed, straight across and not rounded at the corners? After cutting toenails straight across, you can use a file to finish them off and remove any rough edges. If there are callouses on the back of the heel or on the ball of the foot, use a soft pumice stone to smooth out the rough areas. A pumice stone has an abrasive surface and can be purchased in any drugstore. When using a pumice stone, do not rub so hard as to cause abrasions. Just rub gently. Complete removal of the callouses may take several applications of the pumice stone.

Check the toes. If there are corns or bunions or if the toenails seem to be curving inward, be sure that your shoes are the right size and fit properly.

Few things can sap your enthusiasm more quickly than aching feet, and nothing causes outward mental distress and irritability any more than aching feet. You are allotted two feet per lifetime. If problems with corns, callouses, or bunions are not easily corrected by reasonable care, see a podiatrist (a foot doctor). Your poise, carriage, and certainly your disposition and image are greatly improved after a few treatments.

Be sure to bathe your feet daily. When drying them, dry thoroughly between the toes. This eliminates moist cracks in the skin that can result in athlete's foot. Exercising the feet and ankles is also important. Wiggle your toes, flex your feet, and work your ankles in a circle.

Alternating shoes is a good idea. It's advisable not to wear the same shoe day after day. Always wear clean stockings every day. Sometimes a foot powder or spray is helpful, especially during hot weather. Stockings that allow your feet to breathe are best and, of course, light colors are cooler than dark ones.

Next take note of your elbows and knees. If they are rough or look like you borrowed them from the elephant at the zoo, rub a lanolin base cream or thick lotion into the skin. Good old Vaseline is still one of the best and most practical softeners you can use. You should repeat this application several times a day when you are home and perhaps twice in the evening, after work, and at bedtime until the skin softens and smooths.

Love That Skin

Your skin needs constant and loving care. The skin covering your body and face is a dead give-away to your overall personal hygiene health. Your skin is also the first clue of your age. However, the aging process can be slowed down considerably with proper care.

If you have allergies or acne, you must use extra precautions. Various hypoallergenic creams and lotions are available and, of course, cleanliness is imperative. Severe acne and many allergy problems should be dealt with by a dermatologist (a skin specialist). Dealing with a dermatologist takes time and is rather expensive, but it is time and money well spent if you have a skin problem.

Your skin should always be protected from extreme weather. It should be clean and stimulated, with its natural oil replenished daily. Nothing causes you to lose natural skin oils as quickly as overexposure to the sun's rays, which brings on a leathery look and definitely speeds up the wrinkling process. If you are an outdoor worker and cannot avoid long periods in the sun, you should take extra precautions to protect your skin. Things like a wide-brimmed hat, sunglasses, long-sleeved shirts, long pants, extra lubrication, and sun screen lotions are good preventative measures.

Wind is also harmful to your skin. Use a moisturizer or lip balm for protection. Extra care and consideration should be given to a moisturizing lotion for the face and any part of the body exposed to the wind.

As a person grows older, the skin tends to dehydrate. Thus lubricating it to replace natural oils is necessary. Skin also loses its elasticity. This can be helped, also with proper diet, weight control, and exercise. A good facial massage is beneficial. You can do this yourself or ask your barber or beautician to do it for you.

Sometimes skin becomes chapped in abnormal or extreme weather conditions. Extra care must be given these exposed areas. Keep the affected parts of the body well lubricated and, upon retiring at night, use some Vaseline on them.

Skin Blemishes

Even royalty battles the age-old problem of whiteheads, blackheads, and pimples. Blackheads, usually the result of overactive oil glands, attract dirt and bacteria. Whiteheads may be an indication of lack of vitamin A. Pimples result from infection and more often than not can be traced to poor diet habits. There is no better "pimple prevention" than cleanliness. Soap and water eliminate most problems that are not directly related to health or nutrition.

Facials are something to be considered by male and female alike. A facial mask absorbs dirt and grime, tightens pores, pulls blackheads nearer the surface, and enhances circulation. Masks come in a variety, or they can be cheaply made with such materials as raw oatmeal, egg whites, and cucumbers, to name a few.

An extremely important rule is *never to pick or squeeze* a skin abrasion. In no way try to force a pimple out; you are apt to spread the infection and even leave a scar. Not the least important of the squeezing process is that it hurts!

A good mental outlook usually produces a healthy overall look of the skin. Tension and worry can cause blemishes to flourish. Try to keep yourself calm, find some time for enjoyment and relaxation, and don't worry over things you can do nothing about. A tension reduction is another good reason to practice some of your positive attitude thoughts. Look at it this way: A bridge game, a tennis match, a stroll in the park, a ride on a bike, reading a good book, jogging, playing the piano—this kind of "R&R" may keep the pimples from popping out!

To keep blemishes controlled, remember:

1. Cleanliness is essential.
2. Stimulation helps keep cells active.
3. Lubrication replaces natural oils.
4. Protection against the elements is needed.
5. Exercise and good health are necessities.
6. Your mental attitude plays a large role in skin reactions.

Sometimes we get blemishes no matter what. They may be concealed while they heal. Numerous products on the market are flesh colored and at the same time medicated. A liquid or cream powder base can hide a blemish satisfactorily throughout the workday with perhaps a touchup sometime during the day.

Now check for unwanted hair. Legs should be neatly shaved and underarms and face smooth and hairless. There are two common methods of removing unwanted hair. The first is a razor plus lather, the second is a depilatory (a cream, lotion, or foam that dissolves hair).

Use a depilatory with great care. It must be used according to instructions with no deviation. A depilatory should *not* be used by men for shaving the face; it is designed for women's facial hair and hair on legs and arms. Depilatories are usually used on the legs and underarms; however, there are some for removing facial hair. Read the directions and follow them explicitly.

To shave in the bath or shower, first wash your legs with warm water, working up a good lather with soap. Then use a safety razor and gently remove the hair. Don't press too hard or you will nick yourself and remove a lot of skin.

Check for long hair in facial moles or other noticeable moles. Also check the nasal hair; we all have it and, like any other hair, it has to be controlled. Nothing is as distracting as a fluttering nasal hair! Use a pair of scissors with rounded, rather than pointed, tips. Instead of being pulled or plucked, this hair should be clipped as closely as possible to the skin.

Oh, Those Sweat Glands

Perspiration has a strong odor because it contains a small amount of the body's waste material. The underarms have the strongest odor due to the concentration of sweat glands in that area. Never apply a deodorant under your arms until after your daily bath or shower.

Like a good perfume or cologne, deodorants or antiperspirants work with the body chemicals. Sometimes a deodorant that you have been using with success suddenly becomes ineffective because your body chemicals have changed. You should choose a deodorant or antiperspirant that works for you. If one seems to lose its power by midday, try another. It may take several tries to find the one that works best for you. Find one that works with your chemicals so that people don't think you work in a large, unventilated gym.

Your deodorant can be spray, pump, solid, or roll-on. It is a good idea to use a roll-on cream deodorant if it is effective for you instead of a spray. The reason is that you may inhale some of the spray from an aerosol can, and that can be harmful.

Some people might even feel the need to wear underarm shields. If you have a severe perspiration problem, these could protect your clothing.

Always put on clean undergarments and fresh socks or hose every day. These garments are next to your body and absorb the sweat and body odor quickly. If they are fresh each morning, the effect of this absorption is not cumulative.

Being fresh from the skin out helps your outer garments stay fresh longer and last longer too.

Kiss and Tell

On to the subject of good dental hygiene. In Germany, during the middle ages, it was thought that kissing a donkey would relieve a toothache. Some individuals have the kind of breath bad enough to make you *want* to kiss a donkey instead— and that can't be very pleasant at best!

Dentists suggest brushing after every meal. That is the ideal. But you might find it hard to pull a toothbrush from your pocket or handbag at a business dinner and brush your teeth in the fingerbowl. You should brush thoroughly every morning and every evening. Some people brush with ordinary table salt or soda. Dentists generally agree this method is satisfactory. Both are natural whiteners, and both contain an abrasive. And we all know soda is a deodorant. A fold-up

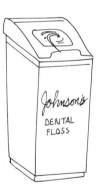

toothbrush is a good investment for people at work and on the go. Dental floss is also a must.

A good mouthwash is a nice way to freshen your mouth after brushing. If your teeth are stained or yellowish, invest in a tube of tooth polish. Do not use it every day, however; it is too abrasive. Use it every other day for a few weeks until your teeth have whitened and then at least once a week.

Also be sure to brush your tongue. This is not a typing error: Brush your tongue! Particularly in adults, the tongue frequently becomes coated. A light brushing on the top of the tongue, as far back as is comfortable, removes that coating and freshens your breath. Be careful not to scratch or injure the tastebuds. Brush gently.

If the taste in your mouth brings to mind the bottom of a bird cage, you can rest assured others are smelling what you taste. If you take reasonably good care of your mouth and still have a problem, by all means see your dentist and/or doctor. This could be an indication of a medical problem and should not be ignored.

There is no way to get rid of *all* the bacteria in the mouth. Even antiseptic mouthwashes do not help much. But you *can* get rid of food debris, simply by flossing the teeth at least once a day and properly brushing the teeth for a long enough time.

Most dentists agree that using dental floss is essential. Dental floss is a fine ribbon of fiber that can be "seesawed" between the teeth. This removes food particles from crevices that cannot be reached with the toothbrush. Floss comes either waxed or unwaxed. Which type you use makes no difference, as long as you use it with regularity.

There is definitely a *right* way to brush the teeth. You must brush down from the top row and up from the bottom row of teeth on the outer surfaces of the teeth. Then brush the same way on the back surfaces. Brushing properly is a little difficult but certainly important. The up-and-down brushing may seem awkward, but it clears away food particles, thus eliminating breath odor and decay. Be sure your brush reaches the backmost teeth, a favorite place for food particles to stay and a place you just can't reach without effort. Next brush back and forth on the biting surfaces of the teeth.

An electric toothbrush can be effective, providing you use it long enough. "Brushing long enough" means three minutes of brushing. You can use an egg timer or your watch to time yourself. You cannot accomplish a thorough brushing in less than three minutes.

If you are a smoker, take even more care than a nonsmoker to see that your breath carries no telltale smoke odor. Naturally, your teeth tend to be yellowish or gray. You must also be extra careful about keeping your hands clean and pleasant smelling.

Have the Hair You Love to Touch

Your hair should always be clean and sweet smelling. Hair can be coarse, fine, frizzy, curly, straight, oily, dry, bleached, or colored. There are many different kinds of shampoos, conditioners, and rinses to suit your type of hair. Each person washes his/her hair with different regularity. A person with exceptionally oily hair has to shampoo much more frequently than one with dry or even normal hair. The problem is not how often you have to shampoo; the problem is to shampoo as often as necessary to assure clean, sweet-smelling hair at all times. Shampoo your hair in the following way:

1. Brush the hair out thoroughly.
2. Massage the entire scalp.
3. Wet the hair with warm water.
4. Apply the shampoo.
5. Lather and massage the entire scalp.
6. Rinse out the first soaping.
7. Reapply the shampoo, this time concentrating on the hair rather than the scalp.

Sometimes you have to "dry clean" your hair, maybe when you haven't enough time, have been ill, or suffer a cold. A dry shampoo can be purchased

at any drugstore. You simply spray it in and brush it out. It works wonders in a pinch and is successful in removing excessive oil, dust, and spray.

Your health and mental attitude play a large part in the appearance of your hair. Taking care of yourself both physically and mentally, as well as keeping your working body parts clean, aids in gaining self-assurance. Nurture your hair with brushing, massage, and shampoo. Like anything else, it responds to tender loving care.

Now you are ready to get dressed and face the day. During the day, freshen up your outlook and your image. At least once or twice, splash a little cold water on your face and comb your hair. Reapply a little powder and lipstick or a dab of aftershave or cologne. You will feel and look refreshed.

If you are wearing perfume or aftershave, consider where you will be going. Match the scent to the occasion. In the office, a very light scent is essential. A heavily perfumed scent soon overpowers those working near you. The more natural you are, the more those around you appreciate the real *you*.

If you are always clean, you present yourself as someone with a great deal of confidence and self-assurance. Our bodies get dirty very quickly, so keeping up with that accumulation of soil and odor from a normal day is a never-ending task. Like anything good, it takes time, and the time you spend with your personal hygiene pays off. Diet, once again, plays a major role in healthy-looking skin, teeth, hair, nails, and sparkling eyes. If you have healthy and clean habits, your whole being benefits in all sorts of wonderful ways. Your good habits show up in your disposition, in your overall appearance, in your desire to attain bigger and better things, and in one of the most important things—your smile!

The Language of Hygiene

Familiarize yourself with the following list of commonly used terms associated with personal hygiene:

- *Antiperspirant*—a preparation that keeps you dry and also destroys unpleasant odors.
- *Cuticle*—the thin dead skin at the sides and base of a fingernail or toenail.
- *Deodorant*—a preparation that destroys unpleasant odors but does not necessarily keep you dry.
- *Lubrication*—a substance used to make the skin smooth and soft.
- *Manicure*—to file and buff nails and to trim cuticles.

The following list of body cleanliness routines should be obeyed with the seriousness of the Ten Commandments:

1. A daily bath or shower.
   a. Allover cleansing.
   b. Special attention to face, neck, and ears.
   c. Hands and feet not neglected.
2. Daily use of a deodorant or antiperspirant.
3. Use of a foot powder or spray.
4. Use of *only* lightly scented colognes or body powders for work.
5. Teeth brushed after every meal, if possible.

The Hygiene Checklist

In the following checklist, place an "X" in front of each of the items that is an essential of body cleanliness:

_____ a. Daily bath or shower.
_____ b. Fingernails polished weekly.
_____ c. Hair spray used often.
_____ d. Undergarments changed daily.
_____ e. Daily use of foot powder or spray.

_____ f. Teeth brushed after every meal, if possible.

_____ g. Females shave legs daily.

_____ h. Men shave daily.

_____ i. Deodorant used even without bathing.

_____ j. Socks changed daily.

CHAPTER **5**

Makeup

Saving face

Men! If you keep up with the trends, what you are about to read does not come as a shock. If you are not aware that men are patronizing beauty salons across the country in increasing numbers, then here and now is as good a place and time as any to find it out. In places like Atlanta and New York, salons claim that 15 to 25 percent of their customers are men. What are they doing there? They are getting haircuts, hair treatments, facials, manicures, and pedicures. Some are covering up gray hair; some want highlights.

The point is, fellas, don't write this chapter off as not being for you. Each concept in this book has more or less value for each person. Don't neglect any part of it. Learn everything you can; then evaluate its implication and application for yourself.

Both men and women should know the basics of shaving and applying makeup. You may not ever think that if you are a man, you would have a reason to apply makeup to a woman. Or on the other hand, if you are a woman, you may be thinking, "Why would I ever have to shave a man?" What if, for example, your parent, your spouse, your brother or sister, or even a close friend became ill or injured and could not care for his/her personal needs. Someone has to administer to those needs, and that someone might just be you! Unrealistic though it may seem, you may be called upon in your lifetime to help a sick or handicapped person. Can you think of a better reason to learn basic shaving and makeup techniques?

You, Your Face

Your face is you. Male or female, young or old, your face is never hidden from view. It is the first focus of attention and the most lasting impression. Your facial expressions are part of your personality. Other parts of your anatomy can be and are concealed by clothing, but your face is out for the world to see all the time. You owe it to yourself to take good, constant care of your face—you're stuck with it for the rest of your life. So treat it kindly and it will return your gift of loving care tenfold.

Here are some basic rules to follow in attaining and maintaining a good complexion:

1. Eat a balanced diet.
2. Have regular elimination.
3. Get sufficient sleep.
4. Avoid frowning or squinting.
5. Get fresh air.
6. Get adequate exercise.
7. Drink plenty of water.

Keep these seven things in mind every day. If you do them faithfully, plus establish a good skin care program, you will be rewarded with a healthy-looking glow all the time.

A perfect complexion is seldom the result of a lucky combination of genes. We are all born with soft, smooth skin. A few lucky people seem to sail through life without a blemish, dark circles, or chapped lips. Or at least we are told they exist! These fortunate, beautiful people, however, do not get off scot-free. They, too, must take excellent care of their complexion and makeup application if they wish to maintain their looks. Most of those who seem to be without blemishes or marks achieve that perfection by using a large measure of common sense and by following definite rules every day.

No magic potions or pills will accomplish that fresh look. It takes daily care and consideration. Makeup is important to both men and women. Creams or lotions should be used to keep the skin soft and supple and to prevent drying and cracking. Soap and water are essential to keep the skin clean and free from blackheads and pimples. Keeping the skin clean also helps to keep the pores from enlarging. While the size of your facial pores is determined by your genes at birth, pores can and do enlarge throughout life, if dirt and grease are permitted to clog them.

When trying to describe a person, you might make up a verbal description like this: "He is six feet tall, with dark hair, dark eyes, olive complexion, wide mouth, straight and narrow nose, small moustache . . ." Notice that only two of the features mentioned, hair and height, are not facial characteristics. This is true of most descriptions. Even a short description usually notes eye color, skin tones, and shape of mouth.

The point is that your face is *you*. Yet, since it is right out there in front, it is exposed to sun, wind, rain, snow, extreme heat, and bitter cold. It is tanned by the sun in summer, chapped by the cold and wind in winter, and exposed to ultraviolet sunlamps and man-made pollutants in between. Every emotion you feel is registered on your face; it frowns, smiles, laughs, and cries. It gets frost-bitten, pelted with cold sleet, baked in the hot sun, and chapped by either hot or cold air.

Your mouth is stretched and pressed, poufed and curled. Your lips are licked, bitten, and stretched. Telltale lines, called crows' feet or laugh lines, depending on your outlook on life at the moment, are quick to form in the corners of your eyes and mouth. Frown lines deepen in your forehead.

Every day of your life your face braves the elements from one extreme to another without complaining. It is shaved, scraped, powdered, lotioned, and lathered. You clean it with soap, creams, and special formulas. Through it all, you expect your face to be soft, smooth, and glowing with good health.

Basic Skin Care

Before delving into all facets of skin care and makeup, let's touch on some general hints or tips. You will discover some shortcuts, substitutions, money-saving ideas.

Keep your makeup subdued. It is best to avoid experimentation with something new on workdays. Because you admire someone who wears eyeliner well, for example, does not mean necessarily that you (1) have the knack to apply it properly or (2) would look good after application. *Be what you are and find what is good for you. Then stay with it.* This does not, of course, mean a change is not welcome now and then.

First of all, cleanliness is essential. Always clean your face well at bedtime; this is a must—no matter how tired you are. It only takes about three to five minutes to cleanse the face properly, and it makes the difference down the road in the appearance of your skin.

Of the many types of cleansers, the choice is up to you after you discover which type is best suited to your skin. Several different types are listed with the function they perform.

1. *Moisturizing cleanser*—a cleanser that contains glycerin, which aids in retaining and absorbing moisture in the skin.
2. *Deep-pore cleanser*—a penetrating cleanser for cleaning clogged pores.
3. *Antiseptic cleanser*—fights harmful skin bacteria.
4. *Cold cream cleanser*—nonliquid emulsion for normal skin.
5. *Estrogenic cleanser*—designed to aid in the revitalization of skin cells that show signs of aging.
6. *Hypoallergenic cleanser*—for individuals with allergies or extremely sensitive skin.
7. *Astringent cleanser*—stimulates and revitalizes skin tissues and tightens pores.
8. *Medicated cleanser*—designed for problem skin, such as acne. Has a healing ingredient.

Warm, not steaming hot, water and mild soap every morning and evening are necessary. The evening scrub is most important since it serves to remove the day's accumulation of grime and dust, as well as the makeup or shaving lotions you have worn during the day. The method of scrubbing should include warm water, lots of soap, and a slightly rough wash cloth. The soap and water soften the grime in the pores and the rough cloth lifts it out. Various creams on the market are helpful in removing makeup.

Use a gentle, mild product to cleanse the skin. A cleanser containing too much acid creates an itchy skin and/or scalp, and it also does not clean as well. If you are using hard water, a high acid cleanser is particularly ineffective; it merely solidifies the dirt and grease on the skin, making it impossible to rinse away. A good and easy way to know if your cleanser contains too much acid is that it will not lather.

After scrubbing the face, you must rinse it well. Rinse thoroughly with warm water—not hot. Dead cells are constantly falling off the skin, not noticeably so, but it is a daily process. Since, however, not all of the dead cells fall away, you have to help the removal process. Special creams and/or abrasive puffs make this task easier. If this procedure is done as it should be, you end up with cleaner-looking skin because it *is* cleaner. This also makes the aging process less noticeable.

Water, as opposed to creams, is essential in cleansing the skin. It replenishes the natural moisture that you are constantly losing in your skin. If you have always cleaned with creams, you can continue using your cream, but, instead of tissuing it off, use a slightly rough washcloth or abrasive skin pad and warm water. Before many days, you see the results of your new cleaning process. The ultimate outcome is a brighter, fresher-looking skin, due to the cell breakup and the removal of dead tissue.

Skin Types

The chemical balance of your body is constantly changing. If, for example, you have been blessed with skin that requires little care, you may not always be so fortunate. You need to constantly look out for changes in your skin that might necessitate changing your skin care program.

There are, naturally, several different skin types—five to be specific. Each requires its own skin care program. The skin types are:

1. *Normal*—use a mild soap and water, or, if you prefer, a cleansing lotion twice a day.

2. *Dry*—needs soap and water, along with a good lubricating cream immediately after washing. Once-a-day cleansing is sufficient for dry skin and at night a good lubricating cream, once again, should be applied.

3. *Oily*—presents a multitude of problems, including blackheads (enlarged pores filled with oil). You must be very fastidious when cleansing oily skin! Rubbing alcohol on a cotton ball may be applied to exceptionally oily areas. You need to cleanse your face often during the day to keep the pores cleaned out, to close them, to kill bacteria, and thus to dissolve the oil.

4. *Combination*—entails a "T-zone," usually an oily area around the nose and forehead, while the rest of your face is dry. Wash the oily area (the T-zone) with soap and water. Use a cleansing cream on the rest of the face. Rinse with cold water to close the pores, and use an astringent on oily areas. An astringent removes the last traces of oily dirt and kills bacteria. It also gives you a refreshed

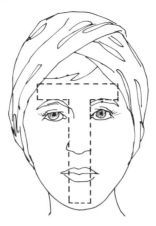

feeling, while toning and tightening the pores. A relatively new product on the market is especially designed for the combination skin. It adapts itself to the needs of the combination skin, moisturizing dry areas and controlling oily T-zone areas. It comes in shades to match your skin tone, so that it can and should be worn during the day.

5. *Problem*—Even with the tenderest attention, your skin can sometimes develop a problem over which you have no control. Some diseases of the skin require the aid and attention of a reputable dermatologist. If the problem is caught in time, a dermatologist can spare you much expense and embarrassment.

Acne is a skin problem that is usually brought on by hormonal and glandular activity. If you are one of the lucky ones, your case of acne might be treated successfully with nonprescription soaps and lotions. Many cases can be treated with good results in this manner, thus avoiding the expense and time spent with a dermatologist. Again, the key is to catch the acne problem before it grows out of proportion. Makeup is helpful in concealing this problem and will make it easier to endure.

Eczema is a skin disorder that is unpleasant, to say the least, and it can cover large or small portions of your body. It itches and burns, and probably the *only* solution is to consult a dermatologist.

Blackheads and whiteheads can and should be controlled by you, and never allowed to get out of hand. *Thorough cleansing* and *proper diet* cannot be stressed enough in the prevention of these two unwanted clingalongs!

Stress can be the cause of many skin problems. ·

Back to taking care of that face of yours. Your skin care involves:

1. Cleansing as the number one rule.
2. Consistency.
3. Lubrication for softness.

4. Stimulation for new cells.

5. Protection—your own insurance of nice skin.

After cleansing your face, always use a toner before you apply lubrication. Allow the toner to dry for a few moments before applying your moisturizer. You can leave the toner on, or splash it off with warm water. Either technique is correct. However, if you splash with warm water, your makeup seems to glide on more smoothly.

Massaging the skin is essential for male and female alike. If you don't feel inclined to give your skin a massage, ask your beautician or barber. Either knows how important it is and is willing to do it for you. Massaging or stimulating the face eases tensions, often helps a headache disappear, and enhances the skin tone. Sometimes a complexion brush can be used for facial stimulation for men and women both. Use such brushes with soap and water in a rotating motion, going up and out along the face.

Another form of facial stimulation is stretching, yawning, making exaggerated vowel signs, and kissing the ceiling with your mouth (an imaginary ceiling, of course). These facial exercises are also good for laughs if you choose to perform them in front of the mirror. A good laugh is a great way to start and end a day.

Massaging the face with a cream actually softens the skin. This allows you to slide across the skin rather than pull it. Always use upward and outward motions, so as not to drag down the face.

Face packs are excellent and should be used once or twice a week. You can make all types of inexpensive home packs, and many kinds of commercial masks on the market do a remarkable job. It is best, however, not to experiment with several types of packs at one time. Try one and stay with it for several weeks before deciding to try something new. Any face pack, after being applied, should be left on for at least ten minutes. It can then be peeled, washed, or splashed off with warm water. A toner should follow, with a lubricant immediately after.

Now that you have cleansed, used a toner, and lubricated, you have prepared your face for a healthy glow, and the little time it took pays off.

Applying Makeup

You get better at applying makeup with practice. There are some very definite do's and don'ts of makeup application. Here are some of them:

1. Never apply blush or rouge in a dab, and do not blend it into the hairline. Blend it over the cheekbone toward the temple.

2. Keep your eyebrow line natural, not pencil thin.
3. Eye shadow should never be "winged" beyond the outer edge of the eye.
4. Apply mascara on upper lashes *only*.
5. Don't make an unnatural line for your lips unless they are extremely thin.
6. A subtle application of makeup is generally a good rule for most individuals to follow.

When you learn your strong and favorable facial features, as opposed to the weak and unflattering ones, you must then decide how to apply cosmetics to call attention to your good features. Properly applied, your makeup can enhance and complement a strong feature, thereby detracting from another, less desirable one. You can learn to highlight your features to give your face more interest. Sometimes having a beautician or cosmetologist point out what is best for you is money and time well spent. A facial and beauty consultation could be very valuable to help you put your best face forward!

Expensive eye creams are fine, but vaseline is probably the best treatment you can give your eyes—and certainly by far the least expensive. It is also the most efficient mascara remover you can buy.

Applying mascara to the lower lashes is nice, but tricky. Unless you are adept at the lower lash application, leave that part of makeup to the experts. A slip of the mascara wand can give you instant dark circles under the eyes. Dark circles can be most distracting, and they certainly can appear without the aid of lower lash mascara! Use a cover-up white base treatment underneath the foundation you have chosen. Simply apply the lighter cream to the dark area and blend it into the regular foundation cream. Use the same technique at the corners of the mouth and nose, blending them in with your base.

Apply blush subtley. A color that blends with your skin tone is best. Powder can soften crows' feet around the eyes and is a natural way to set your makeup. When applying lip color, you can help it stay on twice as long if you again make good use of powder. Put a lip color on, blot the lips, and then pat powder onto the lips. Rub the lips together and apply another layer of lipstick. Cotton balls can be used to apply powder in lieu of a puff, and Q-tips are very handy for removing excess makeup or blending in small hard-to-get areas.

At this point, take a good look at yourself and answer some questions. If you have shortcomings (and we all do), learn the proper way to diminish them, as well as to play your assets up big. Some of the questions you might ask yourself are the following:

1. Does your mouth turn up or down at the corners?
2. Are your cheekbones prominent?
3. Are your eyes widely spaced or close together?

4. Are your eyes deep-set, heavy-lidded, bloodshot, and framed with dark circles?
5. Is your face well scrubbed?
6. Does your skin have a firm and healthy glow?

Your face, despite its constant exposure to weather and man-made pollutants, is actually very tender. Everyone—man or woman—needs to use a lotion or cream to protect that tender facial skin. "Protection" is the key word. Many, many products on the market are made for this use.

Experts, trained in skin care, can also help. Ask your beautician, barber, skin specialist, or the clerk in the cosmetics department of any large department store.

After the aging process takes over, cells no longer renew themselves and revitalize. As a young person, your cell renewal system is automatic and taken for granted. After you reach a certain age, you learn to take *nothing* for granted—cell renewal not the least of these.

What is cell renewal? Just exactly what the name implies. The cells in a young person's skin are automatically refurbished and replenished, thereby giving a young, fresh skin appearance.

As early as 20 years of age, skin begins to lose the natural ability to renew itself. Skin does not look as fresh and smooth as it once did, while you were daily taking it for granted that you would always have skin like a baby! When cells can no longer function as they once did, they need some help from you!

New products on the market are put out by many different cosmetic firms, naturally at many different prices. All varieties of this product are effective as long as they are used consistently and according to instructions. These translucent fluids are quickly absorbed to work deep down, so use them sparingly (drop by drop) over the face and neck. This new product is used after cleansing and before moisturizing.

These cell energizers speed up the skin's own natural cell-renewal cycle by as much as 25 percent. They help you to gain one of the most essential things in skin care: Your skin functions at a younger level and looks its best. Men, don't overlook cell renewal.

Cell energizers therefore can do the following things:

1. Accelerate the normal cell renewal rate.
2. Aid the skin to revive its natural ability to renew cells.
3. Allow skin to function at its best.

When it comes to skin care, men and women have similar problems. So the care and treatments are exactly the same with the exception of makeup removal. The cleansing process, the massaging, the skin types, the exposure to the elements, the abnormal skin conditions—to name a few—all create men and women equal in caring for the skin. Let's sum up the needs of good skin care for both sexes:

1. Sensible eating habits.
2. Adequate rest.
3. A thorough and faithful cleansing program.
4. Stimulation or massage.
5. Skin protection.
6. Good physical health.
7. Good mental health.
8. Skin lubrication.

A Firm Foundation

Foundation can diminish and conceal many flaws. It lends a smooth and flawless look to the skin and certainly makes the application of blush and eye makeup easy. Few people can go without any foundation; there just are not that many perfect skins around.

You may choose from two kinds of foundation: liquid or cream. Each one comes with either oil base, water base, or oil-free. There are likewise three finishes: dewy, matte or semimatte. The kind of foundation you choose is merely a matter of what you prefer—what is easy for you to apply.

Your skin condition determines which base to use. The oily base should be applied with great care. It easily gives a heavy look and really should be used only after a great deal of practice. The water base is probably most popular as well as beneficial. It has little oil in it and is applied with water. It goes on smoothly and helps naturally moisturize the skin. The oil-free, of course, has absolutely no oil and is for those with oily skin.

The most time-consuming thing about foundation is picking the proper shade for your skin tone. It should never give you an ivory or orangish look; it should blend with your natural skin color. Sometimes you can use two different shades and properly apply it to make a very interesting effect.

After choosing the correct shade, you must apply it with great care—never with a heavy hand. If you are using a concealer for dark circles, be sure that it is only a shade lighter than your foundation. A concealer is a stick or cream of a lighter color that can be used to hide blemishes or minimize dark circles. If you choose a concealer that is too much lighter than your foundation and looks too white, you will look like a panda bear! The concealer should be put on in little dots dabbed *beneath* the dark circles, not *on* them.

Apply foundation only after the face has been cleansed, toned, and moisturized. Apply it lightly. Use your finger, dabbing it across the cheeks, along the nose, across the forehead, across the eyelids, and along the chin. Then feather the foundation in an upward and outward motion—never into the hairline and never down the neck. If you have chosen your color properly, you should not be able to tell where your foundation ends. During summer months, everyone has a tendency to darken; so by all means darken your foundation accordingly.

If you have a problem skin, use a medicated foundation to aid in the healing process while making you look and feel better. Tiny lines can be made soft-looking with skillfully applied foundation. There must be an extra light touch in these areas, though, because the lines tend to "catch" the foundation, thereby becoming more noticeable rather than less. Some foundations contain a sunscreen, which certainly is important if you are outdoors quite a bit—winter or summer.

For people who suffer from allergies, many cosmetics offer hypoallergenic foundations. Certainly consider no other kind if you have allergic reactions.

To make foundation perform at its peak, match your skin tone and apply it with a light touch. You are striving for a topcoat—not an overcoat. A slightly damp sponge can be advantageous in applying foundation too. It gives a light touch and produces a sheer finish.

If you use powder, a translucent powder is best—that is, one with no color.

Whether you use powder depends merely on what look you like. It also helps to "set" your makeup so it lasts longer.

Put the Bloom in Your Cheeks

Applied correctly, blush can put the bloom in your cheeks, to coin a phrase. Keep your rouge color in the same color family.

There are three types of blush: dry, cream, or liquid. Again, the choice is yours. Cream and liquid are more easily applied and made to look more natural than dry. However, dry rouge is a quick, sure method used to "touch up" the blush during the day.

Rouge can be used to its best advantage after you have decided which shape face you have. People have either a round, oval, heart, oblong, diamond, square, or triangular face. Here is a simplified version of how to apply rouge for each shape:

1. *Round*—apply rouge toward the center of the cheek.
2. *Square*—form a light "V" with the rouge.
3. *Oblong*—apply rouge to the cheekbone and blend it toward the temple.
4. *Heart*—apply rouge under the middle of the eye and blend it out on the cheekbone.
5. *Triangular*—apply it about half an inch from the hairline.
6. *Diamond*—apply rouge high and smooth it out on the temple, close to hairline.
7. *Oval*—perfect shape—lucky you!

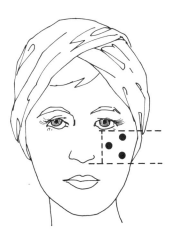

The dotting method seems to be the most preferable method for applying rouge. Put three dots along the cheek bone and then blend it in with the fingers. Don't get carried away with color. Keep it subtle and natural-looking, and it will do wonders to enhance your beauty.

TLC for Lips

The mouth is a very important part of your complete makeup picture. Improper application here can be the undoing of your makeup labors. Few people can go without any lip color at all, but some prefer no color and look great with the natural look. Your lips are a very sensitive part of your face and need lots of tender loving care.

Lips are different from any other part of your body because they do not tan. They will burn, however, and this can happen easily to the lower lip. So take great care to keep the lips moisturized and protected. Many products with sunscreen should be used summer and winter if you are going to be outside for extended periods.

Lips should always be soft, smooth, and moist. They derive moisture from your saliva, but lips that are licked a great deal, of course, are more readily chapped.

Actually, most lipsticks are good for your lips because they contain a moisturizing agent, keeping the lips soft and providing protection. Lip gloss or balm are naturally good for lips and can even be used to emphasize lip color and add a moist look while protecting. A good idea is to apply a lip balm or gloss to your lips before putting on lip color. After a few minutes, wipe off the excess gloss before applying color. This procedure accomplishes three things:

1. Gives added lip protection.
2. Makes lipstick go on more smoothly.
3. Gives lips a smooth, moist look.

Like faces and eyes, lips come in assorted shapes and sizes. Unless you have an extremely pronounced problem with lip size, keep lip color confined to your natural lip line. It's quite an art to be able to outline lips and fill in properly to get a different effect from your lips.

Color is the next thing to decide. Your body chemistry has a great deal to do with dictating the best colors for you. For instance, some reds tend to turn blue or darken; these are not becoming and tend to give a hard look. Applying your foundation to your lips before applying lipstick allows you to blend it with your skin tone and prohibits darkening of the lip color.

If you are using a vivid color and perhaps want to tone it down, apply a shade lighter on top for a pleasing effect. Your rouge and lipstick do not necessarily have to be the same color, but they should blend well with one another.

Another consideration in choosing lip color is the whiteness of teeth. Most people are not blessed with white teeth. Muted colors are best for most people and certainly are more flattering. Remember that orange shades tend to make the teeth yellowish. Apply lipstick properly and logically, and your smile will be even prettier! One small trick (but you have to perfect it) is to lift the corners of your lips ever so slightly with your lipstick to give a hint of a smile. (The hint that outdoes all others a million times over is to refine your very own "real" smile!)

Try not to transfer your lip color from the upper to the lower lip. They are not the same size or shape, so don't rub them together to spread out the color. Use a lipstick brush for outlining and filling in the lips; it gives a glossy look, as opposed to lip color in the stick. If you decide to change your lip line for whatever reason, you must first cover the lips with foundation. Also be sure to change the line ever so slightly. Always covering your lips with foundation prevents lipstick from changing color, and it also blends in with your foundation color more naturally.

The Eyes Have It!

Eyes are the most expressive part of your body. By looking into a person's eyes, you can tell practically to the last detail how that person is feeling—and maybe even thinking. Eyes express sadness, happiness, anger, loneliness, thoughtfulness. They register surprise, fright, horror, anticipation, and excitement—to name only a few easily recognized emotions.

Since the eyes are so important to you and to others, take good care of them. Be glad you have them, be thankful you can see with them, and use them to your best advantage.

Eyes, and the skin around them, are extremely fragile and delicate. Therefore, give great care to keeping the skin soft with moisturizers. Many good eye creams are on the market, and baby oil or Vaseline is also a good treatment for this area. When applying a cream to your eyes, you must have a gentle touch—never *rub* your eyes. It's so easy to break down the skin. Use your little finger to apply cream underneath the eyes and your ring finger along the side. If you use these fingers, you are less apt to apply an undue amount of pressure.

Always, always remove every bit of eye makeup before retiring at night. There are special eye makeup removers on the market. But if you prefer, Vaseline or baby oil, once again, is very effective in removing mascara and eye shadow. These are also a great deal more economical than the expensive removers. How heavy your eye makeup is determines whether one or two applications are needed to remove all makeup. You can tissue the makeup off or use cotton balls to remove all traces.

Plucking the eyebrows can be tricky—and slightly painful. You must be cautious not to pluck your brows so they are thin and skimpy-looking. If your brows are not bushy or grow wild, sometimes it's best not to pluck them at all. A natural brow line is best, again, if they aren't overgrown.

If you decide to tweeze, first press a washcloth that has been wrung out in hot water to the brow. Catch just one hair at a time, and pull it out the direction it grows. Do it quickly. Then dry your tears and go onto the next one!

Brow coloring should be used as a matter of personal taste. An eyebrow pencil is the easiest to use and gives a natural look. Use light, feathery strokes and not too dark a color. Poorly applied brow color sometimes gives an unrelenting look of surprise. You do not want your eyebrows to be the first thing people notice about you.

The Shadow Knows

Eyeshadow can certainly be used to enhance the beauty of your eyes and your whole face. Again, you have a variety of kinds and colors of shadow. You can choose from creams, gels, powders, or watercolor cakes. There are all the colors of the rainbow from which to choose. Just be sure when you have finished applying your color, *you* don't look like a rainbow! It is better to look like the pot of gold found beneath it!

You may wish to match the color of your eyes or the color of your clothes, but most experts agree that browns and beiges are probably the most flattering to all. A combination of colors can be used, such as green or brown topped off with a frosty green. There are any number of flattering color combinations, but you should know how to apply them correctly, or you will look like a circus clown.

Devote some practice time to applying eye shadow. Pick a time when you are going to be home and can experiment with different shades and methods of application.

Try this method the next time you want to try something new. Invest in an eyeshadow brush applicator. Cover your lid completely with a white or very light shadow, extending it above the lid, covering the area to your eyebrow. Next apply whatever color you have chosen, such as an aqua shade. Apply this only to cover the lid area. Then, with a small brush or cotton ball, lightly brush the aqua onto the area above the lid. This hints at the stronger color, but tends to soften and blend.

Next apply a light brown tone over the aqua on the lid and proceed as before with the brush or cotton ball, extending it to the area above the lid. By going over the bright color with a brown or beige tone, you create a more subtle color effect. Nighttime eye makeup can and should be dramatic. Bold colors can be used to good advantage in the evening when you are generally in artificial lighting. You can also consider using an iridescent shadow to create a shiny or sparkling effect.

Create your own color schemes for your eyes, but always do them in good taste. Use your common sense knowledge of color. For instance, blue and pink make a lavender; blue and green produce a teal blue or turquoise. When choosing your eye shadow color for the day or evening, consider these things:

1. The color of your eyes.
2. Your skin tone.
3. Your hair color.
4. The color of your clothes.

Follow the Dotted Line

Eyeliners are worn for three reasons: (1) to make the eyes appear larger, (2) to make your eyelashes thicker, and (3) to make your eyes more expressive. If you have not had any experience with eyeliners, take the time to practice. Start with the inner corner of the eye and keep it as close as possible to the lashes. Brown, once again, is probably a better color than black as a liner, especially if you are blond. Black tends to harden features.

Mascara is a "must" for almost everyone: again, not too black and not too much. Overloaded mascara detracts rather than attracts. A wand mascara seems to be the easiest to apply. After the mascara dries, use a clean wand to separate the lashes for a more natural look.

The secret, then, of good-looking makeup is a faithful skin care program, cleanliness, proper diet, and practice at mastering application of makeup. So, men, if you have read all or part of this chapter on makeup, you might appreciate more the time women spend to improve their appearance. Because men do not wear makeup does not mean, however, that they do not have to worry about skin care.

That Was a Close Shave

Facial cleanliness is a vitally important part of a man's daily ritual. Men have a distinct duty that is comparable to making up by women: shaving.

A man who is not clean-shaven looks unclean. A man can be impeccably dressed, conscientious about his hair styling, generally well groomed (including shoes shined to a high luster), but, if he is unshaven, no one notices all the other positive points of his appearance. He still looks unkempt, shabby, and even careless. Some men are most particular about being carefully shaven on work days, but they choose to "give their face a rest" on weekends and not shave. Well, fellas, if women chose not to wear any makeup to "give their face a rest," weekends could be ugly *and* lonely!

Some men have heavier beards than others; they naturally have to shave more often than those with lighter beards. The man who has great whisker growth probably has to resign himself to shaving twice a day to keep that well groomed image.

You can choose from two shaving methods. More than likely, most men use both methods at some time or other, sometimes using them interchangeably, depending on how they feel. The two methods are the electric razor or blade razor. Take great care with either method to prolong the life of the razor. A straight or blade razor should be cleaned and free of whiskers after each use. The blades should be replaced as often as necessary to ensure a safe, more comfortable, and effective shave. Never shave with a dull blade. A dull blade leaves whisker stubble, pulls the whiskers (which tends to hurt), and can cause nicks and cuts.

Make your choice of method after carefully considering some of the following points:

1. Is an electric outlet available?
2. Is water available?
3. If water is available, is it hard or soft?
4. How much time do you have to shave?
5. How tough is your beard?
6. Is your skin type sensitive or tender?
7. Which provides you more comfort?
8. How dense is your beard?
9. Which one produces the more satisfying effect for you?

Naturally the electric razor is the quicker and more convenient way to shave. Even if your bathroom does not have an electric outlet, some razors can still be used because they are battery-operated. They are so convenient that there is no excuse to have a five o'clock shadow even on a weekend fishing trip!

If the electric razor is your choice, you get a better shave if you use some preparation prior to shaving. Liquids, powders, or lotions available on the market help your razor to glide more smoothly over your face and also give a closer shave. These preshave conditioners produce the pleasing end results by softening hairs, loosening oils, and fighting moisture. Not only do you enjoy a comfortable and clean shave, but you help prevent skin irritation.

If you have a "shave and a haircut" at the barber shop, you get the steam towel treatment. Hot, steaming towels are wrapped about the face and allowed to remain for several minutes. This method lubricates by stimulating the oil glands and at the same time softens the beard and skin. The combination of the moisture and heat allows the razor to glide over the skin very easily and gives a close, comfortable shave.

Of course, the steaming towel method takes a great deal of time, which most men do not have. If steam cannot be used, a man should always wash his face with soap and water first, leaving the face moist. Soap or shaving cream should then be used. Shaving soap is more economical than shaving creams in aerosol cans, but the convenience of the aerosol is sometimes worth paying a little more. Whether you decide to use lather or foam be sure that it has a good foam, has easy application, stays moist, and rinses off easily.

The face has many contours, and there is definitely a correct way to hold your safety razor to get the best shave possible. First, *always use a mirror.* Practice holding the razor between the index finger and thumb. You will learn to angle the razor ever so slightly while drawing it forward using a small sawing movement.

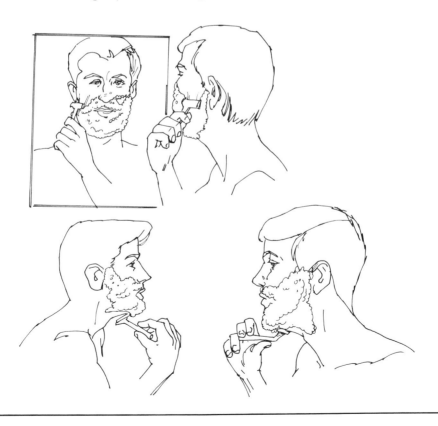

When shaving under the chin, hold your razor in the reverse position. With the razor handle pointing away from your face, hold the top of the handle with the index and middle fingers on top and the thumb on the bottom. You go through many contortions, jutting your chin while working in this area, pulling on your face, stretching, and twisting. All this is done to provide the flattest surface possible to shave clean and smooth.

After your shave, use a good after-shave lotion. This:

1. Produces a pleasing scent.
2. Leaves the skin feeling refreshed.
3. Helps heal small nicks.
4. Helps prevent infection.
5. Helps pores return to normal size.
6. Stimulates circulation in the face.

Let's go over what you have been learning about shaving. Practice the following items to make shaving easier and more comfortable.

1. Always use a sharp blade.
2. Keep the skin and beard moist.
3. Use warm water.
4. Allow the beard to soften after applying shaving cream or soap.
5. Hold your skin taut on the area being shaved.
6. Use a steady, even pressure.
7. Rinse your face well after shaving.
8. Use an after-shave lotion when finished.

Just when you think you are not going to shave for a day or two, reflect on the days of your boyhood when you used to pull up a little stool in the bathroom to watch Dad shave. Remember how you envied him the lather, the actual shave, and the end result of a beautifully shaven face? Now, at long last, you have been given the privilege and the chore of the daily shave.

Your face looks and feels its best if it has a good shave and a smile. The two go hand in hand!

Your face—shaved or powdered, creamed or lathered, roughed or lotioned— deserves care and consideration. You are worth it!

Both men and women must spend considerable time on their faces to look their best at all times. A daily routine of good skin care helps to "Save Face."

Summary Questions

Fill in the blanks:

1. To help maintain a good complexion, eat a _____
   _____.

2. To keep skin looking healthy, get sufficient _____, drink lots of
   _____, and avoid _____.

3. Creams and lotions help keep the skin _____ and supple.

4. Keeping the skin clean keeps _____from enlarging.

5. Small lines around the eyes are commonly known as _____
   _____.

6. Scrubbing the face well is essential, but a thorough _____ is equally
   important.

7. Keeping the skin soft is accomplished by using a _____.

8. The best natural moisturizer is _____.

9. The five different skin types are _____, _____,
   _____, _____, and _____.

10. Enlarged pores filled with oil are commonly referred to as_____.

11. The area across the forehead and around the nose is known as the _____
    _____.

12. A skin specialist is known as a _____.

13. Skin responds to _____, which also helps ease _____.

14. Makeup application should be _____ to give a natural appear-
    ance.

15. Cell energizers speed up the _____ _____ cycle of the
    skin.

16. Cell renewers for both men and women keep skin looking _____.

CHAPTER **6**

Hair Care

Style Awhile

Hair is sometimes referred to as your crowning glory. Al Capp, creator of the L'il Abner cartoon strip, has also called it "Nature's answer to silly putty." It is bleached, colored, cut, and teased. It is pushed, puffed, pomaded, and permanented. It is curled, straightened, frizzed, plaited, up-swept, and pulled back. It is exposed to hot sun, cold rain, sleet, snow, and smog. It is conditioned, softened, smoothed, and sprayed stiff. And, it is expected to shine, bounce, and behave through it all.

Nonsense! Hair is not indestructible. It needs tender loving care and consideration.

Hair is a filament that grows from the skin of a mammal. A filament is a fine thread-like structure or fiber. Hair, therefore, is delicate and easily damaged *because* it is fine, like thread. Unlike thread, however, it cannot be knotted together when it breaks. So before discussing hair styles, let's discuss hair care.

Hair Care

Keep your hair clean. Cleanliness may or may not call for daily shampoos. Oily hair, however, usually calls for frequent shampooing. The test for clean hair is how it looks, feels, and smells. Determine how often your hair should be shampooed and then set a regular schedule for shampooing and hair care—and follow it.

There are three main hair types: oily, dry, and normal. Most hair falls somewhere in between any two of these types, such as normal to dry. Each type of hair has special characteristics and needs special treatment.

Normal

Normal hair needs only to be kept clean and neatly trimmed or styled. Any shampoos for normal hair probably leave your hair shiny and easy to manage. If your hair is very straight or fine, it probably also needs a body wave or permanent to help it look its best at all times.

Dry

This type of hair is characterized by split ends or flying hair. You should use a weekly hot oil shampoo treatment for this. Also, use the shampoos that are recommended for dry hair. Dry hair looks dull and feels brittle to the touch. If your hair is dry from excessive exposure to sun or dry heat, apply a good conditioner after shampooing and leave it on the hair for 25 minutes. Then rinse it out thoroughly to bring back the bounce and shine you want. This treatment should be used about once every week or so to keep your hair in top shape.

Another simple treatment can be done at home, whenever needed. Apply warm, not hot, olive oil to the scalp, using cotton swabs or cotton balls. Part the hair into small sections and work from front to back. Then wrap your hair in an old towel and sleep on it. Shampoo it in the morning and enjoy the shine, bounce, and manageability.

Oily

If your hair is excessively oily, only frequent shampooing is a must to keep it from getting that limp-spaghetti, stringy look, as well as to keep it fresh-smelling. Use a shampoo for oily hair, and lemon or vinegar for a rinse. If you use a cream rinse, be sure to use only a tiny amount and rinse it out well. Cream rinse can build up on the hair strands and increase the stringy look of oily hair.

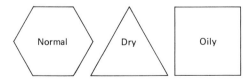

Hair Care in General

Hair care is very simple. Just remember the three "Cs."

1. Clean.
2. Comb.
3. Cut.

    1. *Clean.* Your hair and scalp must be clean. These days, frequent shampooing is more necessary than ever. Some environments increase the necessity of shampooing more than once a week. You live in air-conditioned houses with the windows closed year round. You work in offices with sealed windows and drive in cars or ride in subways, trains, and buses with sealed windows. Smoke, cooking odors, perfumes, sprays, and a thousand other smells of people and daily living settle on the porous cells of your hair and sink in to stay. Smoke, smog, exhaust, and grime assault those cells, when you are outside, and stick to your scalp. Frequent shampooing freshens not only the appearance, but also the aroma of your hair and scalp.

    2. *Comb.* Comb your hair. Brushing does not destroy your hairdo. It makes it more manageable and shinier. It is healthy for the scalp. It strengthens the hair fibers by increasing circulation to the scalp. Whether you brush one hundred, two hundred, three hundred, or a thousand strokes depends on the strength of your arms and the time you have to spend. It really doesn't matter how many strokes. It's the regularity with which you brush that counts.

    3. *Cut.* Last, but not least, is your haircut. Any length of hair is acceptable on both men and women. What is not acceptable is unkempt locks straggling about your face and shoulders like the serpents on Medusa's head. Your hair should have definite shape and form, no matter what length. Your hair should be trimmed and shaped regularly by a professional. A blunt cut is always healthier for your hair, because it leaves just a tiny area of the hair ends exposed. Cutting hair at an angle allows moisture loss and can cause split ends.

    Keeping your hair neatly combed is easy if the stylist has trimmed it to follow the natural shape of your head and your natural part. Every person has an individual head of hair. Cowlicks, waves, and parts follow the direction of the growth of your hair. Following these natural guidelines gives your hair smoother lines and easy manageability, no matter what your hair style.

Dandruff

Dandruff is a white, flaky nuisance that can give a dark suit white polka dot shoulders. It is an embarrassing condition and should never be allowed to get out of hand. It can usually be controlled with vigorous brushing and a regular shampoo schedule with emphasis on getting all the soap residue out. Hot oil shampoos are beneficial, as are some of the special dandruff shampoos. Also, astringents with antiseptic are used very successfully in the treatment of dandruff. Dandruff conditions can be worsened by stress, anxiety, or health problems. Always seek the help of a professional—a barber, beautician, or physician—if the problem is health-related.

Hair Texture

There are three different types of hair texture:

1. *Fine hair*—is sometimes referred to as "baby hair." This type of hair looks best with a medium cut. Too short or too long a cut gives a limp or wilted look. Cut too short, it gives an appearance of being sparse and thin.
2. *Coarse hair*—should perhaps be thinned and worn shorter.
3. *Average hair*—is the ideal for control and manageability.

Making Your Hair Serve Your Appearance

Your hair can be your greatest asset if you take good care of it. You can actually make a slave of your hair—a slave that does your bidding and obeys your wishes if you treat it wisely and kindly.

Look at your face. Is your hair clean and neat? Does it look well-cared-for or just tousled? Does the hair style flatter the shape of your head and face or detract from it?

Hair should always be kept clean and sweet-smelling. Find a hairstyle that is becoming and easily kept. If you are blessed with easily managed hair and do not need to make trips to the beauty shop, so much the better. But if your hair is unmanageable or if you are not particularly adept at handling it, by all means patronize a reputable shop regularly. It's a costly item, but a necessary one in order to look your best.

Hair styling is very important to your overall appearance. The right hair style can do many things for you. A few are listed below:

1. It definitely flatters you.
2. It softens your features.
3. It can cover up some shortcomings, such as too-high a forehead, a cowlick, or an unattractive neckline.
4. It can accentuate and call attention to your better features.

Be individualistic in choosing a hair style. If an afro looks good on someone, it doesn't necessarily follow that it would look good on you too!

Flattering Your Facial Shape

There are many tricks to remember when styling the hair to accentuate your better features or to diminish your weak ones. Imagine each facial shape as a piece of fruit. The round, full face might be a plump grapefruit, the long face a lemon, the heart-shaped face two bananas facing each other, the triangular shape a pear, the diamond a pineapple, the oval shape (which is considered ideal) a perfect delicious apple. Apparently there doesn't seem to be a square-shaped fruit, so envision the fruit bowl as square.

Oval

If you have a long, *oval* face, a side part is more flattering than a center part. The same is true if you have a prominent nose. A hard jawline can be softened by shoulder-length hair curled at the ends; a large forehead can appear shorter by wearing front or side bangs. Since an oval face is considered the perfect shape, try to keep the oval shape evident. For example, do not completely cover the forehead with bangs.

Round

If you have a *round* face, a curly short style is often flattering. Try to avoid shortening the round face anymore than it already is. Avoid a center part and bangs that go across the forehead. A hair style that is built up and about the ears is flattering to the round face. Men should use a side part in lieu of a center part. Sideburns kept at a medium length minimize the round face.

Diamond

A diamond-shaped face has a narrow chin and forehead. It makes good sense, then, to broaden these two features by wearing a bang and not having the hair drastically short.

Oblong

If your face is *oblong,* try for the broadening effect by wearing a bang. Wear an even cut, preferably with no irregular lines. The bangs can be built up to give the impression of a shorter chin. A man should wear his hair full and long at

the sides. Full sideburns are most flattering with this face shape. Blow drying the hair helps to give a long, oblong face more fullness.

Triangular

A face with a *triangular* shape is commonly referred to as "pear-shaped." So your ultimate goal is to give an oval impression. You can achieve this by creating fullness at the top of the head and above the ears. Never plaster the hair close to your head, and the ideal is to not have fullness below the ears. This fullness tends to broaden the jawline.

Square

Square faces are made more flattering by softness around the face. Usually a square face has a shorter forehead; so it is advisable not to wear too much bang. Avoid small, tight curls; they only accentuate the squareness. A low side part helps the square face.

Heart

The widest part of the heart-shaped face is at the forehead, and the chin is narrow. You want to flatter this face with softness and maybe a half-bang to minimize the wide forehead. Keep the fullness of your hair style below your temples.

Individual Criteria

Don't feel you have to follow the crowd and wear your hair exactly like everyone else. Pick a style that is most becoming to you. Some other factors to consider in hair style are:

1. Body
    a. Fine
    b. Coarse
    c. Normal
2. Type
    a. Curly
    b. Wavy
    c. Straight
3. Length
4. Shape of face
5. Life style
6. Color of your hair
7. Amount of time you can or will devote to hair care
8. Amount of money you can afford to spend

Before you choose a hairstyle that is most flattering to you, consider all these points:

1. What is the shape of my face?
2. How does my hair grow?
3. Is the body of my hair fine, coarse, or normal?

4. Is my hair thick or thin?
5. What hair style flatters my age?
6. What does my neckline look like?
7. Is my forehead high or low?
8. What hair style fits my life style?
9. Do I have a long or short neck?
10. What hair style will look best with the color of my hair?
11. For men: Do my ears stick out or lay flat against my head?
12. Where is my natural part?
13. Do I have a cowlick?
14. How is my head contoured? (This is more important for men.)

Don't Brush Off

One of the best friends you and your hair have in common is a good brush. Brushing helps keep your hair dust-free; so it seems logical, then, to keep your brush clean. This should be done on a regular basis and the brush never allowed to become too dirty. A swishing in hot soapy water works on both a brush and a comb. Rinse in hot water—sun drying is great!

When brushing the hair, you can perform double duty if you bend your head forward. In this position, you allow the blood to rush to your head and to the hair roots, thus giving them some extra nourishment. Brush your hair from the scalp to the ends with long continuous strokes. Brush down and out, twisting your wrist with each stroke. If you want double action, use two brushes instead of just one. This allows air to get into your scalp and, of course, brushing makes the hair shiny and healthy.

Brushing is relaxing and, while you are relaxing, you are also lubricating your hair. The right brush is essential. Soft bristles are good for fine hair, and stronger bristles are better for curly or coarse hair. If you can afford natural bristles in a brush, they are ideal, but the synthetic ones are satisfactory. You merely need a more gentle touch using them. If you have a good brush, you do not injure your scalp or hair. Also, a brush should be appropriate for the length of your hair.

Do not rush the brush. Long, continuous strokes are best. Rapid brushing tends to split ends, and it is easy to scrape the scalp. Rapid brushing only gets the hair—not the scalp that is so important for nourishment and stimulation.

Contrary to some beliefs, brushing does not deter the strength of a set or permanent. It does just the reverse, otherwise, a beautician or barber would not use a brush before arranging your hair. Also, some people think that brushing makes the hair oily. This is not true, so brush away—the beauty of your hair depends on it!

The Message of Massage

Massage is important to the health of your hair. Massaging stimulates the scalp and therefore adds to the supple look of youthful hair.

Massage can be done in a circular movement by closing the fingers of both hands. Put them on the nape of the neck and move upward, slowly, until you reach the hairline. To reach the rest of the back of the head, spread the fingers and repeat the circular movement. Use a steady pressure if you do not wish to disturb the appearance of your hair. When you have covered the back of the head, simply move to above the ears and massage toward the crown.

Here is another way to massage. Prop up your feet on pillows and lie on your back across the bed with your head hanging over the bed slightly. Let your fingers crawl up and across your scalp starting at the base of your neck. Be gentle but firm and use circular movements. A massage every day is necessary for very dry hair, but if you suffer from oily hair, massage only before your shampoo. Massaging the scalp twice a week is very important for everyone.

Haircuts

This is definitely the time to seek the knowledge and skill of a professional. Cutting your own hair could be disastrous. If you ruin it, it is a long time growing out. You can take your hair off quickly, but there is no way to restore it quickly. Professionals not only know how to cut and thin hair, they also know what looks best for your shape of head and the contours of the face. If you insist on cutting your own hair, however, do so with great care. Trimming can be done quite successfully if you follow the lines already set by the professional and, above all, use professional *sharp* scissors. Remember, one slip of the scissors can be an irreversible mistake. Proceed with caution.

If you are choosing a new hair style that involves a haircut, remember that what is cut off must grow back. There is a trick you can use to see how you might look in various hair styles. Try on wigs to see if the style you have chosen is flattering and right for your face. This enables you to see how you look before taking the "big cut." Try on several styles in varying lengths. When you have found one or two styles you really like, get some expertise from a professional, a family member, or friend on how they think it looks on you.

Splitting Hairs

There is only one way to eliminate split ends—cut them off! Depending how advanced your split ends are, you may have to trim only a little; for severe splitting, possibly as much as two inches has to go. After you eliminate split ends, always treat your hair gently to prevent further splitting.

Sensational Shampooing

Naturally, a regular shampoo is a must. Cleanliness comes before all else. The trend in young people seems to be daily shampooing. Other hair seems to survive on a weekly shampoo. You will discover what your hair needs by its appearance. Do not allow your hair to get an oily look; on the other hand, a dry scalp and hair should not be washed too frequently. In warm weather, however, if you perspire a great deal, more frequent shampoos may be necessary and are appreciated by your friends and associates.

Specialized shampoos on the market take care of all kinds and textures of hair. Read the labels carefully to see what kind of hair the particular shampoo is best suited for. Then use it according to directions. Shampoos with extra oil make dull hair more shiny; shampoos with oil are for very dry hair. There are medicated shampoos for hair or scalps that suffer a pesky condition, such as scaling, dandruff, psoriasis, or split ends.

If you are going to wash your hair while you bathe, have your shampoo where it can be easily reached. Glass can be hazardous with soapy hands in water, so plastic bottles are a good idea.

Remember in Chapter 4, you read about working up a good lather when you are bathing or showering. The same applies to the hair. First dowse your head with hot water; then apply shampoo and work up a good lather with your hands. Use the same technique referred to earlier with the massage. Your hair should be completely white with the suds for you to know the lathering has been done properly.

The rinsing process is extremely important. Rinse with warm or hot water until your hair literally "squeaks"! This is commonly known as "squeaky clean." Two soapings are necessary for a thorough shampoo and you must rinse until the stream of water is very clear.

A lemon or vinegar rinse can be used if you desire (2 teaspoons to a cup water). They accomplish two things: (1) They cut the soap. (2) The lemon lightens blond hair a little, while vinegar adds lights to darker hair. Cream rinses of all varieties remove tangles, soften the hair, and discourage split ends. After using any solution, rinse well with clear warm water.

To dry, use an absorbent towel by pressing out the hair rather than rubbing. Vigorous rubbing causes strands to break and hair to tangle. Blow drying the hair is an efficient and quick way to dry the hair and, contrary to belief, does not cause a brittle or dry condition. Products are available to spray on before blowing the hair dry to protect your hair from damage.

The proper procedure, then, for a good shampoo is:

1. Brush the hair.
2. Use warm water to thoroughly wet the hair.
3. Rub the shampoo into the hair and scalp.
4. Work up a thick lather.
5. Rinse with warm water.
6. Apply a second shampoo and work up a lather.
7. Rinse the hair until it squeaks.
8. Use a rinse (optional).
9. Towel dry.

A Protective Hair Shield

Some of you already know you only have hair once. When it goes, it is gone! So while you have your hair, take good care of it. Protect it! You protect your teeth, your health, your feet, hands, clothes, eyes; you must also give your hair some protection.

Just normal hair care—that is, shampooing, massaging, and lubricating— is considered protection. Massage, as discussed earlier, improves circulation while exercising and toning the scalp muscles. If the scalp is tight and tense, it is not nutritionally good for your hair. In addition to increasing the blood flow in the scalp's blood vessels, a good massage decreases tension and stress. It also diminishes a headache by stimulating blood flow.

Do you protect your hair against the elements—the hot sun, the extremely cold weather, and swimming? Cover your hair with a cap while swimming. If you sunbathe or are just out-of-doors a great deal, you want to keep your head covered. Even the long cold winter months are hard on hair. The cold, dry air causes the hair to become dry and brittle.

Some of the equipment used on the hair today makes extra lubrication and massage necessary. Blow dryers, back combing, curling irons, hot rollers, tints, and bleaches are wonderful innovations, but extended use of any or all of them is hard on the hair. So protection is the keyword!

Color Me Red

Most people associate the term "DPT" with the shot that small children receive, better known as diphtheria, polio, and tetanus. In the case of hair, however, it could be known as dye, peroxide, or tint. You can color or lighten the hair by a number of methods—with temporary color rinses, more permanent dyes, and hair color removers.

Stay with a color that goes with your skin tone and eyes and that does not make you look brassy or hard-looking. Also consider the most dominant colors in your wardrobe. Unless you are splurging on an entire wardrobe immediately, make certain the new hair color works well with the clothes you are wearing.

If you're covering gray hair, match your natural hair color rather than a darker or lighter color. If you are coloring your hair as a passing fancy, consider trying on a few wigs, rather than going to the expense and time of experimenting to find the best hair color. If you're looking for a drastic hair style change, wigs allow you to test the color on you to see if it is becoming. Consult a barber or beautician; they are highly trained specialists in hair color. You can unbalance nature's plan for you very easily. Yet the time it takes to grow out a ghastly hair color can be agonizing and not good for your disposition.

Permanent or Temporary?

Permanents are, in a way, misnamed. A permanent for the hair is in no way "permanent"—quite the opposite. It is, in truth, only a temporary curl—one of the misnomers of our time!

There are some definite do's and don't's to a good permanent. A "good" permanent is essential, whether it be a salon permanent or a home permanent. A so-called "cheap" permanent turns out to be just the opposite after it ruins your hair. The cheap lotions used in a bad permanent can cause your hair to split, discolor, and dry. If you are going to a shop for a permanent, choose a reputable salon and an operator to match. If you choose a home permanent, *follow directions explicitly*—from application of solution, timing, test curls, rinsing, and winding. No matter which kind of permanent you choose—shop or home— your hair *must* be in good condition to have positive results.

Wigs

Wigs are in—from fun wigs to special occasion elaborate hairdos. There are wiglets, pigtails, pony tails, and page boys. There are braids, curly do's, straight hair, long or short hair, and fuzzy afros. Some cover all the hair and others merely add fullness or accents to your hair style.

No one is forced by fashion or society to accept what nature gave them as "all there is." Men and women are sometimes plagued with the phenomenon called "hair today and gone tomorrow." Men faced with premature balding can choose from numerous styles, colors, and types of hair pieces, full wigs, or toupees. You no longer have to worry that your toupee is ill-fitted, looks strange, or will blow off in a high wind. Our society puts a premium on youth. A man, looking older than his years because of baldness, may forfeit chances for advancement in his career. No one says this is fair or right, but it does happen!

The new full wigs for men can be styled to suit any life style. They can be shampooed at home, pressed almost dry in a towel, hung to dry over night, and combed out for wearing in the morning. There are even sprays available to give more shine and bounce if desired.

If a woman's hair is thin or baby fine and hard to style, she has the choice literally of hundreds of styles and colors. She can always look her best. Women's wigs, too, are available in easy-care "wash and wear" materials.

Modern wigs are not going to smother your scalp because they are con- structed on net-like backgrounds. These allow the scalp and hair underneath to breathe while the wig is worn. If the wig is well-fitted and styled, only you (and your hairdresser) know for sure! If you have to wear a wig or toupee, take some things into consideration. Wigs are like anything else: To get a good one, you must pay for it. Some things you can pay less for and still have look good—but not so in the case of artificial hair. (Haven't you heard the expression said, "That wig came from the five and dime!") Also consult a professional for advice on a proper fit. A hair piece is a major investment—like eyewear. It pays in the long run to have several opinions, perhaps from family members and/or friends.

Be certain that your wig complements your skin tone and is near your natural hair color. After deciding what looks and seems best for you, take care of your new hair piece carefully. It certainly deserves the same tender loving care that real hair receives. It should be kept clean, trimmed, and updated now and then. If you are getting to an age where you might be getting a little grey hair here and there, you might wish to add some grey to your wig. This can be very becoming and natural-looking.

Besides full wigs, there are wiglets, switches, and small toupees.

A *toupee* partially covers the head and, of course, is more comfortable than a full wig. Part of the natural hair should be combed in with the toupee. Most bald men have at least a fringe left around the sides and in the back. This can be incorporated with the toupee to give a natural look.

A *wiglet* is simply attached to the real hair. It has a flat base, and its purpose is to fill out the individual's own hair by blending it in carefully. Experiment and practice blending the wiglet and real hair to produce a natural effect. Sometimes a wiglet is used to add height to an individual's stature. To very fine or sparse hair it gives fullness and thickness. Of course, come as close as possible to the hair's natural color so it is not conspicuous when worn.

A *switch* is used for special effects, such as braids or pony tails. It is a long stem of hair that is used with natural hair. It can be used to give a dramatic evening look creating an elegant up-sweep off the neck.

People often wear wigs for variety and for the creation of a special style. However, many individuals have a loss of hair caused by nerve conditions, medication, medical treatments, or an unusual illness. So wigs, then, are essential for some people's peace of mind and good appearance, as well as a change "for fun" and versatility. If you decide to wear a wig either because it is necessary or because you just want to, remember:

1. Invest in a *good* wig.
2. Match it carefully to your natural hair color.
3. Decide which style flatters you.
4. Keep the wig styled and trimmed.
5. Make sure it is a good fit.
6. Update the style occasionally.
7. Keep it clean.

Sideburns, Mustaches, Beards

Sideburns

Almost all men have sideburns; the length need only be determined by the length of your face. For example, if you have a long face, cut your sideburns a little short. Sideburns should always be trimmed neatly and combed along with the hair. Be certain, of course, that both sideburns are cut evenly so people looking at you do not feel cockeyed. If your sideburns have grown out too far on your cheeks you will need to use your razor—carefully, of course.

Mustaches

Mustaches come in all varieties. You do not have a color choice, but you do have a choice of style. A bushy mustache that covers the upper lip might be attractive, but eating can be bothersome. Nothing is more distracting than a mustache loaded with enough food to carry a family of five through the long cold winter. Mustaches, like sideburns, should be neatly trimmed and combed. A sparse beard growth does not make a mustache attractive; if this is your problem, perhaps you should consider not wearing one at all.

Decide which style is the most becoming for your mouth and lower face contour.

Beards

Your beard is a matter of personal taste and should be neatly trimmed, combed, and kept clean like the hair on your head. When trimming your beard, comb it, and snip small sections until you have it even. To avoid making the beard too short—too fast—take only a little at a time. A beard should not overwhelm your face. It should never give people the impression that you have spent the last twenty-five years herding sheep in a desolate part of the country. Grow your beard in such a way that you call attention to your good features and detract from your weaker ones. Food in the beard is unsightly, so be very cautious when eating.

Summary

You have learned all about hair styles, hair problems, shampooing procedures, conditioners, treatments, brushing, massaging, permanents, hair cuts, baldness, and care of hair utensils. You have learned that you must do some definite things to have well groomed hair. Your hair must be cut or trimmed regularly, and it should be curled or set often enough to maintain style. It must be brushed often and hair care utensils should be washed regularly. Hair must be kept clean at all times, and it should be worn in a style that is becoming to your face and appropriate to the occasion.

There is no good reason, then, for your hair to look "mousy" in its color, texture, sheen, body, or style. Help your hair help you. It can! If your hair is unkempt, your disposition will match. Your hair is extremely important to your overall appearance and your behavior.

The points to remember for healthy, shiny hair are:

1. Being clean, sweet-smelling.
2. Being attractively styled.
3. Being well-brushed.
4. Being adequately rested.
5. Being on a proper diet.

Your hair, in essence, is merely a continuation of your face. If so, then the rules for facial care are certainly adaptable. Keep your hair clean, massaged, and oiled. Condition your hair as carefully as you do your face.

Summary Questions

1. What are the three main hair types?

2. Name the three types of hair texture.

3. A white, flaky substance that gathers on the scalp is known as _____.

4. Name two things that can be accomplished from a good hair styling.

5. Name four different face shapes.

6. Brushing stimulates blood flow to the _____.

7. The scalp is stimulated through _____.

8. A good shampoo includes _____ lathers.

9. _____ is necessary to get the "squeaky clean" results.

10. If you change hair color, it must go with the skin _____.

11. When investing in a wig, a _____ should be consulted.

12. Beards and mustaches should be _____ and _____.

CHAPTER **7**

Posture

Straighten Up

Have your parents ever walked up behind you, grabbed your shoulders, and poked their thumbs halfway through your spine remarking, "Straighten up, you're getting round shouldered"? Or have you ever wished you could walk up behind your parents or someone else and poke your thumb halfway through their spines—for the same reason?

Mentally jab yourself in the spine again and straighten up. One of the most disheartening sights of all time is to see tall persons trying to minimize their height by slumping. It does not shorten them one bit; it just gives them a look of discouragement. No matter how well fitting the clothes, how attractive the face, how fashionable the outfit, how sparkling the teeth, or how flattering the hairstyle, bad posture can ruin the effect. Stomach in, buttocks tucked, shoulders back, and head erect are four good rules to remember.

Another good thing to remember about these four points is that, when they become a habit, they can actually *decrease* the size of the stomach and buttocks. They eventually tighten the muscles in the midsection, thus enhancing your overall stature.

Correct posture, in addition to adding positively to your physical appearance, helps your stamina. Good posture habits keep you from getting fatigued during a regular workday. Besides the short-term physical benefits, correct standing, walking, and sitting contribute generally to good health. By practicing good posture, you allow more room for your organs to function as they were intended.

It also permits more air to enter the diaphragm, thus improving your speaking power.

You do not need to look stiff or uncomfortable when using good posture. You can be quite relaxed and at ease, while standing and sitting correctly. Good posture is a habit to be learned through practice and usage, just as bad posture is a habit to be unlearned (if there is such a word).

Have you ever looked at your back? Is it straight or curved? If possible, look at your feet and legs in the mirror. Are you standing on the outside of your feet or firmly on both soles? Do you tend to plant all your weight on one hip, jutting it out like a carry-along shelf, pointing the opposite foot at a 90-degree angle to your body.

How do you sit in a hard chair, such as at a desk or table? How do you sit in an overstuffed chair or in a car or on a bus? How do you exit from a car? How do you enter a car? And what about stairways? The answers to these questions all reflect how you feel about yourself and how you determine to work toward your own personal development.

Physically, good posture is the nicest thing you can do for your body. It enables you to breathe properly, which is naturally essential to the lung and heart functions. Your spine appreciates the straightness with which you carry yourself, and you will be pleased to have fewer backaches. Pretend it's "be kind to your spine week" and really concentrate on this area. Your shoulders and neck, too, reward you by not aching. Your feet and legs are pleased because you distribute your weight properly, thus making their load much easier to carry. Your chest appears larger, because it just naturally expands. Your stomach no longer has to be called "ol' jelly belly."

As with all habits, good posture must be practiced and used with conscious effort until it becomes as natural as breathing. It encompasses everything you do: sitting, standing, walking, and working. You find that you feel better, as well as look better, when you carry yourself correctly. It is much less tiring and depressing to walk down the street straight and tall than to slump down the street, dragging your feet and hanging your head. Try it the next time you are outside. Walk one block straight and tall, head up and eyes forward. The second block, slump down, round your shoulders and hang your head, watch your feet. Which block was more fun? How did you feel about yourself in the first block? The second block?

Try the next four tests to see how you rate for good posture:

1. *Sit down.* Can you fit both hands, flat, with one hand above the other between the waist and bottom of your chest? If not, you are slouching.

2. *Stand up with your back against the wall.* Your feet should be about three inches from the wall. If you have good posture in this position, your head, shoulders, and buttocks touch the wall and you have only a hand's thickness at the small of your back.

3. *Look at your profile in the mirror.* Drop an imaginary plumb line from the top of your head to your feet. It should bisect you at the shoulder, hip, knee, and ankle bone.

4. *Measure your waist while in your usual stance.* You should be pleasantly surprised with a slimmer measurement, if you pull up your rib cage and measure again. You acquire this muscle control as you practice good sitting, standing, and walking posture habits.

You should be able to look in a mirror and observe your bad posture habits. However, if you have the urge to "cheat" and straighten your back, throw back your shoulders, and tighten your buttocks while you are catching your own image, you will never get a true posture picture. Have someone take your picture with a camera or look back at some previous photos of yourself. You may be astonished at how poorly you stand or sit when all the time you thought of yourself as someone with pretty good posture habits.

Proud as a Peacock

Your posture and carriage present a pretty accurate picture of how you feel about yourself. If you do not want to be noticed, just slump over, duck your head, and let your feet flop where they may. You have accomplished your goal if this is the way you stand. No one notices you, or if they do, it is more than likely for all the wrong reasons.

People slump for a number of reasons. They try to appear shorter, they suffer from fatigue, they may be wearing uncomfortable shoes, they might be discouraged, they lack confidence, or they just prefer to be nonentities. If you are slouching around in this crowd, heed the signals: Start walking as if you are proud, self-assured, vital, and purposeful.

There are some definite benefits to having good posture habits:

1. You look and feel better.
2. You actually speak better, because standing tall permits normal breathing and improves the function of your diaphragm, where your voice originates.
3. Your inner organs have a chance to function properly with the additional room you are allowing them.
4. You will feel and act more self-assured, and you *look* more confident.
5. You diminish aching shoulders, back, and legs to an unbelievable degree.

Like everything in this book, good posture requires practice. You must practice to achieve desired results with makeup techniques. You must practice goal setting. You must practice good management of time. You must practice good manners. You must practice acquiring positive responses. And you must develop a good habit for listening. Likewise, the proper ways of sitting, standing, walking, and holding of your hands must be practiced until they become second nature. You want to attain charm, gracefulness, and fluid body movements. You can master all these things if you are willing to spend some time in the privacy of your own home or apartment, practicing and perfecting your posture.

Use a mirror in helping you to learn and feel at ease with your new rituals of stance, sitting, standing, walking, stooping, and putting your coat on and off.

Walk Tall

Walking tall is a mental as well as a physical position. Be proud of your height, your body, your carriage. Vanity, not pride, comes before a fall. You must have pride in yourself to have self-respect. Pride *is* self-respect. Vanity is self-centeredness.

As for walking, you may not be a poet or a songwriter's inspiration, but you can strive for being "easy on the eyes." Men love to watch women walk— it's just the "nature of the beast." On the other side of the coin, women enjoy watching a man walk. So both sexes seem to need to perfect a pleasing and gliding way of walking.

Watch the way people walk. You see all kinds. Marchers never bend their knees, walking with such determination you can almost hear the beat of "Yankee Doodle Dandy." Ballerinas walk strictly on the toes and the balls of their feet, floating and bouncing up and down to an imaginary "Tiptoe Through The Tulips." Have you listened to the swish, swish of nylons rubbing together as some women walk? Their hips move from side to side. Have you watched the man who turns his toes clear out to the right, throws his head forward, lays his ears back, and gallops to "The Old Gray Mare?"

These examples of people walking, although exaggerated greatly, are still very real and recognizable. At the same time, look for the people you enjoy watching as they walk; observe their walking habits and decide for yourself which kind of walking you want to do.

When walking, graceful and fluid movements are necessary. Do not lead with your head and shoulders as though you were heading into a strong wind. Keep the back straight. The head and shoulders should be directly over the pelvis, and the pelvis should be over the legs and feet. Remember: stomach in, shoulders back, head high. Poise and balance are the core of a smooth, graceful walk. Practice walking in a single, straight line, one foot directly in front of the other, taking steps of a normal length. The exercise is comparable to learning to walk a tight rope. Your direction should be forward at all times, not side to side or up and down.

Do not settle into each step as though walking through deep sand. Your weight should be forward on the balls of the feet as you move forward. Settling hard onto the heels with each step jars your entire body and shoulders, as though you were trying to shake the pictures off the wall. If you must move like an animal, make it a quiet, graceful jungle cat, not an elephant. Your head and shoulders should move with your entire body, not lead, as you walk. When you lean forward from the waist as you walk, you seem to be sniffing out the trail ahead of you.

How fast or slow you walk depends on your personality and the occasion. If you are in a hurry, however, longer steps may help you get there more gracefully

than many short, hurried steps. For everyday walking, look for a gait somewhere between the extremes of strolling and a hurried, harrassed run. Everyone has a natural rhythm of walking that works best for that individual. Determine your natural rhythm of walking; it puts sparkle into your walk and spring into your step.

Practice your walk. You have been walking for years, but you may have just been putting one foot in front of the other. Maybe you have not really been achieving a graceful walk at all. Walking with poise, balance, grace, and fluidity enhances your personal image.

Next, practice coordinating the movement of your hands and arms with your feet and legs. If you completely relax your upper body (do not slouch, just relax), you find that your arms move in a natural rhythm with your feet. As your right foot moves forward, your left arm swings forward. As your left foot moves forward, your right arm follows. This sounds as complicated as rubbing your stomach and patting your head, but it is really only doing "what comes naturally"! Do not swing your arms forward vigorously as though ready to throw a swift uppercut. The swing should be just a low arc, accenting forward movement and helping to balance your natural pace. The arms should not be held stiff and straight but rather allowed to relax. Relaxed, they have a natural slight bend at the elbow. The hands are open, palms usually to the back or slightly toward the body. Fingers are slightly curved, not stiffly open or tightly clenched.

Practice this arm movement with the basic walk. Keep practicing until the movement is natural and relaxed. Stomach in, shoulders back, chin up, and head high . . . and relax.

Correct Stance

When you have arrived at your destination, or even before, you are standing. Standing, too, must be relaxed and graceful with no slumping. You should stand tall and straight, using the basic stance. The basic stance puts a bit more weight on the back foot but keeps the hips aligned. Never place all your weight on one hip, jutting it like nature's answer to a portable TV tray. Not only does this position give you a lopsided look, it tires the back, hips, and legs. If used too often or for extended periods of time, it can cause medical problems with the back muscles and lower spine.

The basic stance is to place one foot slightly ahead of the other, the heel at the instep of the back foot. Place the toe of the front foot at a 45-degree angle to the back foot. The weight rests slightly more on the back leg, but only slightly. Remember to keep the hips aligned and the spine straight. This stance is far less tiring if you must stand for long periods of time. It also is more flattering to the legs. This stance is identical for both male and female. In the masculine stance, place the feet a little farther apart, about shoulder width, but the balance remains the same. Hips are aligned without weight being placed heavily on either side.

Problem Legs

Certain variations of the basic stance disguise less-than-perfect legs. Problem legs are bowed, too heavy, too thin, and knock-kneed.

Be honest with yourself at this point and determine which kind of legs you have. Maybe you do not know for certain how to tell. Perhaps a brief description of each kind of problem can simplify your dilemma. (If your legs are *normal*, your feet, knees, thighs, and calves can all touch each other at the same time.)

Bowed legs. With this problem, your calves do not meet and perhaps the knees do not either.

Heavy legs. You may not be able to tell because they are just too bulky.

Thin legs. The calves probably do not touch, but the knees do.

Knock-kneed legs. In this case, the knees touch and sometimes are considered normal for this reason. However, people with knock-knees usually have too thin or too heavy legs.

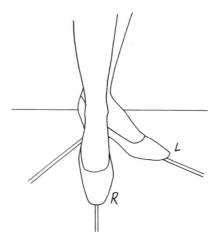

Let's consider each problem individually.

If you have *thin legs*, place your feet in almost the reverse of the basic stance. The back foot is placed at an angle, toe pointed out, heel in. The front foot is pointed straight ahead. The major portion of the weight is on the back leg. This presents a solid picture to the viewer, rather than two thin units.

If your legs are *heavy*, you must create the illusion of one solid line, not two thick lines. Leave a space of two to four inches between the heel of the front foot and the toe of the back foot. The toes of both feet are turned out from the body line about an inch. Place the weight a little more on the back leg.

Bowed legs do not meet at the calf or knees. This may be due either to the bony structure of the legs or to muscle development. In the stance for bowed legs, both knees should be bent. Place the front foot so as to hide the back leg's calf line, by placing it at the heel of the back foot. The front foot is facing straight ahead, the back foot at almost a 90-degree angle. Most of the weight is on the back leg.

Knock-knees are treated like normal legs: put one foot at the instep of the other, the toe at a 45-degree angle. However, check to see if you are standing on the inside of your feet. This can make you look knock-kneed when you are actually not.

When practicing your stance, look in the mirror and see if your:

1. Left foot is at a 45-degree angle.
2. Right foot is pointing straight ahead.
3. Right knee is bent over the left knee and held slightly inward.
4. Left knee is flexed a little.

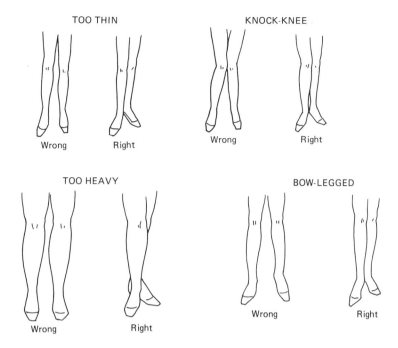

TOO THIN

Wrong   Right

KNOCK-KNEE

Wrong   Right

TOO HEAVY

Wrong   Right

BOW-LEGGED

Wrong   Right

If your stance is correct, you should be pleased with your mirror image. Practice it until it is easy and natural for you. It must become a basic part of your personality, natural and relaxed. Again, remember the basics of stomach in, shoulders back, head held high.

Give Yourself a Hand

Hand positions when you are standing are often awkward. Your arms can hang limply like cooked noodles with no particular life of their own. Your arms should be relaxed, comfortably and naturally positioned for you. Some of the basic positions that put emphasis on grace and coordination are:

- *Masculine:* Arms lightly folded across the front of the body. Be certain, however, that they are not so tightly interlocked that they cause your shoulders to slump forward or make it awkward for you to loosen a hand for gesturing while you talk. In other words, do not look like a cigar store Indian.
- *Feminine:* One arm should be held down at your side, one slightly behind the back. The arm forward is on the same side as the front foot. If the left foot is forward, the left arm should be held lightly at your side, elbow slightly bent,

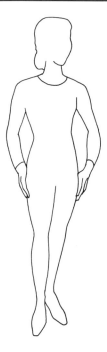

palm just touching the hip. The back arm should be bent, elbow slightly forward, thumb edge resting lightly on the hip.

Again, since you are attempting to present the best possible *you* to all eyes, certain positions for your hands and arms can disguise or hide obvious faults in your figure.

To add weight to *thin hips,* place both hands on the front of your hips, fingers slightly spread, thumbs in back. Bend your wrists slightly backward, and point the fingers in a diagonal line upward. Bring the elbows forward a little.

To make a thicker waistline appear slimmer, place your hands directly on the waistline, thumbs to the front, pointing downward. If, however, you are considerably overweight, do not use this or any arm position that has the elbows bent out from the body in an extreme angle.

People notice your hands because they are there in front of you for all the world to see. Your hands should give the effect that you are inwardly calm at all times—walking, standing, sitting. Even if you are one huge, raw nerve inside, your hands should reflect serenity. They should be held still unless you are gesturing to emphasize a point in your conversation.

Never twist your fingers, locking and unlocking them like a magician's silver rings. Do not clench or unclench your hands. Do not pick at visible or invisible

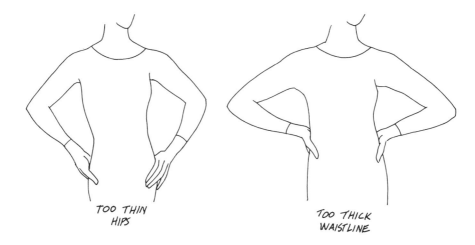

TOO THIN
HIPS

TOO THICK
WAISTLINE

lint on your clothes. Do not twiddle your thumbs. Do not brush at your hair or pick at your face. Do not jingle coins or keys in your pockets.

While sitting, your hands should rest quietly in your lap. When standing, they have several positions from which to choose, and when they find one, they should stay there. Does it sound as though your hands have a mind of their own? Sometimes they almost seem to. Learning to control your hands takes a great deal of will power, perhaps more than any other part of your program. But it improves your outward appearance. Be conscious of your hands at all times. Make them a mirror of your self-control.

Cars, Coats, and Stairs

In a day's time, we do some other things that we do not even think about. But maybe we should give these things a little thought. For example, getting into and out of a car, reaching, going up and down stairs, getting into or out of a coat or sweater. You can plow down the stairs like a horse going to the north forty or knock someone out trying to slip out of your coat. But, with a little sense and a lot of practice, these everyday routine situations can be executed with grace.

Into and Out of a Car

The first rule is not to get into a car head first. Sliding in sideways looks better. Some people are especially entertaining when they are getting out of a car. They struggle for several minutes, trying to emerge gracefully and end up flip-flopping around and finally come plopping out. The new, small compact cars present a

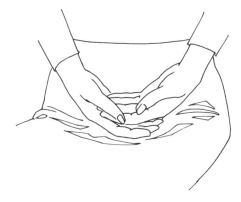

special challenge. So practice while the car is in the garage and you have some privacy.

Step just inside the door with your inside foot first. Bend the knees and keep your back straight. Ease your body in sideways and then swing your other leg into the car. Getting out then should be just as easy if you do this: Slide toward the door, sit forward a little, and put your outside foot on the ground. Use your other foot as leverage and a pusher. Then step out of the car.

Up and Downstairs

You should *feel* for stairs rather than look for them, if possible. Sometimes this is not feasible so you are going to have to look. Try to lower your eyes, not your

head. If you are wearing bifocals, this may not be so easy. But *try!* Keep your head up and your back straight. If you angle your foot, you will be more sure-footed.

In and Out of a Coat

How many times have you thrown your arm or shoulder out of joint and almost strangled yourself just trying to get out of a coat? How many times have you been almost rendered unconscious by someone else flailing coat sleeves around, trying to get into or out of a wrap? It is simple; again, a little practice is wise.

Slip your arm into the right side first and use your left hand to pull the coat over your arm onto your shoulder. Then slide your left arm into your other sleeve. Not so difficult—right? To take it off, shrug the coat off your shoulders and put your arms behind your back until you can grasp the right sleeve with your left hand. *Pull,* do not jerk, your arm up and out. Your left hand is holding the empty right sleeve, so take the ends of both sleeves in your free hand and pull it off.

Sit Up and Take Notice

"Tall" and "rigid" do not mean the same thing. Tall is tall, and rigid is stiff! Sit up tall. When sitting, the small of your back should be against the back of your chair. You may cross your ankles, but never your knees. If you are writing from a sitting position, merely lean forward from your hips. Again, *keep your back straight!* If you remember to keep your back straight at all times, everything else falls into line.

Your feet should be below your body weight. This automatically happens if you remember to keep that back straight. Do not give in to the desire to lead with your buttocks and thighs. Do, however, let the thighs and buttocks carry the load. If you concentrate on keeping the back straight, you will not plop and smash into the chair or sofa.

For ladies, raise your skirt slightly and pull it outward to alleviate wrinkling while you are lowering your body into a sitting position. Men and women wearing trousers should grasp the pant legs just above the knee and give it a gentle tug while sitting. You should not have to arrange your clothing after you are sitting if you take some pains to make the necessary adjustments as you are being seated. Above all, do not fidget after you have taken a sitting position.

You must practice and learn to feel for the chair with the calf of your leg. When the calf is touching the chair, you can be confident it is safe to be seated.

When in a sitting position:

1. Keep your shoe soles on the floor.
2. Do not pull your feet under the chair.
3. Never double cross your legs. That really looks tacky and like your legs should be in a pretzel sack.
4. Keep your knees together.
5. Keep your hands and fingers relaxed and quiet.
6. Keep your feet close together.

Not only do you want to sit properly for your best look, but also for your health. If you have a job that requires a full day of sitting behind a desk, a drafting table, a sewing machine, or if you are a student spending a full school day in session, sitting properly is very important. Your upper and lower legs should form a 90-degree angle at the knees. If your feet are directly under the knees, you achieve this angle. Do not rest your weight on your spine, but rather on your thigh bones. Keep the back straight and stomach in. You will feel more rested, and your shoulders and neck will not hurt if you keep a good sitting posture.

Stooping

If you are going to lift a heavy article, do not use your back. Weight lifters are trained to lift with their thigh muscles, being very cautious never to use the back muscles. Do not bend over from the waist to pick up the object; instead bend your knees and keep your back straight.

You can also injure your back when lifting a light object or merely getting into a bottom desk drawer, reaching down inside a box or crate, or looking into a bottom cupboard. So you must learn *and* practice the proper technique for stooping.

Good posture takes determination and practice, but you and those around you will be extremely pleased with the results. You take on a look of self-confidence and assurance. Others admire your carriage, and you command a new respect.

So, ladies and gentlemen, get gracefully off your derrière, straighten out your legs, pull your stomach in, tuck your buttocks, keep your chest up, and walk as if you are enjoying every minute. Do not forget to breathe and, oh yes, smile. You look great! Let your whole body tell the world you are poised, at ease, confident, and pleased with the way you look. Strive for a graceful walk and fluid movement. You enhance your appearance immediately by consistently using good posture. Practice long and hard until you feel comfortable—sure of yourself—and your reactions are spontaneous and natural. Your attitude about yourself will soar to greater heights than you could have ever imagined.

Summary Questions

1. What are four rules to remember concerning good posture?
   a. _____   c. _____
   b. _____   d. _____

2. What are four reasons that people slump?
   a. _____   c. _____
   b. _____   d. _____

3. Name four benefits of having good posture.
   a. _____   c. _____
   b. _____   d. _____

4. What are four different leg problems?
   a. _____   c. _____
   b. _____   d. _____

5. Name four things you should not do with your hands.
   a. _____   c. _____
   b. _____   d. _____

6. While in a sitting position, what are four things to remember?
   a. _____   c. _____
   b. _____   d. _____

CHAPTER 8

Social Graces

Genteel Is as Genteel Does

Etiquette consists of many things and can be demonstrated in many ways. To get anywhere at all in the business world, school world, or at-home world, you must have etiquette. The dictionary defines "etiquette" as the forms required by good breeding or prescribed by authority in social or official life. Bringing that definition down to plain and simple terms, let's say that *etiquette* is merely being polite. Being polite and considerate should become a number-one habit in your world. Etiquette may be a simple act of kindness or loyalty. It is being thoughtful of another's wishes; it means being courteous and respectful.

Normally children are brought up from a very early age to make proper and courteous responses, such as "please" and "thank you." This is what the dictionary refers to when it states that etiquette is associated with good breeding. Etiquette is certainly nothing you are born with, but rather something acquired and practiced throughout a lifetime.

Politeness and consideration pay off wherever you are. If you were brought up in an environment that fostered respect for others, consideration, and just plain being courteous, you do not have to work as hard at this game of etiquette. If, on the other hand, your environment was one of inconsideration, disrespect, and downright rudeness, your work is cut out for you. Do not put off for another minute learning and practicing respectfulness. Observe those about you in school or at work who seem to be liked and admired and who seem to get ahead. They are *always* polite, having consideration and respect for others.

106

PWEASE?
TANK-YOU!

The Golden Rule—"Do unto others as you would have them do unto you"—certainly goes a long way in telling the story of etiquette. If you show lack of respect or thoughtfulness, and you display rudeness, you most assuredly become the recipient of the same treatment in return.

Of course, genuineness goes hand-in-hand with courtesy. You *must* be sincere with your respect and thoughtfulness. How often have you heard the false tones of a "please" or "thank you" that can literally "turn you off." The way some individuals handle a switchboard with false sweetness, for example, is just enough to make you reconsider calling back again.

Table Manners

You do many things daily that demand good manners. Eating is a prime example of exhibiting good social graces. Rule number one is always to chew with the mouth closed. Noisy eating does as much to turn others away as just about anything. A famous television program once demonstrated the effects of bad eating habits. The program illustrated this by showing several people eating at a counter in a restaurant. Without their knowledge, their chewing and swallowing sounds had been magnified to those around them. The results are deafening and extremely annoying to everyone seated close by. One man in particular shoots a "double whammy," causing various dirty looks to get the "noisy eater" to chew more quietly. Finally, in sheer disgust, he retreats to a far table. This humorous example in its exaggerated form proves that you can turn people away with deplorable table manners.

Table manners should be used at all times—whether at home, at a formal dinner party, in a casual cafe, or even at a picnic. Follow these hard-fast rules concerning table manners, no matter where you are:

1. Never eat in a hasty manner.
2. Never be boisterous or uncouth.
3. Never monopolize the conversation.
4. Never discuss morbid topics.
5. Never be late for mealtime.
6. Never reach in front of another for food.
7. Never fail to "excuse" yourself from the table.
8. *Never forget to compliment the cook.*

Table Setting

An informal table setting includes a fork to the left of the plate, a knife and spoon on the right of the plate with the knife inside toward the plate. The napkin is placed at the left of the fork. A glass sits directly above the knife, and a cup and saucer are placed to the top right of the spoon.

A formal table setting might have two or three forks at the left, and two or three knives and spoons at the right. The knife, fork, or spoon placed farthest from the plate should be used *first*. For example, the fork farthest from the plate on the left is intended for salad, which is served first. Two knives indicate that one is for cutting meat while the other is used for butter. The spoon farthest from the plate is for soup, which is served first. Sometimes a seafood cocktail is served; for this a small cocktail fork is placed to the far right of the soup spoon.

If a salad plate is provided, it is above the forks. A bread and butter plate is above and slightly to the right of the dinner plate.

If, after studying the rules for each utensil, you are still confused, watch the hostess or simply ask someone which one to use.

Remember one rule: Nothing is placed on the table cloth except the things you eat with. Let's say that you have been letting an olive pit lay in your mouth until it is smooth, because it can't go on the table and you don't wish to swallow it. It must go on the side of your plate. You may remove an unwanted object from your mouth and place it on the side of your plate. Do this as inconspicuously as possible. If you drop a piece of food or a pesky pea slips off your plate, the same rule applies; simply lay it on the side of your plate.

If in a restaurant you should discover a fly in your glass of tea or a worm in the fresh broccoli, quietly summon the waiter and send the food back to the kitchen. If something similar happens in a home, do not call attention to it. Your host or hostess would perish from embarrassment. You perhaps could say something like, "The meal is so delicious and I have eaten more than I should. I am too full to eat any more!"

Squelch That Belch

In some cultures, a belch at the end of a meal indicates satisfaction. This is a compliment to the cook that the meal has been most enjoyable. This is, however, a "no-no" in our culture and is considered crude and inconsiderate. A "Thank you, the meal was delicious!" is more appropriate.

General Rules

Food is passed to the right. Foods too hot to be passed should be served by the hostess. In a restaurant, food is served on the left and empty plates are removed from the right.

When eating soup, dip the spoon away from you. Crackers should not be crushed or dunked into soup when dining in a restaurant, but you can enjoy this at home.

When eating bread or rolls in a restaurant, butter only one bite at a time. The exception to the rule is warm bread; then you may butter the entire piece.

Always remove a spoon from a soup bowl, coffee cup, or dessert bowl, placing it on the saucer or plate. Leave unused silverware where it is.

If you must leave the table before the meal is finished, lay your napkin on your chair. A soiled napkin should not be on the table until everyone has finished eating. At the end of the meal replace the napkin, crumpled, at the left of the plate.

Good table manners should be a part of everyday life. If you practice good manners at all times, their use comes naturally to you in formal settings. Table etiquette provides pleasing social relationships.

Where There's Smoke . . .

If you do not smoke or if you are going to quit smoking, you can skim over the next few paragraphs! As for those of you who smoke, the key word is "consideration." Before lighting up a cigarette, pipe, or cigar, be sure to ask those present if it would cause offense. Never light up in a private home without seeking permission first from your host or hostess. If anyone seems to prefer you to refrain from smoking, but is too polite to say so, use good judgment and *do not smoke!* You can always step outside for a few minutes, if you must have a smoke.

Do not smoke on the street, in stores, or on elevators. Not only does this look shabby, it can be extremely dangerous, particularly on an elevator. Smoking in a car or a confined area can be offensive and annoying to a nonsmoker. Rely on your good judgment and consideration, and refrain from smoking in a vehicle. Never smoke in a church.

Nor should you smoke during an interview for a job. You would surely squelch your job opportunity with a prospective employer by "lighting up." Not only could it be offensive to the interviewer, but the curling, swirling, billowing fog can become a distraction as *it* catches the interviewer's attention rather than what you are saying. Another item that can take the interviewer's attention away from you and your qualifications is the building ash on the end of your cigar or cigarette. Will you reach the ashtray in time, or will the ash end up on the new carpet or chair arm? All in all, it makes sense for you not to have to compete with a smoldering leaf of tobacco as well as other applicants.

Never let a cigarette or cigar dangle from the mouth. Do not ever blow smoke through your nose. Those little smoke rings and nose blowing tricks can be reserved for you and your shadow!

Usually the absence of ashtrays means it would be appreciated if you did not smoke. When lighting a cigarette for another person, that person should lean toward your light. Never blow smoke in another person's face. Remember that smoking causes breath odors, as well as odors on clothing, hands, and hair. Give extra care to those areas if you are a smoker. Never speak with a cigar, pipe, or cigarette in your mouth.

Always use only an ashtray or an object provided specifically for ashes or butts. If you are careful to do so, you avoid burns in upholstery, rugs, and clothing. Also avoid flicking ashes; instead, roll the ashes off. If you are in a public building, dispose of your ashes or cigarette butts in the sand boxes provided. Contrary to the belief of some, these boxes are *not* provided for the convenience of the cat population!

Gum chewing, briefly touched upon in another chapter, is undoubtedly better done in private, along with blowing those smoke rings. Chewing gum can be terribly offensive when snapped, crackled, or popped! Perhaps you think you are not guilty of doing any of these things, or maybe you are just totally unaware that you are being noisy. Why take the risk of forgetting yourself momentarily, thus annoying those about you? Chewing gum in any form is unattractive at best; so refrain from chewing at all if you can. However, if you must, never chew more than one stick at a time and always keep your mouth closed while chewing.

Please Excuse Me

Manners apply to almost every situation—every day, every place, every minute. So you must be on your sincerely polite toes constantly. Sometimes a good practice is to heed the old cliches. "It's better to be seen than heard." "Don't speak until spoken to." For example, an individual who must constantly "have the floor"—must be the center of attraction and heard over and above the others—is usually thought of as an egotistical, arrogant, and rude person.

A good listener, on the other hand, is invariably thought of by others as a person who is polite and considerate. Think back on the times you have been around someone who butts in while you are speaking or changes the subject before you are finished speaking. Few things can be more embarrassing or as maddening as these acts of rudeness and inconsideration. Have you ever wanted to add something to a conversation and each time you try to speak, another person drowns you out? After the third or fourth attempt at this without succeeding, you decide to give up.

Etiquette must be applied even at home. Sometimes people forget their manners at home or deem them unnecessary. Are you guilty of this? If you are, it is not too late to shape up. Use your home setting as a practice ground for your thoughtfulness and consideration. The wonderful thing about good manners and thoughtful consideration is that they are almost always contagious.

You must apply all your social graces with everyone, during each day in your work or school environment. A school day goes more smoothly and even more tolerably, if there is mutual consideration between student and teacher, between teacher and teacher, and between student and student.

Certainly an office situation flows more efficiently if there is thoughtfulness for those around you. Consideration must extend to other co-workers, your boss, the public, the postman, and even the inevitable rude individual whose carefully laid-out plan is to ruin the day for you. Rudeness toward you is the real test of your ability to remain calm and at the same time polite. When someone is being exceedingly impolite and inconsiderate, you must call on your reserve to remain polite even though your feathers are ruffled.

While you should remain polite, never let yourself be intimidated or "walked on." You can be firm and continue to be considerate. When you master this art, you have reason to feel very proud of your accomplishment. When that same distraught, rude person leaves your presence feeling better, and even shows

positive signs of being happier, then you can pat yourself on the back for having had a positive influence. When you can continue to say, "I'm sorry you are upset," or "Yes, I understand," when you would rather be saying, "Go home, turkey!" you are becoming a real master at being polite.

First Impressions

Interior decorators refer to the wall that you first see upon entering a room as the "impression wall." A home or business has an impression wall, the first thing seen upon entering. If it is tastefully and pleasantly decorated, it sets the scene for the other rooms. This wall dictates the atmosphere of the setting.

Like the impression wall, the voice that answers the telephone is creating the first impression. It is undoubtedly the key to what people think about your company or school. A pleasant pitch to the voice is essential, as is speaking clearly and courteousness. You can give a feeling of prestige and authority with only a few words on the telephone. The voice answering the telephone builds an image.

On the other hand, an individual who answers the telephone with an overly polite tone of voice filled with insincerity is also disturbing. This kind of voice is commonly referred to as a voice that is "gushy" or "icky sweet." Being sincere is essential; sincerity shows through in voice inflections. A happy medium needs to be established.

For good telephone manners, answer the telephone with a pleasant greeting of your choice and an identification of yourself. If the caller asks to speak to someone else, you may or may not ask who is calling, depending on the policy of your office and the instructions of your superior. Some businesses prefer you not ask for the caller's name if the information is not volunteered. On the other hand, if you are the caller, politely answer the initial greeting by identifying yourself immediately. Make a mental note (or written, if you have trouble remembering) of the caller's name and then *use* it. Everyone is flattered and pleased to be called by his or her name.

Never talk to someone else in the room while you have a caller on the line. The caller immediately becomes agitated and feels his call is no longer important. By the same token, with the situation reversed, do not try to draw the attention of an individual who is talking on the telephone. Complete attention should be given callers—they have the right to your undivided attention. Persons entering the office deserve your undivided attention too, when their time comes.

If you see that you have to delay a call, give the caller the option of waiting on the line or having the call returned. If the caller asks to wait, go back on the line often to show that you have not forgotten him or her. Periodically ask whether the caller wishes to continue holding or have the call returned. Objections sometimes result from being put on "hold" if the call has to be delayed. So do the polite thing and report that the call will be on hold, if there are no objections.

If you have a caller who has been waiting to speak to you, when you are able to answer the telephone, you might say something like, "Thank you for waiting, this is _____," or "I'm sorry you had to wait, may I help you?"

Never talk on the telephone with something in your mouth. This is the height of rudeness. It distorts your speech, and the sounds of chewing and swallowing, magnified, are very annoying to the caller.

Be Ready to Write

Always have something to write with at your disposal. Take notes the whole time the caller is talking to you. A word written here and there allows you to refer to a statement with the necessary recall of the subject matter. If the caller is leaving a message, by all means, take it down word for word. If you must have part of it repeated, *ask!* If a name is left, be sure you know how to spell *and* pronounce it correctly. If you do not know, *ask!* Repeat what has been said before you hang up so that you are absolutely certain you have the message straight. Do not trust your memory for messages. You may think you can remember, but perhaps before you are able to deliver that verbal message, you might have had several other messages and many interruptions.

Your personality shows in your telephone voice. If your personality needs improvement, there is no time like the present to start improving it! In the meantime, practice good voice qualities to improve the image you wish to portray.

Goodbye

When a call has come to an end, always do the polite thing and say, "Goodbye." It is disconcerting and embarrassing to be talking, only to discover that the telephone partner has hung up without saying goodbye. The dial tone does not add much to the thought for the day! Then, the gracious thing to do is to hesitate momentarily after saying goodbye before returning the receiver to its cradle. Have you ever seen someone experiment to see how far away the phone can be thrown and still hit the cradle? This is unkind and unmerciful to the ear on the other end!

Here is a list of some important things to remember about telephone etiquette:

1. Do not interrupt others.
2. Do not let your "good-manner guard" down anywhere.
3. Remain cool and polite when you are confronted with rudeness.
4. Build a positive image on the telephone.
5. Remain unruffled with your voice even though your office might be in a state of chaos at the moment.
6. Have a cordial, sincere tone in your voice.
7. Treat every call as the most important one you have had all day.
8. Take messages accurately and in detail.
9. Never act disinterested in the caller.
10. Always says goodbye when the conversation has ended.

People with common sense and a good feeling about themselves use good manners more naturally. One mark of good manners is the use of the old standbies like "Thank you," "Excuse me," "You're welcome," and "Pardon me." It is also good manners to acknowledge another who has spoken to you in the way of a directive or a question. Acknowledge the person immediately with some sort of courteous response, or even just a nod of the head, or a wink of the eye and a smile. Respond so that the person does not have to repeat the message or to wonder if the message was heard.

I'd Like You to Meet

Have you ever been in a group of people and not been introduced to all of them? The proper thing is to introduce yourself to them with a comment like, "I don't believe we've met." Also, you must have come across someone you have met but whose name you cannot remember. You may, and should, let that person know you have had a temporary memory lapse and the name has escaped you. Asking is certainly better than being miserable until, or if, you figure out who it is.

Why is it so important to make introductions? You may be uncomfortable while being introduced, but in the long run knowing one another puts everyone at ease. A simple introduction might enable you to make further conversation. Sometimes a name is familiar for one reason or another and can possibly open up topics of conversation. At any rate, introductions are necessary, and they should be done properly. A little practice might be needed before you feel at ease with introducing.

There are certain rules to follow in introductions. The name of the person being introduced to a group should be mentioned first. The people in a group should be introduced in the exact order that they are sitting or standing.

When introductions are made involving two people of the same sex, the older person is introduced first, using common sense and discretion. In other words, you would not want to say, "I am introducing you first, because you are obviously the older one here!" Introducing two people of the opposite sex is properly done by introducing the woman first.

It is correct to begin an introduction by saying either, "May I introduce . . ." or "I should like you to meet. . . ." Practice makes introducing easier, and feeling comfortable with introductions is important so as to put all members at ease. If introducing makes you feel uncomfortable, say something about the people, such as "Mr. Smith, I would like you to meet Mrs. Jones. She's a realtor with the XYZ Company. And, Mrs. Jones, this is Mr. Smith. He owns Smith Plumbing and Heating located on West State Street." This gives the people a starting point of information for a conversation.

To put yourself on the receiving end of an introduction, it is polite to answer always, "How do you do?" Only on an extremely informal affair could a simple "hello" or "hi" be used. A good idea to aid in the remembering of the name might be to say, "How do you do, Mr./Mrs./Miss _____." You can also use the first name of the person if the meeting is appropriate to first names.

Sit, Stand, or Shake?

Certain rules of good manners go along with introductions. Men always stand when they are being introduced. Women stay seated unless they are introduced to an elderly woman.

If you are hosting an event, you always stand to greet guests. The handshake is an outward sign of friendship, an expression of warmth and heart-to-heart feelings. A genuine, glad-to-meet-you handshake can immediately put someone at ease. Men always shake hands upon being introduced, and a woman has a choice of whether or not she prefers the handshake. Always respond to a handshake when a hand is extended; it is good manners and can create a cordial atmosphere.

Think of some people you know who seem to have good manners. They are, almost without fail, people with a relaxed personality, and they are gracious in manner and thoughtful of others. They are usually loyal, honest, and cooperative.

You cannot say that mannerly people *always* have these attributes because there are always a few shams or fakes running loose. Some individuals always seem extremely polite, but they can fool you. Some people can "put on a front" of being very mannerly, while in truth they are perhaps ridiculing others—or, worse, using individuals to enhance their position. Sometimes this is evident when an employee is trying to impress an employer, or a student is giving a false impression to a teacher, or a teacher to the administrator. Beware of this kind of person! Such an individual can be destructive and malicious. As already mentioned, sincerity and genuineness are always necessary—good manners being not the least of these.

True Blue

Now explore how etiquette takes the form of loyalty. If you show a genuine interest in the well-being of those around you—if you are truly sensitive to others' welfare—loyalty is a most natural thing. If the boss is exceptionally grouchy and out-of-sorts, try to think, "surely tomorrow will be better." Maybe the boss is not feeling well or has weighty problems to face; the worst thing you can do at a time like this is to discuss the boss's attitude with others. Respect the privacy of the vexed individual, and you might be shown the same kind of respect and loyalty on a day when the situation is reversed.

Correspondingly, always respect the policies and wishes of your company. Learn to handle difficult situations or individuals with diplomacy and tact.

Harmony

Cooperation in a business, school, or office setting is absolutely necessary. Two factions pulling different directions are not only unwise and rude, they can be tragic and obstructive. Helping one another at a particularly busy time, taking

a little extra time to explain something that seems to be a little difficult, or just offering assistance now and then promotes a feeling of goodwill that is essential to a smooth-running operation.

No one likes to be made to feel inadequate or uninformed. So it is only fair to share knowledge that helps everyone. Has a co-worker ever watched you suffer through a situation about which you know nothing and then suddenly pop up and divulge all the missing information, thus making it look very bad for "your side" and very good for the other? Intentionally withholding pertinent information shows a complete lack of cooperation. It is also the height of rudeness, proving nothing and benefiting no one.

Borrow Not

Respect another person's property. Even equipment or materials that are not actually the individual belongings of a person, but are provided for use at work, should be regarded as personal and private property. Keep borrowing to a minimum, and never borrow without first seeking approval. This applies to siblings, roommates, and friends too. Getting into a desk drawer of a co-worker is considered an invasion of privacy and should not be done unless first asking permission. Rearrangement of someone else's desk or books is another no-no. Common sense should win out in most cases; so rely on it. When you have to borrow equipment or supplies, always pay back borrowed articles promptly. If you have had to borrow a typewriter, for example, be certain you leave it exactly as you found it as far as spacing, margins, and tabs. Never leave a typewriter in need of a new ribbon.

Treat all individuals with utmost concern and friendliness: the public you greet, your boss, co-workers, repair people, meter readers, postal workers, custodians, cafeteria workers, and, yes, even those that are difficult to be around. If you need the services of someone, register your request kindly rather than as a demand or order. Equally important, express your gratitude upon completion of the task. Without everyone's working together and cooperating, it can be a miserable situation. Stop and think what a mess you would be in without certain services. When you make a request, be sure that the person complies with your wishes because you have a pleasing manner, not just because he/she has to do it.

Rules of etiquette definitely surround your dealings with superiors or, if you will, your "boss." In the case of the executive, you should always use last names preceded by whatever title applies: Mr., Mrs., Ms., or Miss. Even though you may know one another by first names, use the last name during business hours. You need to put a great deal of value in your boss's judgment. After all, executives do not get where they are without having a great deal of knowledge and skill in the job. Respect and value that judgment that has come as a result of the years of learning and experience.

Make Each Minute Count

Waste neither your time, nor the time of your co-workers and boss. If you do not understand something, for instance, and you have been unable to figure it out, by all means *ask!* Simply ask for instructions; do not apologize for having to do so. Then leave as soon as you understand your instructions.

Always use good judgment about when to ask a question or discuss a problem. If the boss is bogged down and seems to be preoccupied—maybe even a little tense—perhaps asking at a later time would be a good idea. Let your boss be the leader in every respect. Do not assume power or accept responsibility that you really do not have. Your boss sets the routines and patterns to be followed, and these are your guidelines. Also refrain from eating or drinking at your desk; this does not look good to the public or to your fellow workers. In addition to poor appearance, just when you take a bite or a drink, the telephone will ring or someone will ask a question, and you will have to mumble, mutter, and choke your way through the answer.

Some General Rules of Etiquette

1. Always be on time or, better yet, even a few minutes early. But never arrive a few minutes late. Arriving late to work, school, home, or a private function is considered in very poor taste. Punctuality is of extreme importance.
2. Never shout or talk loudly over the telephone. The telephone is an intricate

instrument that amplifies the voice. Don't take away from this marvelous invention. By the same token, speaking too softly into the telephone is just as thoughtless. Talking too rapidly, mumbling, chewing gum, eating, yawning, blowing your nose, or running water while on the telephone are all very rude habits. They are sure ways to keep your telephone from ringing very much!

3. Never interrupt a conversation. Do not keep a running conversation with others in a room while another person is trying to talk on the telephone.

You convey your feelings about other people by the way you treat them. Actually we are all pretty see-through; so it pays to learn and practice thoughtful and considerate gestures toward associates.

Common courtesies are not listed as such, but rather they are unwritten rules. Through your courtesies, you represent your family, your business associates, your schoolmates, your executives or employers, your instructors, your friends, and, most important, *you*. So you must know the common courtesies and obey them just as you would a rule that is written in black and white. Some people are concerned only with smoking privileges, restroom privileges, and how to punch a time clock. This kind of person does not have to worry about the time clock for very long; the job quickly goes to someone else!

So far, simple acts of courtesy—the courtesies that for the most part come naturally—have not been discussed: a gentleman holding a door open for a lady or letting the lady go first through a doorway. A man may precede a woman only when alighting from a bus, train, or plane when there is a chance a lady might stumble; the man might also go first in a crowded room to cut a path for the lady.

Although strained relationships may arise from "women's lib," courtesy is still courtesy. It would be rude for a woman to expect a man to open a door if the man's arms are full of briefcases, boxes, and packages. At the same time, it is no disgrace for a lady to open a door for a man loaded with this kind of paraphernalia.

A lady should always acknowledge an act of chivalry—not just *expect* it! A "thank you," a warm smile, a nod—each shows your appreciation for an open door or an extended hand to help steady you. Most important, remember to show gratitude in some way. Also, another woman can and should hold the door for an older person. Everyone should always glance behind to be sure no one is following before letting a door close.

Interview Courtesies

During an interview, be a good listener. Sure, you are trying to sell yourself. But the part of you to sell is the part that says you are a good listener. You will be given ample opportunity to speak, but one of the most important qualities in a good employee is the ability to listen. This shows your prospective employer four things about you.

1. You are interested in what someone else has to say.
2. It shows you have concern.
3. You are always open to suggestions or new ideas.
4. You are thoughtful and courteous.

Some other points of good manners to observe during an interview are: (These courtesies are presented again at length in the chapter on interviewing. The concept, however, fits very well with social graciousness.)

- Do not ask about salary or vacation periods.
- Do not lean on a desk if you are sitting with one in front of you.
- Do not smoke during an interview.
- Wait until you have been directed to sit down before doing so.
- Use only surnames of your interviewer. Answering "Yes, Sir" or "No, Ma'am" shows a great deal of respect.
- A thank-you note is in order after an interview to let that person know that you appreciated the time and the consideration given you. It is another way of saying "I appreciate your courtesy, and I too am considerate."

To quickly review the social graces, remember that courtesy is consideration, loyalty, and thoughtfulness. It is simply a matter of applying the Golden Rule to each and everyone you meet, wherever you may be.

And now a message from your authors:

1. "*Thank you* for studying this text."
2. "*Please* read on to the next chapter."
3. "*Excuse us* while we write it!"

Summary Questions

Fill in the blanks.

1. Etiquette can be summed up in one word: _____.

2. You must show _____ for others at all times.

3. You should remain _____ when another person is displaying an act of rudeness.

4. If, while eating, you have an unwanted object in your mouth it is permissible to remove it with _____ _____.

5. A pleasant manner used while answering the phone gives a good _____ _____.

6. A voice on the phone should be not only polite, but also _____.

7. It is important to say _____ when a conversation has ended.

8. It is imperative to _____ people who have not met.

9. A man should always _____ when being introduced.

10. A woman has an option of whether or not to _____ _____.

11. Always be _____ toward the feelings of others.

12. For an office situation to flow smoothly, there must be _____ among co-workers.

13. Name four places that smoking should be prohibited: _____, _____, _____, and _____.

14. When setting a table, place the fork on the _____ and the knife and spoon on the _____.

CHAPTER 9

Wardrobe Selection and Care

Costume Caper

Most people are not blessed with great beauty, but beauty is in the eyes of the beholder, it has been said. Single out your best feature—your eyes, cheekbones, or just white teeth—and play it up. Mirrors do not lie; use them to your advantage. Do the very best with what you have been given. Trial and error is a good system, and common sense is your best resource. Be your own most severe critic.

You are not the center of the universe. You are not the sun around which the world revolves. But you *are* the center of your universe. Saying so may sound heretical, but a little selfishness is a good thing. When you know what is best for you in your circumstances, have the courage of your convictions. Do not follow along with the crowd because it is the "in" thing. Fashion is a good example of this. If you know that a certain style does nothing to enhance your appearance, even though the style is all the rage, you are not going to rush out and buy an entire wardrobe in that style, are you? Be selfish. If you feel strongly about something, stick to your convictions. But do use common sense when exercising your selfish right. Deciding you want to wear a beard, long hair, or blue jeans on the job may be a selfish decision, and you may also be looking for another job soon.

Dressing well can actually dictate your personality and attitude at work. If you do not feel good about the way you look, you most certainly do not come across well to associates. Being appropriately dressed for the occasion, for those around, and for yourself is therefore absolutely essential. Dressing well soon becomes a habit and need not take a great deal of time. But the time spent on the care of your appearance is essential and well spent.

Your wardrobe is important. Yet how much money you spend on it is not as important as how wisely you spend those dollars. Your clothing is, again, a matter of common sense. Clothing is extremely expensive, but you do not need to have a lot of clothes, nor do you have to own the very best. Try to buy your clothing when it is on sale. Many catalogs feature wardrobe interchanges; that is, selecting a four-piece outfit that may be used in many different ways. If you stick to basic colors such as greys, browns, navies, and black, you can build more color around them in your accessories—a blouse, scarf, jewelry, tie, shirt, and belt. Pullover sweaters are quite versatile in that they may be worn separately or with a blouse or shirt underneath to completely change their appearance. So mix and match is the name of the game. Learn to blend colors, and use the colors that are most complimentary for you. Fabrics are most important. Get blends of polyester so that you have a minimal amount of care. Because they do not wrinkle, you look fresh throughout the day. This factor saves on cleaning bills, too.

Fashion is ever-changing. Designers do that on purpose to sell more clothes! One year you see flare legs, the next brings tight legs. One year it is calf-high skirts, while the next year is miniskirts. There are short collars, long collars, cowl necks, turtle necks, v-necks, ruffled necks, dolman sleeves, set-in sleeves, full coats, slim and fitted coats, wide neckties, extra narrow ties, bold colors versus pastels, belted jackets, and then loose jackets. How do these add up? They add up to lots of money, if you want to stay looking fashionable. So take a look at being fashionably dressed and at the same time at keeping the cost down to a mild roar. You need not shop at the most expensive stores. Doing so is fun, if you are able, but most people do not fall into this category. One very smart thing (and an almost necessary thing in this age of inflation) is to take advantage of sales. Merchandise is on sale because, for one reason or another, it has failed to sell. Usually the price has been too high to begin with and perhaps its season is coming to a close. The store, wishing to move this merchandise, drops the price considerably. If you spot an article of clothing you would like to purchase but cannot afford, watch for it to go on sale. Of course, you are gambling while you are waiting for the price to come within your range; someone else may buy it. If this happens, you can console yourself with the thought that perhaps you were not supposed to have it in the first place!

Beware the merchant who orders special merchandise (cheaper to begin with) for a so-called sale. Spotting these items is fairly easy. Steer clear; you will not save a thin dime.

How you put your clothes together, how you accessorize your outfit, and how your clothing fits all give the appearance that "you paid a little more." Purchase clothing that can be mixed and matched. Take into account the colors, the textures, the styles in order to best utilize the interchanging process.

There are two schools of thought on price of clothing. Some people prefer very expensive articles, while others would rather spend less and have more variety. Depending on the size of your pocketbook, of course, the choice is yours. Ask yourself these questions before buying any wardrobe item:

1. Does it look like something I wear?
2. Does it fit well?
3. Will it go with the things I now have?
4. Can I afford it and, if so, am I justified in buying it?

Fashion has gone far beyond the things that used to be considered "no-nos." Some of these things are now definitely accepted. Stripes, for instance, never were mixed with polka dots; now you find both in the same piece of fabric. Men used never to wear a figured or striped tie with a figured or striped shirt; now this is a great look, if done in moderation and with good taste. The secret is in how tastefully the two are mixed and blended. This effect sometimes takes a few trial-and-error practice runs—and perhaps even a little constructive criticism from a friend or family member.

The same goes for color. Navy blue and green, used together, used to be thought of as extremely unattractive. Now they are beautifully worked together. Pink, red, and orange are not thought of as particularly compatible; however, with good taste, they can be used exquisitely as a combination. Again, good taste and common sense are necessary in being attractively dressed.

Colors

Color is an important ingredient in planning a wardrobe. Many color experts now perform color analysis on both men and women. If you have the time, money, and inclination, you will enjoy and benefit from consulting one. These experts have sound advice on what color is best for you. They look for the colors that best complement your skin, eyes, and hair. They emphasize the importance of wearing only the best colors for *you*, thus eliminating the need for a large wardrobe. Not to dwell on color analysis, a wealth of material may be obtained on this subject. Live demonstrations are available, seminars are given, and any number of good books are on the market.

However, this consultation is expensive, and, if you cannot seek this professional advice, a little experimenting sometimes helps. You don't have to do this expensively; try using your color in jewelry, a tie, a blouse or shirt, a scarf, or anything worn close to your face. Yellow, beige, grey, orange, and purple pose some problems as opposed to shades of blue, brown, and green. Some colors look wonderful on someone else and may be your favorites, but they might be unattractive on you. Some colors give the skin a sallow (yellowish) appearance; by all means, avoid these. Bold, bright colors are fun to wear but must be tastefully worn. Pastels are beautiful. Earthtones are exciting to use, and even a monochromatic color (one color) can be very interesting.

You can create a magical look about your appearance if you remember some common sense rules about color.

1. Bright or light colors enlarge body size.
2. Dark colors tend to diminish body size.
3. Big plaids, checks, polka dots, or prints enlarge body size.
4. Small plaids, checks, polka dots, or prints diminish body size.
5. Light tops detract from dark bottoms; this is a good rule to remember if you have large hips.
6. Black reduces figure size; so do browns, navies, dark greens, or smokey greys.
7. White denotes crispness and reflects light; so it is cooler. It tends to make a figure or feet appear larger.
8. Choose colors that go with your skin tone, eye color, and hair.

Much Shoe-Do

The old cliche, "Put your best foot forward," means no scuffed shoes, and a run in your stocking is a veritable sin. No matter how much care and attention go into the makeup, dress, or hair, a run in the hosiery catches the eye before anything else. Certainly the old, tired excuse that you did not have that run when you left home is most often just that—an excuse, and a very feeble one at that! Keep an extra pair of stockings at work because snags are inevitable at times.

A man who has a hole in the heel of his sock looks dowdy—all over—no matter what the rest of his attire tries to portray. So when those socks get thin and you can't darn, throw them away! Men should avoid wearing white socks with dark pants. This gives a very slovenly appearance.

Shoes are a valuable accessory. If they are tempered with good taste, they can give a wardrobe an appealing finish. If, however, shoes are explosive in design and color, they can make a wardrobe look appalling. You surely have heard the comment, "I bought these shoes and then didn't have a thing to wear with them!" So a whole new outfit had to be purchased to wear with them. This is the *wrong* way to go at it. Your wardrobe must come first and your accessories last. If you spot a pair of shoes you think you would like to buy, be sure of four things:

1. You have something to wear with them.
2. They will go with several items.
3. They go with your lifestyle.
4. They fit properly and are comfortable.

Shoes are very expensive—in fact, the most expensive—accessories. If you are buying them for school, get the best ones you can afford, and get a color that is fairly neutral and that goes with most of what you have. Beige, bone, or taupe are all colors that go with just about any color.

Watch the material from which your shoes are constructed. Be sure it is durable, practical, easily cleaned, and, at the same time, attractive.

Always be certain your shoes are clean and polished. Dusty or dull shoes can completely ruin your overall appearance. Keep a polishing rag handy to free shoes of dust, and renew the polish or lustre. Never have rundown heels on your shoes. Besides looking very bad, they are not good for walking. Avoid fad fashions in shoes. Some of the fads are over almost before you finish paying for the shoes. You spend a great deal of needless money on fads. Few people can truly afford this kind of expenditure, nor can it be justified.

You can prolong the life of your shoes if you put a good polish on them to lubricate them before ever wearing them. Always keep the tongue of a shoe straight, and use a shoehorn whenever necessary. If you do not have a shoehorn, use the bowl part of a spoon. This keeps the counters (backs) of the shoes from breaking down. Shoe trees are good for allowing the shoe to maintain a good shape, particularly if a shoe gets wet. Ideally, the tree should be slipped inside the shoe while it is still warm from your body heat. If you are prone to foot and shoe odor, a cottonball soaked in alcohol and rubbed inside the shoe helps this problem.

Nothing is more offensive than foot odor. Keep your socks fresh daily, your feet clean constantly (powdering helps keep them dry), and try alternating shoes every other day, if possible. Also, keep your toenails neatly trimmed and clean. If, after faithfully performing all the necessary foot care routines, you are still plagued with foot odor, perhaps you should consult a podiatrist (foot doctor). In the meantime, do not remove your shoes in the presence of friends!

Purses and Wallets

Handbags perform several functions for you. You want your handbag to blend with your dresses, pantsuits, coats, shoes, and change of season. You also have to decide how much you want your handbag to hold, how large a bag you should carry in proportion to your size, whether you prefer a shoulder strap, clutch bag, or regular carrying handles.

A neutral-colored bag is best, of course, if you are limiting yourself to one or two bags. Remember that the bone, beige, and taupe colors are the most practical. Leather, naturally, is very durable—also very expensive. Canvas bags, when popular, are cheap and washable. Handbags should harmonize with shoes, but they do not necessarily have to match. The harmonizing should be carried out through fabric and texture, as well as color. Larger people should carry a very large handbag and *never* with very short skirts. An evening bag need not be very large at all—just large enough to carry the barest essentials.

Men have a large selection of the kind of billfolds to choose from. They must consider what size billfold fits the pocket without stretching it. Some billfolds, a bit wider than the conventional size, are designed to be carried in the breastcoat pocket. There are trifold billfolds, as well as billfolds with zippers, snaps, or button closures. The one that seems to be most popular is the fold-over type. A leather billfold wears the longest without a doubt in comparison to any of the other fabrics, and it pays in the long run to select a very durable billfold covering, since they are used constantly.

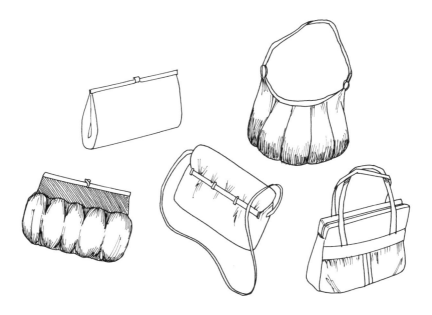

Sharp Scarves

A scarf, if not overdone and tied well, can complement an outfit. Some people do well with scarves; others do not. Know your limitations. If you fall into the latter group, perhaps you should consider wearing some other kind of accessory.

Scarves may be worn in a variety of ways. Probably the easiest way is around the neck of a suit, blouse, shirt, or dress looped inside the lapel and used to cover the buttons. Either a string of pearls or a chain that is not too heavy may be wound around a scarf. A long scarf may be worn around the neck and over the shoulders, with each end tucked into the waistband to give a suspender look. You can loop a scarf to the side, wearing it cowboy-style or tied into a bow and pinned to the neck of a suit or dress. Scarves can be criss-crossed and pinned with a pin or flower. Scarves can be braided (you need three, of course), and used as a belt. Have the right length for however you wish to wear your scarf, and remember to blend and harmonize colors, patterns, and textures.

Bows are popular. The same thing goes that we mentioned about scarves: If you are not handy with a scarf, avoid wearing them; if you cannot tie a pretty bow, admit it! If you fall into this category, try practicing the following five easy steps, and you should be able to tie a perfect bow with a little practice. To tie a pretty bow, you must be able to move the ties from the top underneath, pretty much as a man tying a bow tie.

- Cross the two ties, right over left. Take your left hand and pull the top tie under, then over the bottom tie. The top tie is the right one and the bottom tie is the left tie.
- With the left hand, reach up under the top tie. Pull up the bottom tie to make a loop. Hold it with the thumb and forefinger of your left hand.
- Still holding the loop in your left hand, take the top tie in the right hand and put it around and under the loop you are holding in the left hand.

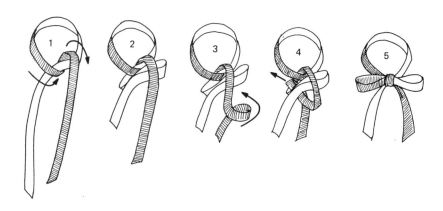

- Pass the top tie behind the loop that you are holding in your left hand.
- Change hands. With your left hand, pull the tie that you have started through the back. Pull the other loop to the right with the right hand. Pull both these loops gently through.

It's a Frame-Up

There are so many kinds of eyewear, and the styles are constantly changing: countless shapes of frames, colors of frames, no frames at all, and tinted lenses. Tinted lenses definitely ease eyestrain, particularly if you work under fluorescent lighting. Have an eyewear professional advise you as to what is best for you. Take into consideration the contours of your face, your eyes themselves, and your coloring. Never let eyewear overwhelm your face. You want to be able to see, and you want others to be able to see *you*—not just your glasses. Take your time when deciding on frames; they are an expensive investment and should be the most flattering frames possible.

Ties

Your tie should always be clean—no tell-tale spots or soil from your workday or lunch. It should never be wrinkled. Most ties hang out smoothly if they are untied and hung up properly when not being worn. A knit tie tends to stretch when hung up; so rolling it is better.

Be sure your tie is tied properly and neatly. Some fabrics tie more easily than others and therefore look better when tied. The windsor knot, basically a large size double knot, seems to be the most widely used. It looks the best when worn with a widespread collar with medium to long points. A windsor does not go well with a narrow, long point type of collar. It can be used with or without a dimple. If you are going to be wearing a shirt with a tab collar, bear in mind that the tie fabric should be a lighter weight and the tie should be slender. A bulky tie results in a bulky knot that is much too large for a tab collar.

To make your tie tying easier, see the diagram on page 129 for instructions for properly tying the windsor knot. The ties in the pictures are depicted as if you were looking in a mirror.

1. With the long or wide end of the tie about twelve inches longer than the short end, cross over as in Figure A.
2. Next bring the wide end around and behind the short end, then up and through the neck loop and around in front of the short end, as in Figure B.

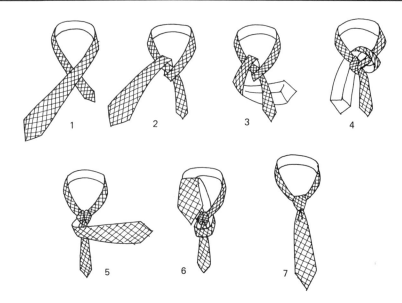

3. Then bring it around back of the knot and cross to the opposite side, as in Figure C.
4. Now bring it up across the front of the knot and through the neck loop, then cross to the opposite side, as in Figure D.
5. Now bring it across the front of the knot, as in Figure E.
6. Next bring it up through the neck loop in back of the knot, as in Figure F.
7. Last step: Put the wide end through the knot and shape, as in Figure G.

The focal point of a man's dress is his tie. Just as vertical stripes tend to lengthen a short figure, in a tie, they lengthen a short, round face. Conversely, a long thin face can be complemented by polka dots or circular patterns. If you are wearing a bold pattern in your suit or shirt, the tie should be plain in color and pattern. You want to create a contrast, not a clash. If you wish to wear a wildly patterned tie, be sure your shirt is plain and your suit's design is moderate.

The pattern of the tie, then, should be coordinated, as well as its color. Bow ties can be worn by young as well as old, but a man with a broad face should probably consider the conventional tie in deference to the bow tie. The bow tie tends to add width to the face. Tie tacks or clips, used by young men as well as by older men, look very fashionable. They are worn low on the tie—not more than 5 to 6 inches from the bottom of the tie. Women, also, can wear a tie tack or clip on a collar, lapel, or turtle neck.

Jewelry

To answer the question, "Am I wearing too much or too little jewelry?" apply this rule of thumb: *Never* overdo your jewelry. If you think you might be wearing too much jewelry, take some off. No jewelry at all is better than too much.

Costume jewelry is greatly a matter of personal taste—yellow gold, white gold, pastels, bronze, torquoise, brilliants, pearls—the choice is endless. You can enhance your appearance, complement your hairdo or flatter your facial features by proper use of jewelry. Earrings can pick up the color of your costume or your eyes, and can give a bright, airy atmosphere or create a romantic design. Pins can be worn in different places for accent—use your imagination! Pins can be worn on a belt, a scarf, a ponytail, a long sleeve, a pocket, a cuff, on the shoulder, or on a ribbon tied around the neck.

Your size should dictate the size jewelry you wear. Large people should wear plain, chunky bracelets, while smaller people should wear more delicate and fragile bands. Dangling or very large bracelets should never be worn to work or to school. Not only are they totally out of place, but their jangle can be very distracting and they can be dangerous around some office machines.

Necklaces come in all lengths, sizes, and colors. A choker should be worn by a person with a long slender neck. A longer necklace with a vertical line will add length to a short neck. Again, large chunky necklaces should be left for the larger individual. Single, unadorned fine chains are popular among young and old, large and small people.

Rings should be proportionate to the size of the hands. A person with long slender fingers looks best wearing a ring with stones set in a horizontal direction.

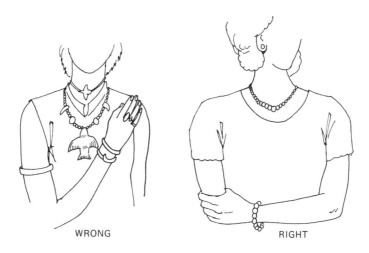

WRONG   RIGHT

This design calls less attention to the extreme length of the fingers. If a person has a short stubby hand, stones set lengthwise are best. This creates an illusion of longer fingers. A high, dome-shaped ring might be worn on a large hand; a round or horizontal setting is best for a long slim hand.

These are some things to avoid when choosing jewelry:

1. Colored "fake" gems that sparkle (except for evening wear).
2. Jewelry that does not coordinate with the color or type of costume you are wearing.
3. Too much jewelry. Wearing no jewelry at all is better than overdoing it.
4. Jewelry that is proportionately incorrect for your size.
5. Lots of jangling bracelets for work or school.

The Basic Wardrobe

Basic clothes are the wisest buys. Basic, in this case, means clothes you can dress down for work or school, and dress up or add to for a more festive occasion or evening wear. A basic wardrobe does not consist of fads, but of clothes that are in style.

Sleeveless apparel, such as jumpers, one-piece jumpsuits, sweaters, or dresses, can often be worn all year, even in extreme climates. The sleeveless look is appropriate and comfortable in hot weather and adding a blouse or sweater underneath the garment makes it suitable for colder days. Choose fabrics that are wearable throughout the year; silk, lightweight wool, or synthetics are good examples.

A basic suit and coat are necessities. The suit can be worn all year if it is a suitable color and fabric. If you have purchased a quality suit, it should wear well for three to five years. A basic coat should be a neutral color such as black, brown, or navy. In regions of climatic extremes, a zip-out lining and detachable hood are good investments. Blazers are very popular and are a good investment also. Buy one you can wear all year, keeping in mind color, texture, fabric and style.

Suits can be mixed if you have purchased compatible and harmonizing colors and textures. Buy a beige suit for a dress occasion and a brown suit for business. Then the beige jacket can be worn with the brown pants and the brown jacket with the beige pants for a more sporty look. The shirt can be worn with or without a tie and a vest or vest sweater can be added for a different look.

Sports jackets are extremely popular and can be mixed with the suit p For example, a tweed, plaid, or checkered jacket of brown, grey and beige e mixes with the brown or beige slacks from the two suits. Sport coats, too, be dressed up or down and worn all year. Never be afraid to experiment with mixing and matching. Use your imagination and courage to derive a great deal more pleasure from your wardrobe.

Fit and Fitting

Clothing sizes can be unpredictable; not all makes or brands are sized the same. You may wear a ten in one garment of a certain brand, but require a different size in a similar garment of a different brand. You may be sufficiently out of proportion to require one size for your top half to accommodate your shoulders and chest and another size for the bottom half of your garment to accommodate hip or thigh size and length of legs. Therefore, you must try on a garment before purchasing it. Sizes can be deceiving.

Your blazer or suit should fit well. A good test is to move your shoulders forward and stretch your arms forward to see if the back spans or the armhole binds. Your jacket must fit properly on your shoulders for it to hang correctly. Collars should hug the neck and should not gape. Shrug your shoulders and see how the collar falls.

The fit of a skirt is very important. Be sure the hem doesn't dip in under the seat. A skirt fits well if it does not strain when you sit down, if it fits over the hips and stomach, and does not wrinkle around the waistline or belt.

The waistline on a suit or dress should match your waistline. If it does not fit properly, it will make your whole body appear out of proportion. Sleeve lengths are important too; the sleeve of a suit should hit the wristbone. A suit coat should be long enough to cover the seat of the trousers. Trousers of proper length should have a slight break over the instep but hang straight in back. Trousers with or without cuffs are in fashion.

Style

Good taste cannot be bought. Some people are born with it, some acquire it, and some go bopping around forever wearing red shoes and a plaid skirt or suit with a flowered blouse or shirt.

How you dress often dictates how you act and gives an impression of wanting to succeed. Long, long ago Adam and Eve decided that we should wear clothing— so dress tastefully and buy the best you can with what you have to spend. Give the impression that you care how you look and that you wish to succeed.

Your clothing should be impeccable—that is, spotlessly clean and well pressed. Even an ultra-expensive garment can look tacky if it is soiled or wrinkled.

Your undergarments should be appropriate for your outer garments. They should not show or cause bulk anywhere.

Your garments should be well fitting and fashionable. Remember that fashionable does not necessarily mean the latest in style. The basic wardrobe should be in good taste and versatile—something you can make fashionable. Take your personality and figure problems as well as your figure assets into consideration when buying a wardrobe. Select carefully to derive the most benefit.

Bulge Battle

Perhaps you are fighting a weight problem. The sooner you decide to help yourself or to seek help, the sooner you will be able to achieve your desired weight. Many different diets, plans, exercises, health clubs, and literature on losing weight are available. Never be too proud or stubborn to ask for help. To stop eating when you are hungry is difficult. Sometimes joining a group where others are also trying hard to lose weight can help. In these groups you learn to lose weight sensibly and to maintain that weight so that you can enjoy a good figure and good health. Find a support group if you need one.

Organize your lifestyle to help you achieve your goal. Plan your activities carefully, sensibly, and continuously. Instead of going to that double feature movie and eating buttered popcorn, join an exercise class. Spend one or two evenings a week toning up your muscles instead of softening your will power. Plan activities that will allow you to spend your leisure time someplace where food is not the center of attraction. Organize your clothes closet so that you will not be discouraged when you have lost only part of that excess weight and suddenly find you have to buy an intermediate wardrobe.

Be sure you do not fall for the fad diets. You need a balanced daily diet to get all the necessary vitamins and nutrients. Organize your meal planning so you will not be so hungry between meals that you must have that double chocolate fudge sundae with nut topping before you faint. Plan your meals to be filling, but not to fill you out. Instead of keeping potato chips and candy bars on hand, buy celery and carrots. Do not simply put the packages of carrots and celery in the refrigerator; cut them into carrot sticks and celery sticks. Keep these in the refrigerator in bowls of water and when you feel like you could eat the porcelain off the refrigerator door, chew on the carrots and celery instead of chips and sundaes. The vegetables will cool your throat and ease the hunger signals. Not only will this help you lose weight, but it is better for your teeth, too.

If you are unable to find an exercise class nearby, or if the price for the local health club is out of reach for you, organize an exercise class for yourself. Among your personal and professional acquaintances you should be able to find at least three or four who are willing to join you in simple exercise. Meet at least once a week and help each other. Here you are using management skills of organization and direction.

Exercise comes in many different forms, not just calisthenics. Dancing is wonderful exercise; swimming, aerobics, weight lifting, running, and walking are other alternatives. Instead of exercising twice a week you could form a bowling team and exercise on Tuesdays and bowl on Thursday evenings. Do whatever fits easily into your lifestyle and life plan.

The operative word is *plan*. Plan it out and then follow that plan. You must control your lifestyle before it controls you. Set up definite controls to ensure that you will achieve that desired weight loss. Plan your leisure time so that it helps, not hinders, your plan. You need not cut all social activities out of your life; rather, you must choose carefully what you really want to do. The choices you make must fit the final objective you have set for yourself. You do not have to be cruel or insensitive to others, but you must be hard on yourself if you are to achieve your goal. You can join your friends at the local pizza house, but limit yourself to a single slice of pizza rather than the whole pie. Educate your thinking about food so that you will know how much you can fit into your diet without ruining your plan. If you find yourself eating too much at certain times, perhaps your plan will need a little correction. If you overeat on occasion, be prepared to exercise harder and longer to compensate for the extra calories. Your motivation is the final objective you have set for yourself.

Get into shape. Feel good about yourself, and it will show in everything you do. It will show in your personality, your grooming habits, your way of dressing, and most of all—your smile. No one is ever well dressed without a smile!

Summary Questions

1. Place a check (√) mark on the blank in front of each item below that must be worn in the office.

   a. _____ Low necklines or mini skirts

   b. _____ Undergarments appropriate for outer garments

   c. _____ Spotlessly clean and well pressed garments

   d. _____ Bold, bright colors

   e. _____ Well fitting clothes

   f. _____ The latest in fashion

2. Place a check (√) mark on the blank in front of each item that you consider when planning and choosing your wardrobe.

    a. _____ Your personality

    b. _____ Fabric and upkeep

    c. _____ Color, line, and style

    d. _____ Your figure problems

    e. _____ Number of garments in wardrobe the item can be worn with

3. Name four factors to watch for in selecting colors.

    a.

    b.

    c.

    d.

4. Be honest and mark with a check (√) mark the column that best describes your habits.

	Always	Sometimes	Never
1. Do you avoid lounging at home in your work clothes?	_____	_____	_____
2. Is your tie neatly knotted?	_____	_____	_____
3. Do you wash undergarments and hosiery after each wearing?	_____	_____	_____
4. Do you avoid wearing white socks with dark pants?	_____	_____	_____
5. Is your clothing free from stains or spots?	_____	_____	_____
6. Do your clothes coordinate attractively?	_____	_____	_____
7. Do you wear a fresh shirt daily?	_____	_____	_____
8. Do you protect clothing from perspiration stains?	_____	_____	_____

	Always	Sometimes	Never
9. Does your tie harmonize with your shirt and suit?	_____	_____	_____
10. Does your outfit coordinate with your hair, eyes, and complexion?	_____	_____	_____
11. Is your suit pressed, and are the pants well creased?	_____	_____	_____
12. Do you check hosiery for runs and snags before wearing?	_____	_____	_____
13. Are your socks long enough to avoid exposing bare skin when you sit?	_____	_____	_____
14. Do you check garments for split seams, ripped hems, or loose buttons before wearing?	_____	_____	_____
15. Do you have nonwashable garments cleaned often?	_____	_____	_____
16. Are your socks smooth and free from wrinkles at the ankles?	_____	_____	_____
17. Do you keep shoes brushed, polished, and in good repair?	_____	_____	_____
18. Do you wear a deodorant or antiperspirant?	_____	_____	_____
19. Do your shoes harmonize with your clothing?	_____	_____	_____
20. Do you carry a clean hand-kerchief?	_____	_____	_____

Let's recap some of the things you have learned in this chapter. Do not over-dress—not even in the evening. Too much of anything is not good and that goes for jewelry, makeup, cologne, and too much skin showing! People have a tendency to behave the way they are dressed. If you find you act *too* casually in pants, for instance, make a concerted effort to be less casual and more profes-sional. Dress tastefully and appropriately for the occasion. Keep within your budget. Choose accessories that are functional and complement your outfit. Take special care of your garments. Pick colors that suit your body and your lifestyle. Treat your body with respect—fat is neither attractive, nor healthy. You owe it to yourself to feel good about your body. Look your best at all times for your professional and personal development.

CHAPTER 10

Image Dressing

Dress to Impress

Whenever people meet, or observe one another as they pass on the street, they make judgments about each other based on appearance. The fairness of making judgments based on such flimsy evidence as clothing alone, can be debated from now until doomsday. The fact is, snap judgments are made. Because they are made, you must give some thought to them.

You may be an exception. You may not judge appearances as quickly as most people do. Then again, you may. In order to realize how easily the mind makes rash decisions based on appearance, try the following exercise. The example in this activity is extreme, but it is intended to start you thinking about and discussing the appearance factor.

The situation is this: You are standing on a street corner when five people walk down the sidewalk toward you. They are attired as follows:

1. The first person is wearing a T-shirt, jeans, boots, and a hard hat.
2. The second individual is in a business suit.
3. The third is in a police uniform.
4. The fourth individual is wearing a sweater and slacks.
5. The fifth and final pedestrian is dressed in an army uniform.

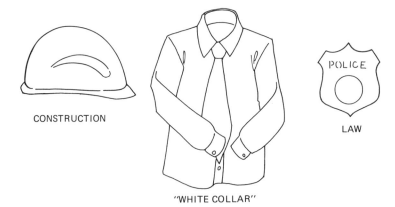

CONSTRUCTION

"WHITE COLLAR"

LAW

Keeping in mind that you were presented an exercise with catches, carefully examine your first thoughts concerning these five people.
What pictures or images do you get?
What is the occupation of each?

1. _____
2. _____
3. _____
4. _____
5. _____

Rank these people according to how readily you would trust them. Give the one you would trust most a "1" and the one you would trust least a "5."

1. _____
2. _____
3. _____
4. _____
5. _____

Rank them again according to who makes the most money and who the least.

1. _____
2. _____
3. _____
4. _____
5. _____

Rank them again according to who has the most education and who has the least.

1. _____
2. _____
3. _____
4. _____
5. _____

As you drew your mental picture of these people, it was probably obvious from the information you had that the person in the police uniform was a policeman. The individual in the army uniform was in the armed services. The wearer of the T-shirt, jeans, boots, and hard hat was a construction worker. The person wearing the business suit probably worked behind a desk somewhere, and the person wearing the sweater and slacks was possibly a student or someone out for a casual afternoon of shopping. The point is that clothing does conjure up a preprogrammed image in your mind.

Prepare yourself for a surprise. Just before these people were paraded by your imagination, they exchanged clothing. The person owning the police uniform had exchanged for the jeans, T-shirt, boots, and hard hat, and so on. Then consider this final twist: All of these people were women!

Do you feel cheated? Do you feel you were not given enough information at the outset to accurately deal with the situation and the questions? You should! You were tricked, but this was merely a tool to enable you to realize how often you and others make appraisals based on little more information than you had here.

Did you find that your mind jumped to the unwarranted conclusion that all of the people were men? If you did, don't worry. Most people think that way.

You can't easily change the way people think, but you can understand how they think and use this knowledge to control what they think about you. Now take away the element of surprise that these people were all women. Take away the possibility that they exchanged outfits and start over. Each individual is now a woman; each individual has on her rightful attire. Would you change any of your answers? Probably not.

Packaging

Most people agree that you can't judge a book by its cover. What's inside is what's important. The same thing is true of people. The true character of a person cannot be judged by superficial observation.

While these statements are true, it is also true that designing book covers is a big business, because the book cover makes the first impression. Similarly, a person's first impression is made through visual contact.

A good looking, appropriately dressed individual might turn out to be a creep, while someone who appears sleazy might be the most loyal, sincere, brilliant, interesting, and entertaining person you could meet. Nearly everyone recognizes the truth in these kinds of statements. So why spend your time and effort coping with several chapters devoted to the proposition that you must look good to be successful? The answer is simple. Looking successful, by itself, will not *make* you successful. However, looking successful will greatly enhance your opportunities to prove what you can do. Your appearance speaks for you first. Use this fact to tell others what you want them to know about you.

To understand this idea, consider four items:

1. A $5,000 diamond ring
2. A $1.00 bag of peanuts
3. A paper sack
4. A beautiful package tied with ribbons

First, put the diamond ring in the paper bag and the peanuts in the attractive package. Which *appears* to be the most desirable? Now, reverse the items, placing the ring in the attractive wrapping and the peanuts in the plain sack. The point becomes obvious that intrinsic worth and attractive appearance should be coupled to get the maximum value from both.

Millions of dollars are spent by American businesses every year to develop packaging to make products more appealing. The object is to compete with all of the similar products that are rivals for the consumer's dollar. The competition is to catch the eye, to make the best first impression on the consumer. Then the task is to maintain that impression through easy identification. The package attracts attention, provides distinctiveness, and influences attitudes.

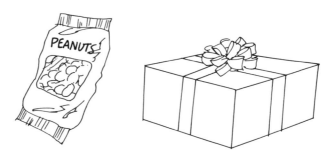

You are trying to sell the one product that is unique to you, the one product that is unlike any other . . . *yourself.* You are selling yourself to an employer for wages. You are selling yourself to the social group whose acceptance you want. Since you are selling yourself, shouldn't you pay close attention to the package you are delivering? Reflect on the diamond ring and the peanuts in the earlier example. If you believe you are a diamond, don't go around packaged like a peanut!

Symbols and Culture

Symbols are any objects in the environment used by the communicator to convey meaning. Symbols can be words, pictures, physical objects, gestures, and more subtle cultural variables. Symbols take on meaning through learned associations with real objects. Shapes, textures, materials, colors, and other dimensions of packaging take on meaning largely in relation to learned associations, deeply rooted in cultural influences.

Color conveys meaning. White, for example, is associated with purity and cleanliness, whereas green is usually associated with the out-of-doors. Red is interpreted as warm, harsh, or exciting. Black carries the connotation of authority and power. The symbolism of colors is often derived from the people who traditionally wear them and the occasions at which the colors predominate. For example, white conjures up the picture of a bride and weddings; red could be associated with firemen and fires; black is most commonly worn by the clergy and by judges.

Shapes also evoke meanings that many people agree on. For example, pyramid shapes are associated with masculinity, strength, and aggression, while round shapes are associated with femininity, softness, and gentleness. Materials have meanings, too. Metal, for instance, is linked to coldness and strength.

Conformity

The matter of knowing how to dress—how to package yourself—can be interpreted as playing the game. Do not think, however, that this is merely a ruse or a phony effort to be what you are not. If you are truly uncomfortable in the clothes you wear, you convey this feeling through body language showing that you feel like a fish out of water! You give all kinds of signals that you are out of your depth. For example, a man whose collar is too tight runs his finger around his collar and stretches his neck and chin in an obvious effort to gain relief. A

woman whose pantyhose are on backwards leaves no doubt as to what is causing her discomfort!

You put on hiking clothes to go hiking. You put on mountain climbing clothes and boots to climb a mountain. You put them on. You get used to them. You make sure they are comfortable, because you know you need the right attire to accomplish the specific task you are preparing for. Climbing the mountain to business success is no different. Wear the uniform, and wear it comfortably. Try to look like you belong to the group you want to be with, or you will end up being with the group you look like you belong to.

Of course you have the right to attire yourself in any way you choose. However, if you want to play football, the first step is to dress like a football player. If you don't, you'll never get a chance to carry the ball. You have to get in the game before you have the opportunity to prove you can score. To score in sports or in business still takes ability, but the proper uniform can get you the opening to display that ability. So if you look like a successful business person, your opportunities to become successful are greatly enhanced.

Dress codes in the business place are not as rigid and obvious as they once were. People have been more vocal about their right to be individuals. Every person has the right to tell the world or the boss, "I am going to be what I want to be, do what I want to do, and dress the way I want to dress." However, the rest of the world or the boss has the same right to answer, "That's OK—just do it somewhere else!"

If you are the kind of individual who wants to express individuality to the exclusion of all consequences, then getting ahead, because it means conforming, is not that important to you anyway. Consequently, you won't be disappointed when you don't get ahead. However, if you are concerned with upward mobility—socially or on the job—clues are all around to assist you. The simplest and most obvious clue is to keep an eye on your superiors at work. They dress in a manner they feel is appropriate for the business. Follow their example because what they

see as appropriate dress for them is no less correct for any other representative of that business.

Actually conformity in appearance is everywhere. You choose the style to which you conform. If you are so naive as to believe you are expressing your individuality when you put on a T-shirt, jeans and sneakers, then look around, because several million other individuals have stolen your individualism. You are not on your own in your three-piece suit, either. Clothing stores throughout the country sell them every day. If you really want to be a nonconformist, try this one: Join the Hell's Angels and wear a three-piece suit to the next meeting, or secure a position as a young executive and then show up for work the first day in cut-offs. Ridiculous? What do you think?

The point is, dress codes *do* exist in the mind—if not on paper. Whether you are talking about the army, the police department, the executive suite, or a beach party; each situation has its own uniform.

The uniform or costume sets the stage. Consider attire coupled with the motion picture industry. People employed in that make-believe industry painstakingly work to make their product believable. Movies set in a specific time in history require special costuming. If you are attending a western, your mind image expects to see ten-gallon hats, boots, guns and other normal trappings typical of cowboys. So what do you get? You get ten-gallon hats, boots, guns and other normal trappings associated with cowboys. You probably do not even consciously notice that things are as they should be. The surroundings are believable and your mind does not have to cope with incongruities of costume that might interfere with your grasp of the story line.

Imagine the character of Moses in *The Ten Commandments* wearing a black leather jacket. Picture the gracious, luxurious plantation living depicted in *Gone With the Wind*, with those Southern ladies and gentlemen attired in loin cloths and grass skirts. Now reverse the clothing of the characters in the *Odd Couple*. Place the character of Oscar, who is depicted as sloppy and disheveled, in a three-piece suit and Felix, the perfectionist, in wrinkled, grease-spotted, torn, and uncoordinated clothing. Not only would your mind be confused by their appearance but their attitudes and lives would be inappropriate to their visual personalities.

Is clothing really so important? If your study of this chapter does not convince you that it is important, ask others. Ask successful business people you trust and respect. Somehow you must begin to realize how easily judgments are made on first impressions, and how much that first impression is based on sight. Perhaps the following exercise will help you to see the importance of the visual contact in making judgments.

Think back to when you were a youngster. Your acquaintances were mostly people you knew through your parents, people they spoke to on the street or in the grocery store. Perhaps your first recollection would be of an uncle or aunt or other relative. Make a list of ten or fifteen of these people. They should be people you do not see often now. Once you have completed the list, think about the people and make notations beside their names of what you remember about them. If you are honest, you will note that you have both positive and negative thoughts about each one. Also, you picture each attired in the way you usually saw them. Other people have these thoughts and mental pictures of *you* filed in their minds, just as you do of them.

Why so much emphasis on clothing? Because it is a powerful force working either for you or against you. Dressed properly, people receive courtesies without asking for them. They get quicker and more lasting attention and more favorable glances from persons of the opposite sex. Colleagues, prospects, clients, and friends listen more closely to what they have to say.

Many individuals suffer more than they realize from poorly chosen clothing, unshined shoes and disheveled hair. Perhaps you have to look like you belong at the top before you get there. Even if you never get there, if you dress properly you always look to others like you belong there. Hopefully you agree that this is not a bad image to have.

What Is Your Image of Yourself?

Find a mirror (full length) and stand in front of it. Take a good, long look. Then sit down and try to separate yourself from the reflection and analyze what you saw. What judgments would you make as you think about the person you saw? What impressions did you get from that reflection? Would you like to socialize with the person you saw in the mirror? What kind of a job would you offer that mirror image? Where was that person going or where was that person coming from, based on the appearance you observed? What kind of person was in the mirror?

Now that you have answered the first set of questions, here are three more for you to tackle:

1. How do you really look to yourself?
2. Did what you saw reflect what you think of yourself?
3. Did it reflect what you want others to think of you?

Do not use the common excuse for not looking your best, "Well, I look as good as or better than anyone else in my group." What should be important is, *"Do I look the best I can?"*

Up to this point, the emphasis has been on the importance of dressing correctly and looking your best if your objective is to make an impression in your business world and social life. If you are convinced of the significance of clothing yourself correctly, you are beginning to ask questions such as, "How do I dress correctly? Where can I get some specific ideas?"

This book provides some pointers, but remember that its purpose is to give you enough information to make you want to learn more on your own. There are several excellent books on the market by people who have thoroughly researched how women and men can clothe themselves to create an exact impression.

For now consider these ideas. Remember that mental conditioning was reflected in the expectation of how the cowboy would appear in a western movie. You may recall also that other dimensions such as color take on meaning in relation to conditioned associations rooted in cultural influences. A clergyman wears black and a nurse wears white, for example. You may even have drawn more conclusions on your own by now. You might have thought that the most powerful image you could create would be with a black, three-piece suit. You would be on the right track.

The best place and time to dress in this manner is when you are invited into the office of the president of a company. You might go there to sell the president something. You might have an idea or suggestion worth presenting. You might have an interview for a job or for a promotion. Why would you wear this powerful outfit? You are on the president's turf facing the power of that office. You need all of the first impression power you can muster to be on nearly equal terms, and to create the impression that you belong.

Regional differences influence the style of dress also. In the eastern United States, more conservative dress is accepted. In the southwest, the same attire may be viewed as too formal. Remember the earlier suggestion that you keep an eye on your superiors. What they consider appropriate is probably appropriate for other employees. Someone in your life who really loves you and really cares, might be your best advisor when it comes to making you look good.

Wise Shopper

Before adding to your wardrobe, thoroughly check what you already have. Research where you are going to shop. Stores have personalities just like people. Ask people whose appearances you admire where they shop. Read newspaper ads closely. Then start shopping. Go into stores and look around. You will not be the first person to tell a salesperson you are just looking. When you go into a store looking for something new to buy, go in looking good. The only way to look better is to start by looking your best.

Salespeople are business people. They have sized up a great many shoppers. You too can play the game. Look at fabric; look at style; look at fit. Do not look at price—at least not at first. Price is important to you, as it is to nearly everyone. No one wants to pay more than is necessary for an item.

Picking out a salesperson to be your ally is as important as picking out the clothing. When you have chosen your salesperson, be honest about your needs, the amount you want to spend, and what you are trying to accomplish through your appearance. This person can keep you informed when new lines of clothing arrive or advise you of special store events, like reduced prices on the clothing that interests you most. Put yourself in the role of the salesperson, rather than the consumer for just a moment. If you, as a salesperson, do your job well and give your best, most honest advice to your customer, you will earn your customer's appreciation and repeated business.

Price is an elusive concept. You may be able to buy more clothes if you pay less for each item. Yet, something that is a bit more expensive will probably last longer and look better, so it might be the better value in the long run.

Never miss a sale at a quality store. Even if you do not have an immediate need, you could pick up some quality merchandise that will cost less now than in six or nine months when you will need it. The best way to save money on clothing is to take care of what you have. Dressing incorrectly in the business world can cost dearly in terms of financial and job security.

When you find a suit you like, grab the sleeve and hold it tight for a minute. Then let it go and see if it goes back into shape. If it does, you know it will hold a press. If it stays creased and wrinkled, you will probably look after a half day of wear as if you slept in it.

Button, button, who's got the button? You do, of course, or at least your outfit may. Even buttons can reflect your taste. They can match or contrast, they can be thick or thin, they can and do hold your pants up. Make sure they are always tight and trim.

Jacket linings should be smooth to avoid tugging or friction when you put on a jacket over a shirt, blouse or sweater.

Earlier you decided a black, three-piece suit was the tops in power, and it is. Another power piece for men is the vest. When wearing a light colored suit to denote a more relaxed or friendly image, remember the vest can supply some of the power sacrificed in color.

Hangers are important. A shaped wooden or plastic hanger is best. Do not use a wire hanger to hang your suit.

Cotton shirts are best. They look cool and rich. The drawback is that they need ironing. Permanent press fabric would seem to be the answer; however, after a few washings, they too, should be touched up with an iron for a crisp, smooth look.

Light, soft colors are best when picking out a shirt. The most standard colors are white, pale blue or pale yellow. Other pale colors work well. Solid colors are more formal than patterned shirts; however, conservative patterns are completely acceptable.

It would be a good idea to have several shirts to go with each suit. Several means at least two, but three would be even better. With several shirts, you avoid the appearance of having only one outfit, and you have plenty of time to launder them.

Neckties also are part of your overall visual communication. Be sure they are delivering the same message as the rest of your outfit. When tied, your necktie should meet the top of your trousers. Keep the color of your tie darker than either the suit or the shirt. How many ties do you need? About two or three per suit—the same as with shirts. Give ties a rest between wearings; they will hold their shape better. When you take off your tie, give it a shake before hanging it up to help get rid of wrinkles. Let your ties breathe and do not wear the same one two days in a row if you can avoid it. Also avoid leaving them tied and slipping them over your head.

Shoes may not make you, but they can break you. Dark brown and black shoes are the most acceptable, as you may have already decided yourself. A dirty shoe is never powerful. It makes you look unfinished. Clean and polish shoes often—before each wearing, if possible. It is a good idea to invest in shoe trees; they help your shoes hold their shape between wearings.

Lately a great deal of emphasis has been placed on color. As was suggested in an earlier chapter on wardrobe, there are experts who can give you a color analysis to determine the colors that look best on you. Pamphlets and many good books are available that even contain fabric samples.

Fashion should not dictate a wardrobe, but it is essential to select clothing that is suitable for your promotion. Yes, it is true that proper clothing will produce an image powerful enough to help you get ahead. Women, for instance, can look feminine and still dress to succeed in business. Pin stripes for both men and women are extremely popular at present. When wearing pin stripes a woman should be cautious not to take on a masculine look. A frilly, feminine blouse can be worn effectively with pin stripes. Most men do not like women to have a masculine look, so the feminine, softer look is the wiser choice and can still command authority, if done properly.

For women, suits are undoubtedly the most effective at giving a look of authority and success. Slacks can be very smart looking, but they will never replace the smart look of a dress, skirt or suit in the business world.

The two best fabrics are wool and linen. However, there are many synthetics that create this same look and if they are done well, they can be as effective as the real thing. It is a well known fact that *real* linen is very hard to keep pressed, so a good imitation is great. The pattern should be either a subdued plaid, a tweed or a solid. A plaid blouse, for example, would be an excellent choice for a solid suit.

Navy blue and black are very practical colors and lend a feeling of power, and gray has been proven to create a sense of efficiency. Women who try to create a sexy look with their wardrobe naturally appear to be less authoritative. The two do not go hand-in-hand in the business world.

Survey and observation have revealed some startling facts about color. We will cite one example to show how strongly color and color combinations dominate the impressions we give. Let's examine the gray suit. A white blouse with the gray produces authority, while a black blouse increases the look of authority so much that you can actually cause offense to some executives. Wearing a gray blouse with the same gray suit, however, destroys the image of authority almost completely. A very feminine color, such as pastel blue or pink, creates a soft look that makes it difficult to give a power image. A pale yellow also will lessen authority, but will be more apt to give the impression of someone who can be trusted and easily liked. Strange as it may seem, color is extremely important in image dressing.

You, and only you, can give others the impression that you would like to better your position. You can do this effectively by the proper choice of wardrobe.

Remember that what you have studied here are merely the basics of how to enhance your appearance. There are many refinements and fine points still to be discovered and considered. For example, while the bulk of this chapter concentrates on business appearance, there is a wealth of information on how to make clothing work for you in a leisure setting. Even in the business context, several items were not even touched on, such as selecting the right wallet, briefcase, jewelry, handkerchiefs, scarves, hats, gloves, belts, and yes, even umbrellas. If you have never considered the total you before, with regard to your appearance, the present is the best time to begin.

Although clothing has been the focal point for this chapter on image, clothing is not the only factor. Your appearance consists of more than clothing.

Do not forget a word of the preceding information that dealt with your health and body. You need soap and water, exercise and diet, manicures and pedicures, and special care for your eyes, your teeth and your hair.

For men, it also means a few more things—like beards and mustaches. Observe what kind of image is created by the skills of movie makers using the beard or mustache. Think long and hard before you let your facial hair grow. No matter how you picture the final stages of the growth of a beard, the simple fact is that at the outset, you are going to look like a bum! Therefore, choose a time when you will be least noticed, such as when you have a two-week vacation. Put the worst behind you while you have the fewest observers.

A beard is a mask of sorts, and is often interpreted as being worn by someone who does not wish to be recognized. For some people, it may detract from your credibility. A mustache is more widely accepted than a beard. In any case, the main thing to remember is that you must keep your beard or mustache trimmed neatly. Treat facial hair the same as scalp hair and shampoo it regularly. Allow more time for the morning toilet, as trimming will become part of your daily chores. Be careful when eating and drinking. Carrying part of your breakfast on your face until lunch can be only disgusting.

If you fear that it will be a struggle for you to pursue the business image you want, because you think it will not feel natural, then consider these few words of advice. Like any other habit, you have to cultivate the habit of wearing suits, ties, and appropriate accessories. All the other trappings become easier with time.

Have you heard others speak of people making the job, or of the job making the person? The same thing is true of clothing. The person wearing the clothing becomes what the image in the mirror projects. People tend to become what they are thinking. The mental pictures you hold will greatly influence your direction and achievement. This idea is applied to your appearance because the image you expose to others is the image others believe you have of yourself. The more often you get feedback about this image from others, the more comfortable you become with it yourself.

Summary Questions

True/False

_____ 1. People are not judged by their appearance.

_____ 2. People cannot be accurately judged for their *true* character by their appearance.

_____ 3. Only expensive clothes look really good.

_____ **4.** Being dressed appropriately for a task allows more personal comfort and greater ease of performing the task.

_____ **5.** White is considered a warm color.

_____ **6.** Red carries a connotation of authority.

_____ **7.** It is not necessary in the business world to conform to styles of dress; instead be individualistic in choosing styles.

_____ **8.** Observation of how the boss dresses will be a helpful clue in your choice of clothing.

_____ **9.** A powerful image can be created with a three-piece black suit.

_____ **10.** Men can increase the power of their appearance with a vest.

CHAPTER 11

Communication

Smoke Signals to Satellites

Communication has progressed from sign language and smoke signals to T.V. signals bounced off satellites. Communication is an integral part of everything that happens to everyone, every day: the study of it approaches an attempt to understand infinity.

As youngsters, you learned communication in the form of language, spelling, punctuation, sentence structure, and the use of nouns, verbs, adjectives, adverbs, and the other parts of speech. Literature, both prose and poetry were part of your studies. Shortly thereafter, you discovered that emphasis and inflection were additional dimensions that could change the meanings of words. By now you know that sounds like a snarl, a yelp, or a scream have meaning. A lifted eyebrow, the shrug of a shoulder, a wink, a sigh, and the swing of a hip all carry messages. Colors convey messages and moods. The ways and means of communicating are unlimited.

Feedback

Feedback is crucial for effective communication. Through feedback people begin to see themselves as others see them. (Remember the "as others see" cartoons in Chapter 1.) Feedback lets you know what others receive as a result of your communication.

KNOWN TO OTHERS	Area I	Area II
UNKNOWN TO OTHERS	Area III	Area IV

The Johari Window is one popular method of helping people visualize the process of giving and receiving feedback. The Johari Window is a model created and developed by two psychologists, Joseph Luft and Harry Ingham. It is used in training supervisors, teachers, and industry trainers to improve communication. The Johari Window is pictured in Fig. 11-1.

Areas one and two of the window deal with things that other people know about you, while areas three and four are things about you that are hidden from others. Areas one and three represent things that you know about yourself, areas two and four are things that even you are not aware of.

Area one, then, is the area representing things that both you and others know about you. In this box are things like: You and others know you are a teacher. You know you like your hamburgers with onions and tomatoes and so do others (particularly those who have to stand close to you!).

Area two contains information that you do not know about yourself, but others do. Things that you rationalize might be included here. You may, for example, believe you are conservative with your money while others perceive you as cheap. You may fail to perform activities that others expect from you. This often happens when you lack self-confidence. For example, others may feel that you have a good singing voice, but you think your voice is poor. As a result, you do not volunteer for the choir, and others are disappointed in you.

The third area is the one that you keep to yourself. You know, for instance, that you are about as tender-hearted as anyone can be, but you don't show that side of you to anyone. You may act as if a baby crying does not bother you, while inside you are just longing to pick up and comfort the little one.

The fourth and last box is what neither you nor others know. Perhaps this is what is meant by the expression that you are playing over your head—perhaps a reserve area shows up only under unusual circumstances. The subconscious or unconscious area has been referred to as the unused potential in each individual.

For quick reference, name the areas as in Fig. 11-2.

```
                        SELF
              KNOWN              UNKNOWN

              Public              Bad Breath
               Self                 Area


              Private
               Self              Potential

```

Now think of the panes as rooms. These rooms have movable walls and any room can expand or contract to accommodate your growth as a communicator and as a person. For example, see Fig. 11-3.

In this configuration you are allowing for better communication. You have allowed feedback to reduce the size of your "bad breath area" by listening to someone who made the effort to inform you that your onion sandwich at lunch lingers like the Amityville Ghost. This area shrinks when you become more open with things that you were too timid to let others know about you. You expand your private self when you trust others, which is easier when they also share their private selves with you.

These walls are in motion constantly as you communicate with different people. As you grow in knowledge and experience, your entire window grows. Different sections grow at different times, depending on the knowledge you acquire. When you are told something in confidence, your private self expands. When you are permitted to share this knowledge, your private self shrinks and your public self expands once again. The Johari Window model is a means for you to better visualize what happens among people in the communications mech-

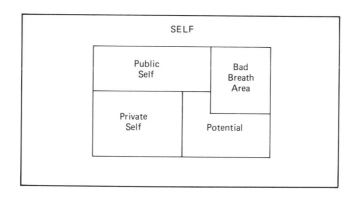

anism. Consider what happens as you communicate, and apply this knowledge to become more considerate and understanding in your communication with others.

Blame It on Communication

A man's wife was slightly hard of hearing. If not spoken to in a slightly louder tone than normal, her immediate response would invariably be, "What?" In order to turn this slight impediment into a communication advantage at dinnertime, the man would, in a slightly softer than normal tone, ask his wife, "Do you want to go out to eat or *what?*" Her reply, naturally, would be . . . "What?" As a result he got a lot of home cooked meals.

Is it any wonder that communication, with all its facets, is a subject that gets so much attention? A *lack* of communication has been cited as the major cause of problems for corporations and other organizations, as well as for interpersonal relationships. Better communications is recommended as a universal remedy. These statements seem to oversimplify a complex problem involving a great many factors, but the simple solution rests with each individual. All of us must learn all we can about communication. Through this learning, we can begin to compensate, adjust and better understand the communication process. The focus should be double-edged. Communicate not only to be understood, but also *not* to be misunderstood.

You know it is necessary to communicate when you decide you want to work for a common goal with someone else. Perhaps you and a friend want to attend a movie together. You have to agree on which movie, when to go to the movie, how to get there and other details. This planning seems automatic and simple, but you must coordinate through communication.

Coordinated effort toward common goals in business as well as in personal relationships is impossible without the communication of thoughts and ideas, attitudes and feelings. Communication is the core of all human activities. All facets of human behavior are involved in one way or another with the sending and receiving of information. All of the other concepts you study—from attitude to interview—involve communication. Therefore, communication is essential to everything you strive to accomplish.

Communication Is More Than Tools

If communication is so vitally important, why is there such a lack of it? The reason is that communicating is taken for granted.

The tools of communication bombarded you from your cradle days; your parents prodded you to speak, "Say Ma-ma and Da-da." You learned much earlier, however, that the right tone or squeal produced food or the toy you had tossed to the floor. So you learned to speak and to write; you studied spelling and punctuation. You gathered these tools and then assumed you could communicate.

Communication itself is as much a concept to be studied as the tools we use. The goal of communication is understanding, total understanding. The message receiver and the message sender must perceive the message in precisely the same way.

Transmitting messages is reasonably simple, once you have mastered the tools of writing and speaking. However, the act of telling often leaves a wide breach between the sender and the receiver. Trouble begins with the basic fact that one human being is trying to transmit a message to another human being.

In communication you are not dealing with words only, you are also dealing with the emotions belonging to both the sender and the receiver of the message. A clear message does not ensure that the receiver of your message agrees with the message content or has the same emotional response as you did when the message originated. Does this sound like "gobbledygook"? It probably does. However, as entertainers have said, "You ain't heard nothing yet."

Good, clear, understandable communication is difficult to achieve. The only human being over whom you have any real control is yourself, and so changes must begin with *you* changing *you*. You must work to be a good communicator.

One- or Two-Way Messages

One question you need to consider is whether you are a one-way or a two-way communicator.

A one-way communicator sends ideas but the receiver has no opportunity to indicate a response or request clarification. One-way communicators look at what needs to be communicated from their own viewpoint only and think that if the ideas are described and if the receiver is *told*, then the job is done. If the communication is interpreted incorrectly or the receiver is not convinced, the sender just cannot understand what went wrong.

A two-way communicator permits a response. The receiver's response allows you to check on how the message was received. Do not settle for finding out *if* the person you are communicating with understands; rather, find out exactly what that person understands. Most people when asked, "Do you understand?" respond, "Yes," simply because they do not want to appear to be slow thinkers or unsure of themselves. If you ask, "What do you understand?" people must give an explanation of what they received by restating what you said. This method is not a perfect solution, but it will be a big help in a great many cases, since you are getting an explanation rather than a one-word answer.

Feedback is what you are aiming for, because you need feedback to know what is going on in the mind of the person with whom you are communicating. You might receive suggestions as you continue the two-way brand of communication. Such suggestions may make the original idea better or provide a faster way to attain your original goal.

Two-way communication recognizes that everyone in the conversation has needs. The basic need is to be part of what is going on and to be involved rather than simply to be told. If two people are arranging how to spend an evening together, it will be a much more enjoyable evening if both give input about where they want to go and what they want to do. If the communication is job-related, you can be sure that the work will be more enjoyable if everyone involved had a change for input. All of us, employees, friends, or lovers, dislike being ordered around. To be a good, effective communicator you must be a two-way communicator or you really have no communication at all.

Effective communication is a fundamental force in the development process. In every kind of business, in every personal relationship, your success with self-development is related to the ease, clarity and appropriateness of your communication. Your development cannot take place without successful communication, because you need to perceive and understand how other people think and feel. You need to be able to communicate with each person you contact. In business, this means subordinates and superiors, and at home, it means spouse, parents, and siblings. In social settings you must communicate with friends, relatives, and acquaintances. The person who continues to make communication mistakes is soon lacking a job and friends. In baseball it is called having two outs—one more and you can head for the showers.

Don't Assume

The practice of making assumptions is human and natural; however, it is as volatile as nitroglycerin. A breakdown of the word in a joking manner is, however, a very accurate explanation of how dangerous assumptions can be. It has been said that, "When you *assume,* you make an *ass* out of *u* and *me.*" What are some dangerous assumptions? Five assumptions that cause many communication problems are:

1. Words have the same meaning for everyone.
2. Body language has the same meaning for everyone.
3. If a difference of opinion is expressed you must force your point of view.
4. Logical explanations should do the job.
5. The only reason for having a discussion is to present your point of view.

In analyzing these five common assumptions, reflect on words and their meanings. Open the dictionary and the first thing you notice is that most words have more than one meaning. Try this little test on yourself and on your friends. Take the word "car," or if you prefer, "automobile." Picture a car in your mind. You will probably picture your car or the car you wish you owned. Everyone else will do exactly the same thing. If you were in a room with 100 people when the group was asked to picture a car, and you could look into each of those 100 minds, you would see 100 different kinds of cars.

Now think about the communication of this situation: The boss walks into the office one morning, and on arrival, it begins to rain. The boss stops at the desk of a relatively new employee and says, "I left the windows rolled down in my car; would you mind running out and rolling them up for me?" "I'll be glad to," answers the employee, heading for the door. The boss leaves for a two-hour meeting. The employee gets to the parking lot, but doesn't know which car belongs to the boss.

Does the employee roll up every window that happens to be down in every car? Does the employee roll up the windows in one car and hope it was the right one? What happens? Any number of things can happen, with any number of results. These will not all be explored here but your imagination can come up with many. One thing happens for certain—the employee is getting very wet trying to decide what to do!

Better communication should have taken place at the outset. The boss should have described the car—the make, the model, the color, and even the license number. The employee should have asked for these details. If the details had been given, the employee should have been asked to repeat them to be sure the message had been received correctly.

Are logical explanations alone sufficient communication? The first question you need to ask yourself is "Whose logic?" or "Whose rationalization?" Don't assume that the facts as you see them are the facts as other people see them.

When you assume that expressions of differences call for you to force your viewpoint, then you tell others that your communication is phoney. All you want is agreement with a predetermined decision. You communicate a lack of respect for others' opinions if they disagree with yours. Resentment and un-cooperative people result. The objective of discussion should be for everyone to listen with open minds to everyone else so that mutual objectives can be reached.

Scared? . . . You Bet!

You can be sure that the people who are presenting this material are as scared as _____. (Fill in the blank with your own word or phrase.) Experts say that as high as seventy percent of all communication efforts are misunderstood, mis-interpreted, rejected, disliked, or distorted. You now have some idea of why we have used repetition and examples for greater clarity. We are attempting to lower the odds of being misunderstood or misinterpreted. The self-tests and questions are our method of getting some feedback from you, rather than simply hoping that you do understand and leaving it at that.

Barriers

Barriers to understanding can be compared to litter that blocks your path to any destination. You can overcome these barriers by recognizing what they are and what they can do to distort the original intent of a communication.

All kinds of understanding are needed in the people business. You must understand the complexity of individuals, other people's moods and feelings, and the words and actions of communication. All these kinds of understanding must take place at once, because each individual brings to the communication process different experiences, attitudes, values, interests, motives, assumptions, emo-tions, preconceived notions, attention span, vocabulary, and inferences. Col-lectively, this conglomeration of components comprises the complex concept of communication. Put this list together and it forms a frame of reference and

determines how a person perceives and interprets all communication. You have this frame of reference and so does the person you communicate with.

Is it any wonder that business people are continually complaining about communication problems? The larger the business, the more widespread the communication problems. Consider the chain of command that requires information to be directed upward and downward through a large corporation.

You may remember playing "telephone." One person thinks of a phrase and whispers it to another person who whispers it to a third person, and so on until the last person in line says the phrase aloud. When spoken, it rarely resembles what the first person said.

Perhaps you have heard the expressions, "Those two people seem to be on the same wavelength," or "The chemistry between those two people is right (wrong)." The wavelength or chemistry referred to are their closely matched frames of reference. Most of the components that make up their frames of reference are the same. Communication is much easier when most components are similar.

To crack a barrier, you must consider and accept the other person's frame of reference and then communicate in those terms. See things through others' eyes to communicate your thoughts.

Emotional States

The emotional state of a person can be another barrier to communication. This example shows how:

Before work in the morning, the boss woke up with a headache, stepped on a marble on the way to the bathroom, found no soap, and went downstairs to find burned toast. One daughter fell down the front steps and broke her ankle, the car would not start, and the spouse backed over the prize rosebush getting out of the driveway. The boss finally arrived at the office, slammed the car door none too gently, and broke a window. Then the secretary resigned—and this was the day you had planned to ask for a raise! The question is: Are you going to have any trouble communicating?

Your Expectations

Does this situation remind you of comedy routines you have seen when a person wants to borrow something but already knows what the answer will be? Suppose Bill is going to ask Bob if he can use his cabin on the lake for the weekend. Bill starts from his office saying to himself, "I know Bob doesn't like to loan anyone his cabin, but maybe this once he will." A few steps later Bill is saying, "Bob has always been known as a tight-wad." A few steps more and Bill thinks, "Bob probably won't loan me the cabin; he has never liked me anyway." Then Bill thinks, "I don't like Bob that well either, and his cabin isn't that great anyway. Who cares if that selfish tight-wad won't loan me his cabin?" He is almost there when he thinks, "I don't want to spend a weekend in that dilapidated old cabin." He finally reaches Bob and says, "Keep your crummy old cabin, you skinflint— who needs it anyway?" Bob's answer is to simply stand in silence—stunned and confused.

Selective Listening

People tend to select what they hear rather than pay attention to everything communicated. Of course they select what is interesting to them.

Semantics

This barrier, described earlier, has to do with the varied meanings of words. Words are only symbols and represent different things to different people.

Technical terms

Almost every line of work has a set of technical words that have meaning to people in the same line of work but mean little or nothing to anyone else.

Wrong Choice of Media

Suppose that your letters to a friend usually discuss only trivia. The letters contain items of the day, a few jokes, and light-hearted subjects. Whenever you have something important to convey, you pick up the telephone and call that friend. Just this once you decide to write about something really important. Your friend becomes confused. You did not call, as you usually do about something important, so your friend might assume that the matter is not important. Therefore, inconsistency of means can confuse communication.

Put this example in an office setting, where suddenly an important message arrives by memo, when prior experiences have conditioned employees to expect important messages to be delivered in a meeting. The result could be a major disruption in performance with many dollars lost.

Overkill

Overkill consists of sending so many messages that no one is paying attention any longer. You've heard the expression, "just talking to hear yourself talk," or the story *The Boy Who Cried Wolf.* The moral is: If you talk or send messages just to be doing it, when you have a really important message, no one will be listening.

This list represents the basic, most common communication barriers. People create these barriers. Because there are so many people creating their own special brands of barriers, and improvising even on those listed, the job of identifying all the possibilities would be an unending task. We hope that, armed with this information, you will create fewer barriers for yourself and be better able to cope with the barriers others create as well.

Final Thoughts

Communication is the essence of human relationships. When people communicate effectively, their lives are more meaningful and satisfying. Relationships with co-workers, children, family, and friends improve.

Communication is more than passing thoughts, ideas, and information. Communication is the means by which people sell, ask permission, give orders, persuade, boast, advocate, love, apologize, question, and more.

Many things happen during any communication because both the transmitter and receiver are including feelings and nonverbal actions in the communication. Both are responding to attitudes and gestures as well as to the spoken or written word. These nonverbal communications include body language, which is discussed in the next chapter.

Dealing with people is difficult. They have many emotions and experiences from birth to the present. All of us have different ideas about the world based on our view of it.

Do you know someone—perhaps yourself—who cannot take criticism or a compliment? Perhaps you know people who think they have no faults or to the other extreme, that they possess no talents. Reasons for these attitudes are behavioral. Positive reinforcement may be required to pave the way for positive communication. The chapter entitled "Transactional Analysis" gives you additional insights into how and why people respond as they do in the communication process.

Armed with this information, you should be able to shoulder the responsibility for being a good communicator. When you run into a bad communicator or a negative communication experience, you should begin to analyze the reasons for the bad communication. Consider what you have done or said which has caused someone else to react negatively. The natural reaction is to blame the other person. Even though the other person *is* to blame, consider what you did to contribute to the situation; then figure out what you could have done differently. Learn from the negative encounter so that you can relate better in your next communication.

The more you know about yourself and others, the easier it will be for you to develop personally—both in your business life and in personal relationships.

Communication can be compared to a huge puzzle with thousands of pieces. The more of those pieces you can fit together, the better communicator you will become. One large important piece has not been given to you yet. It is so important that an entire chapter has been devoted to it. That piece and the chapter are concerned with *listening*. Listening is so natural an act that it hardly seems worth a chapter, but because it *is* such an automatic, taken-for-granted function, listening skills are neglected. You will have the opportunity to explore the importance of listening and developing these skills shortly.

Summary Questions

1. Explain one-way communications.

2. Explain two-way communications.

3. Give examples from your own experience of instances when you were a one-way communicator and instances when you were a two-way communicator.

4. List three assumptions that produce communication gaps.

5. *"Emotional states"* is listed as a communication barrier. Give an example of why and how they can make communication difficult.

6. "Communication is the essence of human relationships." Do you believe this statement? Why or why not? Explain in your own words.

7. Why is feedback so important?

8. Draw the Johari Window. Now draw your personal Johari window as you believe it to be.

9. Name and explain four assumptions that hamper communication. Give an example of each.

10. Why is understanding so important to effective communication?

11. Name, describe, and give an example of three communication barriers.

CHAPTER 12

Body Language

Every Little Movement

What is language? Language is a means of expressing oneself by written, oral, or other means. Language makes it possible for people to communicate with one another—to make suggestions, give directives, and express ideas. Language is capable of conveying love, hatred, fear, horror, sadness, happiness, and depression. Language can get you into trouble or out of trouble; it can make friends or it can break up a friendship. It can entice or discourage a member of the opposite sex.

Language does not consist only of oral and written forms. Body movements can express all the things that other forms of language express—a little more quietly, but just as emphatically. Body movements and facial expressions are means of letting others know how you feel.

Body language is a reflective or nonreflective movement of part or all of the body, that delivers an emotional message to others. As a matter of fact, ninety-three percent of all communication is nonverbal, so you can see that we come across to others primarily through body language.

However, body language and spoken language must go hand-in-hand. One without the other will not give full meaning; they depend upon each other. The study of body language is a new and exciting science called Kinesics.

The human face is the most widely used part of the body in Kinesics. In this science of body language, studies have been made which prove that facial characteristics themselves say a great deal. For example, a fine, narrow nose might indicate sensitivity; full, bushy eyebrows usually denote power and authority. A person who is not out-going often has a small mouth. These statements, of course, are not always true.

Movements of hands, head, feet, shoulders, mouth, eyes, nose, eyebrows, and legs can actually convey complete thoughts. Your body is very versatile. It has so many functions, one of which is that it is a logical place to hang your clothes. It reproduces the human race, which is in itself a miracle, and another talent. This talent is what is commonly known as body language. All people use this form of communication, but are often unaware of its impact on others. One example is the act of folding your arms. Folded arms may be a sign of foreboding, of saying to someone, "I won't let you in." The folded arms position probably would not be a good one to assume when conferencing with the boss. Folded arms can indicate a lack of confidence or self-consciousness. Hands on hips is generally indicative of anger.

Fingers are used a great deal and the manner of their use tells a story. Consider the thumb twiddler. Thumb twiddling usually indicates boredom and inattention. The twiddler is probably thinking that the person speaking should relinquish the floor. This thumb rotation is a rude and unnecessary gesture. Thumb twiddling also indicates nervousness. If you have this habit, try to break it before you give a wrong impression.

Boredom can easily be detected from body language—a stifled yawn, a roll of the eyes, a shrug of the shoulders. No verbal communication is necessary to show that you are bored or disinterested.

A crook of the finger and quick backward movement of the head gives a summoning sign, "Come here," or, "I want to talk to you." Body language can be used alone—without any sound to accompany it, but most people use body and facial movement in conjunction with other forms of language.

Signs of stress are often revealed through body language. Drooping shoulders, for example, can express depression, sadness, or defeat. Another example is a person who pounds a fist on a hard surface, or shoves a fist into the palm of the hand, or uses an open palm to hit the temples at the side of the head.

Eyes Are Communicators

In some cultures, casting the eyes downward is a sign of respect, while in American culture, lack of eye contact can indicate dishonesty or lack of pride. In the United States, eye contact is considered necessary and is a habit to be practiced and polished. Nothing is more favorably impressive than the ability to keep eye contact.

Eyebrows are very expressive, depicting sadness, amazement, anger, puzzlement, worry, or fear. They can express, "I told you so!" Have you ever noticed

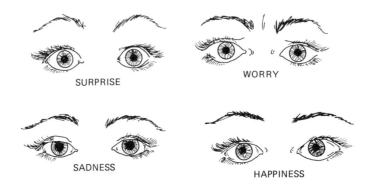

SURPRISE   WORRY

SADNESS   HAPPINESS

people rolling their eyes and lifting one eyebrow at you? Look out—this can mean, "Count me out," or "Boy, you *are* stupid!" Do not *ever* try this one on your boss. Have you seen the gesture that throws the shoulder shrug in with the eye rolling and eyebrow lift—it means, "You drive me nuts!"

Some studies say there are thirty-five different positions of the eyelid. When you combine these with the movements of the eyebrows, the number of different signals you can transmit with your eyes and the skin around them is unlimited. The eyes can show understanding, wonderment, sadness, surprise, fear, sympathy, love, hate, happiness, or anticipation. They can transmit more emotion and thoughts than any other one part of the body. They are a mirror of what is going on inside. In truth, it is the face surrounding the eyes that relays the nonverbal messages. If a person's face was completely bandaged, for instance, with only the eyes showing, those eyes could tell very little. Without the use of surrounding facial muscles, the eyes alone cannot tell the story. The eyelids have a great deal to do with eye messages; they squint, narrow, blink, and widen. Eyebrows, too, send many messages. Use the same pair of eyes and place brows in different positions and you can tell stories of surprise, grief, horror, apprehension, happiness, mockery, hurt, adoration, or fright. The face is capable of showing many emotions and extending countless nonverbal messages.

It is important to manage your eyes. A stare, for example, can break another person, and should be reserved for an inanimate object rather than another human being. Look at people long enough to let them know you see them, but do not stare, as this might be an intrusion on their privacy.

Eye contact is a facial gesture that is used both favorably and unfavorably. Take special notice of yourself and others and see if you observe this behavior: Two people who obviously do not know each other approach each other in an uncrowded space. They maintain eye contact from about 15 feet away, but as they move closer, they drop their eyes or simply look away. Why does this happen? Most people wish to inhibit a direct line of communication with total strangers.

This reaction is sometimes referred to as an awkward eye. You will see this awkward eye response in crowded or confined spaces, such as elevators, buses, or waiting rooms. We use the awkward eye when meeting strangers, indicating that we prefer to keep on "stranger" terms.

Have you ever tried desperately but without success to hail a cab or catch a waiter's eye? Some of these people must have taken lessons on how to avoid eye contact, and to remain unavailable to serve you. As a student, have you ever avoided an instructor's eye in hopes of not being called upon to recite? As an instructor, have you avoided eye contact with a student who annoys you or perhaps asks questions for which you have no quick solutions?

If you look away from others when conversing with them, you might be indicating that you are unsure of what you are saying. On the other hand, people who look away while you are speaking to them might be indicating that they do not agree with you or that they are not interested. If you look at the person you are speaking to, you display confidence in what you are saying. A person who looks at you while you are speaking is probably interested or in agreement with you.

Gestures

A person can acknowledge understanding or agreement by a simple up and down motion of the head and a smile. On the other hand, it is possible to express disagreement by doing just the reverse (a back and forth motion of the head and a scowl). These are the simple acts of shaking your head yes or no. Surely you have seen a person brushing his hands together to indicate a job finished.

Think about how many wordless gestures a minister uses to indicate what the congregation should do next. He gestures for the congregation to stand, to sit, to sing, to read, to kneel and to give generously when the collection plate is passed!

A movie director uses body language predominantly to direct films. If you bind the director's hands and feet and put blindfolds on, it would be next to impossible for him to proceed.

A policeman uses a great deal of body language. He gestures for you to be silent, to move in a specific direction, to put your hands up, to back off, or to come forward, and of course, the fact that he is armed makes these gestures more emphatic and easier to follow!

An individual scratching the head or stroking the chin can express deep thinking or attentiveness. Of course, prolonged head scratching may also mean that a return to Chapter 4 on hygiene would be advisable to review the importance of a good shampoo!

Placing a hand over the heart might suggest that a person is convinced or sincere or honest—or experiencing heartburn!

People indicate all sorts of shapes and sizes with gestures of the hands and arms. Demonstrations of size such as tall, short, huge, tiny, skinny, or fat can be made. Round, square, triangle, diamond, or octagon shapes can be demonstrated just by gesturing with the arms and hands. It is possible to express disassociation by turning the back to another person or by placing the hands and arms on the face. By leaning away slightly from an individual, we may give the impression of not wishing to associate or participate.

Standing too close to another person might tend to make that person uncomfortable and ill at ease, or to put that person on the defensive. The person's posture will often let you know that you have committed this error.

A common gesture that most people are unaware of is wiping the index finger between the upper lip and across the nostrils. Disbelief or observing something obscene can prompt this gesture. An individual indulging in an untruth or an exaggeration will draw his index finger beneath the nose. This simple gesture might also have a simple explanation—that the person forgot to carry a handkerchief!

Some individuals are "touchers," "pokers," or "elbow jabbers." Touching can be an effective way of demonstrating sincerity, friendship, or love. Elbow jabbers are extremely annoying; they usually jab when least expected, often to gain attention. Poking is not desirable, but is done for emphasis, to call attention, or to point to a direction or an object. Patting usually denotes fondness, but should be used with discretion. If the touching, patting, poking, or jabbing is not done with good taste and judgment, another effective gesture might follow— that of a face slap! A hand placed on a shoulder with the thumb pressing determinedly into the shoulder is an effective way to control aggression.

Body language is a popular topic these days, but it is certainly nothing new. It has been around since time began. Think of silent movies—whole movies were built around body language when there was no sound available. Gesturing was exaggerated so that the viewer would be certain to understand and to catch the meaning of the drama.

Referees and umpires make good use of gesturing, since they cannot rely upon being heard. The strikes and balls are gestured in baseball, and penalties are gestured in football, basketball, soccer, volleyball, and other sports. The referee in a boxing match holds up the winner's hand and gestures the counting of a knockout. Traffic policeman use their bodies to direct traffic. Orchestra and choir directors rely solely on their arm and hand gestures when conducting. A railroad engineer signals in lieu of verbal communication. Construction workers, too, use a variety of gestures in the course of a day's work. Continue with this list and see how many more people rely on body language to help them in their occupation or profession.

Body language can be useful and successful if used properly, or it can be unbecoming and unnecessary. Consider the contestant on a give-away show who jumps, skips, hops, undulates, turns in circles, claps the hands, and generally creates an impression of stupidity. A great deal of thought and common sense should be given to the use of gestures.

Who Nose?

Your nose, too, indicates certain expressions. Flared nostrils can indicate anger or fear. Quivering nostrils sometimes portray eagerness or anticipation.

Your Lips

Lips come in many shapes and sizes—thin lips, fat lips, full lips, big lips, and some smart lips! A lip biter signals insecurity, worry, or anticipation. Tightly closed lips or thin lips might signal strength. Persons who thrust their lower lip out indicate doubt, pouting, or defiance.

The mouth has a function even more important than shaping words; the mouth *smiles!* A smile can be the difference in how well or how poorly your message is received. If you are serving tables in a restaurant, your smile can mean the difference between tips or no tips. It can mean the difference between winning the election or going down in defeat, or the difference in people wanting to know you better or not getting to know you at all!

Hands, Feet and Legs

Think of the many messages that are conveyed with the hands. "I love you," "Don't be frightened," "You did a good job," "It will be over soon," "I understand," "You have my sympathy," "Don't worry," "Congratulations," or "Keep up the good work," can all be conveyed by a touch, a pat, or a handshake. Some cultures are more prone to touching, patting, and shaking hands.

Think of these gestures made with hands: the "V" for victory sign given with just two fingers; drawing the fingers across the throat meaning "It's over,"

or "Cut," or "Finished;" making a circle of the thumb and forefinger, meaning "Good, okay, right," or "I understand." Feet and legs indicate certain things, too. A person who sits with legs crossed might suggest an orderly mind. A tapping foot might indicate anger or impatience.

Posture is another transmitter of body language signals. People who hold their muscles tensely may be saying "Leave me alone." A person with an unnaturally straight ramrod back might have a very rigid personality. Bowed shoulders may indicate sadness, weariness, or a heavy burden. Raised shoulders might hint at fear and squared shoulders suggest responsibility.

Consider dancing, particularly ballet, where most of the meaning of the music comes from the body language of the dancer. The dancer's body language can impart an idea of love, hate, grief, happiness, life, death, or fear. The body is the sole interpreter of thoughts and ideas. It is the only means of communication.

Think about the Indians; much of their communication was done through body language. They relied heavily on the use of gestures, both of the face and body. Consider their signals to fight, to be silent, to run, and to crawl and their rain dances and their worship. They relied on body movements rather than on verbal communication.

The study of Kinesics is very interesting and very complicated. No one gesture will *always* mean the same thing, or even only *one* thing. For example, folded arms do not always mean, "I am unsure of myself," or "I won't let you in." Crossed legs do not always suggest tightness or withdrawal, but might convey a leadership feeling. The name of the game is to observe and try to receive the signals people intend to send. Observe yourself—do you stand, sit, or walk the way you really feel or the way you think you *ought* to feel? Watch yourself and others—it is an interesting game, and you will learn a great deal about "ye and thee." After all, there is nothing more interesting than people; so try to be as observant and alert to their signals as possible. Remember the saying, "Reach out and touch someone." Try it. You may be able to help someone who is in need of your support.

If you have never visited a nursing home, there is no time like the present. Visit the elderly if you want to see body language working overtime. (You will also see many bodies that have already worked overtime!) An elderly person who fondles an article or reaches for a hand to hold, is probably giving a silent plea for help. That person feels desperately lonely and needs companionship. Many older people cannot speak at all. These people might make use of as many gestures as they are physically capable of. They might pat the seat of a chair, for example, to say, "Please sit by me," or they may tap fingers on a table to suggest, "I am hungry," or point to a book to plead, "Please read to me." Their eyes say, "Please don't go yet," or "I remember when," or "Come back again soon," or "Thank you," or "I am so lonely," or "Please . . . just let me die."

It is essential that your body language transmit what you really want others to know or feel. Therefore, you must really observe how you present yourself. Start observing how other people attempt to transmit their signals.

Signs of Love

Body language is used in the matter of love, too. This is not something that we recommend for use in your classroom or office, but we will touch upon it lightly.

Men and women give all kinds of indications and intentions sexually, through body motion—the way they sit, stand, walk, pose, and use their eyes and tongue. For example, hips that are thrust forward with legs spread slightly apart, are a fairly obvious sexual signal. The eyes give all kinds of signals. One common signal is to narrow the eyes slightly while lingering with eye contact. The eyes can promise many things. Individuals arouse excitement by touching the tongue to the lips as a sign of availability.

Of course, in the case of body language and sexuality, it takes "two to tango." Signals of love can be misinterpreted and they must be answered properly to make it work. If the overtures are one-sided, a slap on the cheek might occur, and don't tell anyone you read it here first!

Interpretation

Have you ever heard someone say, "It wasn't so much *what* was said, but *how* it was said." Therapists probably use this concept more than anyone else. A therapist or counselor gets a hidden message from a sagging posture, crossed hands, and dull eyes.

To believe you hear the whole story simply by observing body language is a fallacy. Likewise, it is impossible to hear the whole story by listening to the spoken language only. With verbal communication only you might hear the story, but miss some important meaning or interpretation.

Observe two people engaged in conversation. When asking a question, the speaker invariably moves his or her head upward at the end of the question. The eyes open wider; sometimes the hand moves upward too. This seems to indicate that the other person should speak and give an answer.

It is advisable to try to understand body language. Think how you might avoid an unpleasant situation in the office with your boss, or in the classroom with an instructor, if you are aware of certain signals that indicate irritation or anger. Most people tend to use the same gestures repeatedly. You might be able to determine that another office employee is having a difficult time emotionally by facial expressions or posture.

Think back to the last time you watched a comedian do an impersonation. The sound of the voice is imitated, but it is the gesturing, however exaggerated, that is the real clue to the identity of the imitated person. Political figures rely heavily on body language, as do religious leaders, actors, and day-to-day workmen; all of them use all kinds of gestures. Hitler gestured to the extent that he would almost knock himself out of the podium. (What a shame he didn't!)

Large or small groups of people are interesting to observe. Watch three people sitting on a couch. The two at the ends will turn in to enclose and include the member in the middle, at the same time, excluding others. They might cross their legs, providing even more of a barrier. This turning inward is referred to as "bookending."

Observe a couple of the opposite sex who have no choice but to sit face-to-face very close to one another. This can happen on a bus, plane, train, or at a social gathering. If the couple does not know each other, they might cross their arms and legs and lean away from each other as if they are protecting themselves. You might find it interesting, educational, or amusing to experiment with some arrangements and observe the results.

Something else that often happens in large business gatherings is that those with the most importance, prestige, or highest status place themselves at either end of the group. Sometimes those with more importance or status adopt a different body position than the rest of the group, setting apart their importance.

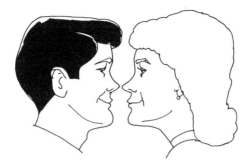

Often when one member of a group shifts, the whole group shifts in a like manner.

Radio, where only voices were heard, left a lot to be desired. More than half of the ideas people hope to communicate are conveyed through body language as well as voice. Without body and facial movements, comedians do not seem humorous, politicians may not seem sincere, preachers may not seem emphatic, and no one seems very animated. Empathy for others, too, is more easily shown by proper use of body language.

Have you ever heard someone say, "I couldn't talk without my hands!" Try it! Then try to concentrate on not moving your head at all—not even to nod up and down. Then try not to move any part of your face except your mouth while talking. You will find it extremely difficult to deliver your message effectively, and you may find you need more words to express your thoughts. Without the use of gestures, you may find it extremely difficult, if not impossible, to transmit a message.

Sometimes you can avoid an unpleasant confrontation with another individual if you observe from their facial expressions that they are displeased with you, or that they don't like you. Pick up your body language and retreat!

I CAN'T THINK OF A THING TO SAY!

After studying this chapter on Kinesics, we hope you become more aware of your own body language and try to control it to better express yourself. Use it to your best advantage.

Enjoy watching others and observing their body language while trying to analyze what message they are trying to convey and what kinds of people they are.

Use your body language as a special gift. Let it help your lungs and voice box tell your story. Hopefully others will become more comfortable in your presence because of your facial expressions. Practice positive gesturing and smiling and enjoy the rewards.

You might be able to help someone who desperately needs help and can only deliver this message nonverbally. Be observant of your friends, family members, co-workers, boss, acquaintances, and those whom you do not know at all. Be ready to respond to their needs and with your own skillful body language, perhaps you can tell them "I am here—what can I do to help?"

Summary Questions

Use a, b, or c to indicate the best choice of words to fill the blank.

1. Body language is known as _____ communication.
   a. verbal
   b. visible
   c. nonverbal

2. A speaker behind a podium who uses no gestures delivers a(n) _____ message.
   a. emotional
   b. dead
   c. exciting

3. The facial feature that exhibits the most effective body language is the _____ .
   a. mouth
   b. eyes
   c. nose

4. A bowed head and lowered eyes might indicate _____ .
   a. pride
   b. humility
   c. submissiveness

5. Looking a person straight in the eye indicates _____ .
   a. boredom
   b. hate
   c. honesty

6. Leaning _____ another person might indicate willingness to communicate.
   a. away from
   b. toward
   c. to the side of

7. Arms held close to the body suggest _____ .
   a. acceptance
   b. welcome
   c. foreboding

8. Stooped shoulders might indicate _____ .
   a. rejection
   b. happiness
   c. strength

9. Forcefulness is displayed with a _____ pounding on a surface.
   a. clenched fist
   b. foot
   c. head

10. Boredom might be shown by _____ .
    a. yawning
    b. shifting feet
    c. twiddling thumbs
    d. all of the above.

CHAPTER **13**

Transactional Analysis

You may have come across transactional analysis (T.A.) under such titles as: *I'm OK—You're OK, Games People Play, T.A. Games, Scripts People Live, Reality Games* and others. Transactional analysis is a system of analysis that was developed from the work of Eric Berne, a prominent psychiatrist in California. Berne authored the book, *Games People Play*. Through transactional analysis, millions of people have become more aware of how to control themselves, their emotions, and their social interactions.

Is T.A. a tool used in psychiatry? The answer to this question is a definite yes. However, the important thing is that T.A. has been put into terms that the general public can understand and is usable and adaptable for daily living.

Why is this subject included in personal development? One reason is that it has been so widely read. Another reason is that it is a means of communication. It gives you insights into your own potential and a realization of what happens during transactions you make each and every day with other people. You can call these transactions conversations.

Once more, remember that this chapter is only to expose you to this means of self development. Everything you need to know about T.A. is *not* contained here. We introduce you to the concept because it is helpful in your personal development and personal growth.

All Three of You

The first thing you should know as you begin to explore T.A. is that you are not alone. You have no less than three personalities with you at all times. Transactional analysis tells us that all people have three persons operating within them. Since these people are within you, an introduction is in order. They are your *Parent* state, your *Adult* state and your *Child* state. These states show themselves in the way you think, feel and act.

Now that you have been introduced to these personalities, you should get to know them better so that you can recognize them as they appear in your behavior.

The Parent in you feels and behaves in much the same way that you believe your parents felt and behaved when you were a child. Think about that for just a minute. What is important is not the way your parents actually felt and behaved, but the way you *believed* they felt and behaved.

What does the Parent side of you do? It does just exactly what you think it does:

1. It makes rules and regulations.
2. It gives you your set of do's and don'ts, your concept of good and bad, should and shouldn't, can and can't, and all the other musts, nevers, have-to's and ought-to's.
3. It sets limits.
4. It gives advice.
5. It disciplines.
6. It guides.
7. It protects.
8. It judges.
9. It criticizes.
10. It keeps traditions like God, country, hot dogs, and apple pie.

Your parents, guardians, or whoever influenced your formative years, determine to a great extent how you view the authority of parents and society. You must be aware of the existence of the Parent nature. Begin to separate what makes sense to you and what doesn't, in order to function in the reality of here and now. In other words, sort and update your feelings, attitudes, and behaviors in order to make decisions based on what you know will work. Take all of this information and use it to live your own life in a more meaningful way—not as a carbon copy of someone else.

The Adult part of you gives you your cool. The Adult could be described as cold and calculating, like Mr. Spock in the popular television series "Star Trek." He was analytical, unemotional, and logical. This part of you is nearly machine-like. It computes, stores memories, and uses facts to make decisions. This part of you functions like Mr. Spock, without emotional entanglements.

The Adult side of you engages in these kinds of activities:

1. It gathers data on itself, the Adult function and on the Parent and Child natures.
2. It analyzes how the Child feels and what it wants.
3. It considers Parent feelings and reactions.
4. It sorts alternatives from this data-collecting process.
5. It plans steps in the decision-making process.

Planning in the decision-making process should be a familiar concept for you because it is the same process you explored in your study of goal setting. It includes identification of the desired results, the process of attaining those results, the steps necessary to achieve those results, alternative actions if the results are not achieved, and starting over and repeating the cycle to achieve the desired results.

You have heard the saying, "The exception proves the rule." This simply means that nothing is true in every circumstance. The saying applies here, for when the Adult is defined—or the Parent or Child—the definition applies to *typical* situations in which most people recognize themselves, but there are exceptions. You may recognize that some, but not all, of the definitions or functions apply. Each person's Adult, for example, has a unique way of functioning and may or may not go through the process of decision-making as just described. Parts of the process are probably typical of you and other parts are not.

Now, look at that third person in your personal triple play, the Child. You are thinking ahead correctly if you think it represents your feelings as a small girl or boy. Your Child is all the wonderful things it has always been and is still right there with you. This side of you is trusting, joyful, natural, innocent, loving, creative, fun-loving, and adventurous. Since you have some of the same feelings and behaviors you had when you were little, you can also be angry, rebellious, and frightened under the influence of your Parent nature.

Do you find this concept complicated? It *is* complicated, but necessary. You need some understanding of human psychological makeup as you communicate. You must be able to grasp what is really happening as people interact, in order to adjust yourself to the people around you.

Each of these three personalities within you is important. None is better than another. They are equal, and when in balance, they work together for a productive life.

Transactions, communications, or interactions occur between two human beings, each with three selves involved in the action. When you interact with another person, you are dealing with one or more of three personalities. The same is true when someone communicates with you. Is it any wonder human beings find it difficult to communicate? A conscious realization of all that is happening in even the most simple conversation, can help you become a better communicator. You can be aware of what adjustments you can make to be understood more clearly. Your awareness will also make you more tolerant in receiving information from others.

The simplest transactions occur when your Parent addresses another person's Parent, when your Adult talks to another person's Adult, or when a Child to Child communication takes place.

This state of communication is termed parallel communication. Crossed communication occurs when your Parent addresses someone else's Parent, but their Child responds. Another kind of transaction happens when there is activity by more than two of these people simultaneously. This is called an ulterior transaction.

Stroking

A great deal more information is available about transactional analysis. What you have read should whet your appetite to learn more about T.A. The remainder of this chapter will expose you to other terms associated with transactional analysis.

One such term is "strokes," or "stroking." Stroking is how one human being acknowledges another human being. Some ways of stroking are:

- Saying hello
- Waving the hand is a similar vehicle that is, of course, an action rather than a verbal means of communication.
- Smiling (a strong form of recognition and a very positive stroke)

A stroke is not necessarily a positive communication, however. Stroking is recognition, and can be given in many ways, even by walking up to someone and saying, "I hate your guts!"

Everyone needs strokes; all of us crave recognition. However, people's abilities to receive those strokes vary greatly. You know people who cannot accept a compliment gracefully. Some people do not see themselves as deserving a genuine compliment, and may become suspicious of people who compliment them. Instead of graciously accepting the compliment with thanks, such a person responds with a negative or embarrassing comment. This sort of reception discourages any future compliments.

To analyze this phenomenon, you need to understand the four basic positions. The Child in you has a unique way of seeing and experiencing. The four basic viewpoints or positions of the Child are:

1. I'm OK: You're OK. (a healthy position)
2. I'm OK: You're not OK. (distrust and suspicion of others)
3. I'm not OK: You're OK. (depression)
4. I'm not OK: You're not OK. (dissatisfaction with life in general)

Strokes are of different types: positive strokes, negative strokes, conditional strokes, and unconditional strokes. Strokes are vital for physical and mental well-being. Throughout life you need stroking. As a baby, you were stroked physically; as you grew up, verbal stroking was substituted for physical stroking.

The positive stroke indicates "I'm OK, You're OK." The negative stroke sounds something like this, "You did a lousy job," or "Since you can't do it, I'll find someone who can."

A conditional stroke rests on performing or refraining from some act, such as, "I could really like you if you baked an apple pie," or "I'm not going to like you very much if you break my favorite vase." An unconditional stroke has no strings attached. "I like you," or "I love you," implies "just the way you are." Giving positive unconditional strokes is important. Making others feel good about themselves makes you feel good as well.

People who become more accustomed to negative strokes than to positive ones begin to reject positive strokes and will even go out of their way to collect

GET THE FLAVOR?

negative strokes. They begin to believe that they do not deserve positive attention and are uncomfortable when it is given.

Use Your Understanding

Familiarity with the concepts of transactional analysis can and should make you a more responsible person. If you know what is happening in conversations, you should be more conscious of controlling your emotions when there is a breakdown in communication. A little knowledge can be a dangerous thing, and a little knowledge of T.A. is all that you have. Never use what you know to manipulate or try to change others. The person most easily changed by you is you. T.A. should make you more aware, more knowledgeable, and more able to cope with yourself in your business, social, and personal life.

The Fun Begins

A lot of little fun things start going on within the realm of T.A. that are fun to read about, but not so much fun when you consider what people are doing to themselves. Some of these things are referred to as stamp collecting, rackets, rituals, pastimes, and games.

Stamp collecting is the process of storing up feelings. People store up good or bad feelings and use them to do things that they probably would not do otherwise. You collect these stamps from yourself, or from others; when you get enough, you cash them in for a reward or prize. When you collect enough bad feelings from being insulted or hurt, for example, you can turn them in for things like a free drink, an outburst of temper, or a day off for sick leave. When enough good feelings are stored, you might trade them for things like a new shirt or blouse, or an evening out.

Stamp collecting is a method of helping the Child in you to feel OK. If you honestly believe in the position, "I'm OK: You're OK," then you are not a stamp collector. You do not need crutches or excuses for what you feel and do. You have made the decision to be OK, and you are OK, no matter what happens.

Do you recognize the parallel between this idea and the recommendations in the section on positive attitude? You must take charge of your attitude, and only you can decide to be a positive person.

Rackets are habits of feeling bad. The habits were learned from your parents; they are not your feelings in reality, but you act as if they are. If you experienced family tensions as a child, if your parents acted depressed, confused, guilty, nervous, or angry, and if the adults did not take action to eliminate tension and pressure, then chances are you learned a racket. Both rackets and stamp collecting come from the "I'm not OK" position, which your Child character uses to avoid taking constructive action.

The Time of Your Life

Time is the common denominator for all living things. Therefore, what people do with their time becomes extremely important. The element of time enters the discussion of T.A. because you choose to fill your time with happiness and laughter or with anger and sadness. Within you is the ability to use all the hours, minutes, and seconds you have to make your life good, warm, and loving.

Time management is important as you reach for personal and career goals. This will be discussed in a later chapter.

To focus on the application here, review the four basic positions for seeing and experiencing yourself and other people:

- I'm OK, You're OK.
- I'm OK, You're not OK
- I'm not OK, You're OK
- I'm not OK, You're not OK.

Which of these attitudes do you have *most* of the time?

How you feel determines how you spend your time. The reverse is also true: how you spend your time determines how you feel. You, and only you, are in control.

In our discussion of feelings, we can speak about six ways people spend their time. These six ways are:

1. Withdrawal
2. Rituals
3. Pastimes
4. Activities
5. Games
6. Intimacy

Withdrawal is not always bad, depending on how often you withdraw and why. We all need some quiet time to be alone with our thoughts. Nothing is wrong with being a good friend to yourself. You can even be alone with your thoughts in a room full of people. You have to determine how often you use withdrawal. Ask yourself whether you are running away from the world or just enjoying some time alone with your plans, hopes, and dreams.

Rituals are usually superficial transactions between people. "Hello," "good-bye," "how are you?" "I'm fine, how are you?" are examples of rituals. With rituals you touch other people and people touch you—but with a minimum of feeling.

Pastimes are a safe way of passing time. Now there is a sentence that took a lot of thought. Nevertheless *it is* factual. They consist of safe talk—the kinds of conversations you would use at business gatherings or parties. Examples of this kind of transaction would be "Hasn't this weather been beautiful?" "Have you taken the personal development course? So have I, and I thought it was . . . !" People who do not get involved in pastimes have difficulty at parties and other social situations. Pastimes make you feel good and can be fun.

Activities can be a useful means of using time. One very useful activity is working to earn a living. Writing about T.A. is an activity; learning about it is another. Weeding the garden, cooking, cleaning, and playing golf are activities you might engage in. Sometimes you choose your activities and sometimes your activities choose you.

Games. Shakespeare said, "All the world is a stage and we are the players." Players we are! The games that we play are many, and everyone plays sometime. Games sound like fun and an "OK" use of time. *Be careful.* Reflect on what you are doing to others and to yourself. Games can hurt—really hurt.

When you are being criticized or picked on you are in an "I'm not OK" situation, which makes you a *victim.* (Victim is a term from T.A. vocabulary.) When you do the picking or criticizing, you are the *persecutor* (another T.A. word), telling someone else, "You're not OK."

You might try to be a *rescuer,* and enter someone else's argument trying to help. What you are saying is, "I'm not OK, but I can make it right for you." You will probably be told to butt out. If you really want to set yourself up to feel *not* OK, this is one way to do it.

Why play games that hurt? Remember that all people need to be touched, recognized, and acknowledged. A crummy relationship is better than no relationship at all. Games are played not to hide your "not OK" feelings, but to prove that you are not the only person who is not OK.

One of the most easily read books about games is called *T.A. Games, Using Transactional Analysis in Your Life,* by Adelaide Bry. The ideas behind various games, the names of the games, and their objectives are described. One game is called NIGYSOB; the idea is to "get even," and it proves you are not OK. The name, NIGYSOB, stands for "Now I've got you, you son-of-a-b——." The object is to catch someone in a situation where you can say, "I told you so," or simply "Gotcha."

It works like this: When someone is going to the store ask them to pick up something for you. When this person returns, having forgotten the item requested, you can say "Gotcha!" You have the opportunity to make that person feel stupid and to exact a price for the blunder. Remember, though, that you could easily be in the other person's shoes.

A great many games are available. Some are described in Adelaide Bry's book. Most of these games are designed to prove that someone is not OK.

How Do You Play?

You have options. You can play or not play; you can play intensely or not so intensely. You can choose to play often or only occasionally. The best choice is never to play a hurting game, but to play only good games—seldom and lightly.

The best-spent time is spent in intimacy. *Intimacy* is the expression of "I'm OK, you're OK." The experience is between two human beings who are vulnerable and open to each other, because they give themselves to each other. Can you be intimate all the time with everyone? No!

Intimacy is being close to someone. It is being you, honest, caring, and sharing. You are intimate with your children, your parents, a sibling, and a special person you love.

What could be more intimate than sex? The answer is: a great many things. In fact, at times sex may be no more than a ritual—not actually intimate at all. It can be simply a pastime or an activity. Sex born of loving, caring, and sharing, however, can be the ultimate intimacy.

T.A. can be an extremely interesting subject and some of you may even find it exciting. Remember that one purpose of this chapter is to give you enough exposure to T.A. to stimulate you to learn more.

Another purpose is to make you more aware and more tolerant. Be tolerant of others and of yourself when engaged in transactions or communication; realize just how your communications are delivered and received. When you become aware of all the personalities acting within you and within those you communicate with, you should become more patient and understanding. Your awareness of game playing adds another dimension that you must consider when dealing with others.

With knowledge comes responsibility. You know what options and choices you have. Deal wisely with yourself and with others. If you want to make changes—make them within yourself. Try always to see yourself and others as being OK.

Summary Questions

1. List three things you have said or done recently that were well thought out and based on facts (Your Adult in action)

2. List three things you have said or done recently that your parents might have said or done. (Your Parent at work)

3. List three things you have said or done recently that represent your childhood behavior. (Your Child coming through)

4. What kind of advice would each of these personalities give to a friend who asks advice about buying a new car?
   a. Your Parent
   b. Your Adult
   c. Your Child

CHAPTER **14**

Assertiveness

Step Up—Not Over

Have you ever heard the saying, "It's never too late to teach an old dog new tricks." If you are an old dog reading this chapter, you are in luck, but it would be better if you are beginning to form *good* habits, attitudes, and practices. These things are necessary to become a successful part of the business world. One of the most valuable assets you have, or wish to attain, is assertiveness.

Many people mistake assertiveness for aggression. The difference between the two is plain, but some people have difficulty sorting it out. Aggression means dominance—often without regard for the feelings or rights of others. Assertiveness, on the other hand, means *knowing* your rights and standing up for those rights. A fine line exists between the two, and it is important to learn the difference early so that you will do the most good to yourself and the least harm to others.

Assertiveness begins or fails to begin when you are a child. Like your attitudes, personal hygiene, social graces, ability to manage time wisely, body language, and goals in life, assertiveness begins in childhood.

Assertiveness is useful in any setting—in the business world, at home, at school, in counseling, housekeeping, sports—even when trying to catch a spouse! Think carefully about what rights you have. Do you have the right to express an opinion, to have an innovative idea, and to share that idea? Do you have a right to have desires or wants and do you have the right to make those wants known? The answer to all of these questions is unequivocally, "Yes"! So what are you waiting for? Now is the time to make those nonassertive bones responsive and practice some assertive behavior.

Being assertive involves many different behaviors and some of these need to be exercised frequently and practiced often. Be aware of others; be able to put yourself in their position. Understand how they feel and what they think. Be empathetic. Sometimes it is necessary to set aside your goals temporarily to help another individual.

Being assertive means being forceful. Strong eye contact, a strong or persuasive voice, and straight posture are signs of assertiveness. Facts to support your convictions help you to be assertive.

Being assertive means showing *genuine* enthusiam. The words genuine and sincere cannot be stressed too often. Without sincerity, you cannot get to the top.

Being assertive means being able to exert the rights you have and to stand by those rights without feeling guilty or apologetic.

Being assertive means being persuasive and convincing. Persuasive people can convince others about an idea or goal without using negative phrases or ideas. Assertiveness is demonstrated through optimism. Attempt to point out positive qualities or abilities another person possesses.

Being assertive means not being unnecessarily apologetic. An assertive individual never stretches an item of information or distorts facts. In other words, a truly assertive individual is a pretty nice person and one who is going somewhere—right to the top!

Some overly self-confident, overbearing, egotistical individuals may think of themselves as being assertive, when in truth they have only mastered the first three letters of the word.

Now that you are aware of some characteristics of assertive behavior, let's talk a bit about the different types of behavior. When you are familar with these behaviors you should know why you prefer to be an assertive person.

An assertive person can clearly and positively express an idea, opinion, or desire, without violating the rights of others. The assertive person can say "no" without feeling guilty and still respect the feelings and opinions of others.

Persons who display nonassertive behavior have little influence. They feel their opinions do not count and their ideas matter very little. They are often resentful, easily hurt, frustrated, and hesitant. They are afraid to give a negative response to anyone for fear of being thought rude or pushy. They are frightened and lack self-confidence, tiptoeing around trying not to hurt anyone. Instead, they themselves are trampled upon and hurt by almost everyone!

The other extreme is aggressive behavior. These people dominate and lack concern for those around them. The feelings, rights, wants, and opinions of other people have little or no importance for aggressive people. They state facts and opinions clearly and emphatically, but with little or no concern for the feelings of others, issuing orders rather than offering constructive suggestions.

Think about the body language that normally accompanies each of these types of behavior. The body language of assertive behavior consists of direct eye contact and well-balanced posture. Hands usually make relaxed movements. An aggressive person's eyes are cold, staring, with little or no expression. Posture is rigid and movements are stiff and rude. Usually the feet are spread apart and hands are placed on the hips. The hands of an aggressive person are often clenched, with many jerky finger gestures, fist pounding, and pointing. These characteristics are reminiscent of Hitler, who demanded respect, but commanded intense hate.

The body language of nonassertive individuals is distinctive, too. The eyes are averted, downcast, and sometimes pleading. Nonassertive people usually lean against something for support and nod their heads a great deal. Their hands are fidgety and nervous.

Observe the behavior of different individuals you know. Invariably the body language coincides with the type of behavior an individual exhibits.

You began to form your behavior patterns as a child, under your parents' influence. The parent who can give direct and clear instruction without "passing the buck" gets more response and cooperation than a parent with a different approach. A parent who gives clear direction is imposing a standard of assertive behavior. That parent does not give examples of what the "other" kids do.

The parent who transmits fear and anxiety to the child and feels guilty for telling the child "no" exhibits nonassertive behavior.

The aggressive parent tries to shirk responsibility, blame others, or use fear of punishment as a means of discipline. An aggressive parent gives a cold, calculating command with no explanation of why it must be done. Sometimes a parent or spouse who is aggressive at home is very passive and nonassertive at work or vice versa.

Parental behaviors exert considerable influence on a child, who later imitates and implements them. If you did not come from an assertive environment, you will have to learn to change your attitudes in order to become assertive. The most desirable behavior, the one that will help you succeed, is assertive behavior. If you are either nonassertive or aggressive, you have your work cut out for you.

If you are nonassertive, you must begin to feed on your successes—however few or small they might be. Forget your failures; they can only be constructive when you have learned something from them.

Learn to accept a compliment graciously, build up your own self-image, and shake your negative side. You can do this through body language, verbal contact, appearance, and a positive attitude. Set goals for yourself—some that you can accomplish easily and some more difficult ones. The goals you attain easily will give you a feeling of success and build your self-image. Give yourself an incentive to change your behavior; motivate yourself to change! Know what your rights are and begin to assert them. Practice is the key to changing your behavioral pattern.

Pick out people you admire and know to be assertive. Pattern yourself after them; observe the way they look, act, and project themselves. Try to adopt some of the same techniques and attitudes these people show and adapt them to your situation. Build yourself up within. Think of the many things you do well. (If this is something as apparently insignificant as cleaning windows, make note of it.) Perhaps you have a nice smile, white teeth, large veins for donating blood, a nice hairline, a love for old people, or great patience. Do you sketch a little, play the piano, have mathematical ability, or type well? List anything at all that might make you feel good about yourself. You must like yourself and take pride in yourself and your accomplishments. Make a list of your strengths and your weaknesses. Sometimes seeing these in black and white will startle and jolt you enough to motivate you to do something about your weak points. No time is like the present to begin. Make that list.

List Your Strengths and Weaknesses

Strengths	Weaknesses
1. _____	1. _____
2. _____	2. _____
3. _____	3. _____
4. _____	4. _____
5. _____	5. _____
6. _____	6. _____

Observe

If you are not quite sure what type of personality you possess, observe your attitudes, your body movements, your reactions, and the responses you evoke from those around you. If people seem to like you but take advantage of you, you are probably nonassertive.

If you are well liked and respected, you are probably an assertive person. If no one seems to like you, nor you them—if they do not care, and neither do you—then you are an aggressive person.

Have you been around people who are totally insecure about their surroundings? Imagine an insecure instructor. This instructor will always be the first to respond to a memo or questionnaire from the immediate supervisor. This teacher comes early and stays late and makes sure superiors and peers know it. The insecure teacher has poor discipline habits in the classroom because of nonassertive behavior. This teacher "butters up" the person in command and never disagrees with that person—or with anyone else. Sometimes the teacher finishes sentences for whoever is speaking. This practice is supposed to give the impression that the teacher fully understands what is being said, but it is rude and disconcerting to the person speaking. This insecure teacher never says "no," and consequently is asked to do tasks that others have the intestinal fortitude to turn down.

Consider the case of an individual who appears loud, arrogant, and in love with self. This person probably seems aggressive, but may actually be covering up a low self-esteem, saying, "Look at me—I'm good, I'm great—aren't I?" These people need to be loved too.

Some people are blessed with handsome features but find it difficult to cope with life and need to build self-esteem. Each person has some handicap to overcome in developing assertive behavior.

People in many occupations rely on assertive behavior. A writer is one of these. In all types of writing—personal letter writing, business letter writing, newspaper writing, poetry writing, and story writing—it is essential to know your subject and to be assertive in several ways. You must never violate the rights of others, and you must be direct, factual, concise, and straightforward. You must be sensitive to your readers and never apologize for your writing. Humor shows that you enjoy your labors and sometimes makes it easier to give an impression of assertiveness.

Think of the importance of assertive behavior for the sanitation worker in this situation. A barrel has been left behind unemptied for three pickup days. You decide on the fourth day to approach the garbage hauler. You might say something like, "Is there some reason this barrel is left unemptied time after time?" If the hauler is nonassertive, the answer might be, "Boy, I don't know— I haven't been on the route very long (he's only the owner.), but I suppose we could dump it." If his behavior is aggressive, he might growl, "This barrel is full of rocks, cans, and grass. It's too heavy to lift, and I'm not going to. Furthermore, *you* wouldn't want to lift it either." The assertive hauler, on the other hand, might say, "State law prohibits us from picking up a barrel exceeding _____ pounds, and this barrel obviously exceeds that limit. However, if you'd care to get on one side, the two of us can carry it to the truck and dispose of it."

Think about this example of using assertiveness in an office setting. Your office is arranged as the efficiency experts suggest. The arrangement has been in place for several years and by now everyone has forgotten exactly why each item is placed where it is. The boss, forgetting the original reasoning behind the office arrangement, returns from a seminar where "change" was the primary theme. Being a person of action, the boss decides a change is in order.

The first target is the secretary's office. This morning the boss returns and announces, "We are going to change the office around." The boss is a real plant nut, so plants begin to take over the rearranged office. If this were a war movie, the announcement would be, "Damn the torpedoes, full speed ahead!" Adapting this to the office situation, you could say, "Damn the efficiency. Bring on the plants!"

File cabinets, storage cabinets, work tables, chairs, and counters are shuffled to accommodate the new decor. Potted plants, hanging plants, climbing vines, and a palm tree arrive. Efficiency seems forgotten, sacrificed to accommodate what could be a second home for Tarzan. The palm tree takes center stage to satisfy its thirst for sunlight, and casts its work-hindering shadows over the secretary.

To complicate things further, assume that the secretary and the receptionist share the outer office. One covers for the other during lunch, coffee breaks, particularly heavy periods of work, and trips to the restroom. Now, with the abundance of fantastic foliage, these two compatible employees can no longer even see one another. Their visual contact is blocked by the plants and the furniture that was rearranged. The two secretaries can't reach each other's telephones without leaving their desks and trotting around the two file cabinets—which takes approximately three rings of the telephone.

Another problem is that the reception area where customers wait is no longer visible from the office. There is a completely blind spot where neither the secretary nor the receptionist can see people who enter the office. The secretaries must shift their eyes and bodies, stretch their necks, and reach out to part the tangled green forest, restraining themselves to keep from whooping like jungle men, "Me Tarzan! That you, Jane?" Efficiency has been greatly cut down. Eye contact is gone; body language is lost. Voices in the wilderness have become the primary means of communication. Visual contact with the counter is nonexistent.

This proves to be a disadvantage to the customer coming to this office. A

person may stand for some time, shuffling feet, trying to attract attention. More deliberate actions ensue, such as coughing, spitting, sneezing, and finally shouting, "Me Jane—you in there, Tarzan?"

Finally, you decide to call joking attention to the havoc and inefficiency caused by the plants. After several weeks, this has done nothing but evoke a few chuckles. You decide it is time to use assertive behavior.

Keeping in mind the important elements of assertiveness, rehearse what you want to say before approaching your boss. Be sure you are factual and can back your facts with proof. (You certainly will not need to exaggerate—the situation is bad enough!) You must be tactful and persuasive at the same time.

You first ask for a few minutes of your supervisor's time, at the supervisor's convenience. Be sure you keep eye contact throughout and have control of your voice.

You might try this approach: "I have postponed approaching you about this, hoping that the situation might correct itself. Since it has not, I feel I must speak to you about it. I feel the efficiency of our office has been cut in half since bringing in all the plants. We cannot see people coming into the office, nor can they see us. We cannot see each other. We cannot reach the phone on the other desk and this had been a big time saver. These are some of the more obvious disadvantages, but there are other, equally annoying ones."

Now that you have been straightforward and stated your case emphatically and persuasively, give your ideas for a possible solution. You might say something like this, "I have two suggestions for solving our dilemma. Undoubtedly the greenery helps the appearance of the office and gives it a warm touch, but let's go to smaller plants and rearrange the office to reinstate its previous efficiency. Then we could enjoy the plants and improve efficiency at the same time." You might add that one of the very large plants could remain, but in another corner. You should have measured the area and the base of the plant first so that you know this arrangement is possible.

You have now assertively stated your case and offered a possible solution, and substantiated both with facts. Your chances of getting the plants moved are good, once the boss has been approached in this assertive manner. Your self-assertion has accomplished these three things:

1. The plants have been moved.
2. You have kept the good will of the staff.
3. Your boss respects you because of your assertiveness.

Think of all the people who can and should use assertive behavior. Anyone in the business of selling—whether it be merchandise or ideas—needs assertiveness. This category includes a great many people because almost all of us have to sell ourselves or an idea at some time. Attorneys rely on their assertive abilities, if they want to win their cases.

Doctors and dentists rely on assertive behavior when talking to patients or when consulting with other physicians. Think about the dental hygienist who rubs you the wrong way by being aggressive, or the one who makes no impression at all by being nonassertive. Then think of the really good hygienist who makes you want to brush properly and even floss.

The hygienist who is nonassertive might say, "We could brush or floss with more regularity, couldn't we? But I know you don't have much time to do this, and I understand completely!" The aggressive hygienist might say, "Fella, don't ever come in here sporting that much plaque again!" The assertive hygienist might approach the patient in this manner, "I can see you've been trying to floss and brush, but you're missing some important areas. I'm going to show you how to floss correctly and explain why it is necessary to do it this way."

Managers, librarians, mothers, fathers, teachers, administrators, beauticians, barbers, body men (that is—automobile bodies), nurses, judges, custodians, secretaries, athletes, government officials—all rely heavily on assertiveness to have an impact on others.

We have mentioned doctors and lawyers—now let's talk about the Indian Chief. The Indians have always expressed many things through body language. Visualize two Indians deciding whether or not to go to battle. Picture an Indian using nonassertive behavior, literally beating around the bush afraid to shake his head "no," shrugging his shoulders. The assertive Indian stands assuredly with folded arms, because his mind is already made up and can't be changed. Last, the aggressive Indian does not care what the others decide—he is already out hunting scalps!

The three different types of behavior—assertive, nonassertive, or aggressive—are also suggested by vocal inflection. Tone of the voice affects messages; the same words can have different meanings depending on the inflection and tone of the voice. For example, the word, "oh," can say many things.

- "Oh!"—surprise or discovery
- "Oh,"—trying to think what happens next
- "Oh?"—doubt—"Oh, yeah, prove it!"
- "Oh . ."—denoting "It's *so* cute!"
- "OH - -"—impression of sadness

Other one-word expressions that have different meanings, depending on voice inflection are so, what, and why. Try to think of other words, and how they are said to give an aggressive, nonassertive, or assertive meaning.

An amusing true story that comes to mind involves two wealthy, elderly widows. They had always been very frugal, saving their money for something—they did not know what. Neither woman had any family to whom to leave savings, and an attorney friend thought it a shame they did not spend some of their money on themselves and do some traveling.

After many weeks cajoling and using assertive skills, the attorney finally convinced the two women they should throw caution to the winds and travel. They agreed to go to New York City and admitted that it was something each had secretly wanted to do.

The attorney made the travel arrangements, sparing no expense. They were to fly first class and reservations were made in one of New York's finest and most expensive hotels. Before they left their small town in Iowa, they were given all kinds of good advice about what to do and what not to do in the big city.

They were advised not to go walking after dark, not to go alone anywhere (even in an elevator), to keep their purses close to their bodies at all times, not to visit freely with strangers, and to be always on their guard.

The two ladies took the advice to heart and started on their trip. They had a superb flight and arrived at their luxurious hotel, awed by what they had seen. They were on the 40th floor of an exquisite hotel and after getting unpacked and refreshed, they decided to go down to the lobby and look around.

They timidly went out into the hall and rang for the elevator. After a short wait, the door opened and they stepped inside. On the elevator with them was a large, muscular man with an equally large, muscular dog on a leash. They crammed themselves into a corner, remembering the advice given by their friends not to visit with strangers, and remained there quietly. The elevator door closed and the elevator started moving. The man with the dog gave a command, the single word, "Sit!" The two ladies, already feeling extremely uncomfortable and intimidated, immediately hit the deck. Once seated, they looked at one another and realized simultaneously that the command had been intended for the dog— not for them!

They were humiliated and embarrassed, but decided to ride it out sitting down. What they did not realize, was that the man felt equally embarrassed. None of them knew what to do to rectify the situation. Picture what this must have looked like when the elevator opened in the lobby—a man, a large dog on a leash, and two old ladies sitting on the floor! If one of the three had used an assertive behavioral approach on the elevator and laughed off what had happened, it would have eased the situation considerably.

You might be interested in knowing the conclusion of this incident. When the two ladies went to the front desk in the lobby to pay their bill at the end of their stay in New York, the innkeeper told them it had been paid in full. It seems the gentleman on the elevator with them was a nationally known big-league baseball player and felt so badly about having intimidated the two women, that he paid their bill. His aggressive behavior and tone of voice toward the dog turned out to be costly in this case.

Manipulator or Manipulatee

Another topic of importance is that of manipulation, which has not been discussed so far. Aggressive behavior can be manipulative. You must be able to identify manipulation and protect yourself. You do not want to be manipulated nor should you be guilty of manipulating others.

There are many kinds of manipulation in an office setting, for example. One secretary can manipulate another secretary into doing an unpleasant job. Managing time so that the task will have to be done during your lunch break is one way to do this. A parent can manipulate a child's life while the child is very young and even after the child has become an adult. Manipulation is not always intentional, but it violates the other person's assertive rights.

Are You Angry?

Anger is something we all experience, and although it is not particularly attractive, it is as normal as breathing. If you express your anger in a healthy manner, it can be constructive. Anger used properly can allow you to stand up for your rights or beliefs. It can improve a strained relationship with another person and give new understanding to a situation.

Anger can keep you from performing your job efficiently. Aggressive anger might "get it all out," because you are lambasting someone, but it puts more distance between two people in a relationship. Do not vent your anger by seeking someone on whom to lay blame. Words once said cannot be taken back. When something is said in aggressive anger, the damage is done and is sometimes irreparable. If you belittle and hurt another, you will "lose face;" you will lose your self-esteem. Always remember that words spoken in anger cannot be retracted. Apologies can be made and forgiveness granted, but the bitterness and humiliation of the spoken words linger and hurt.

Another way to express anger is nonassertively. Most people do this by giving the silent treatment—clamming up. You accomplish nothing by remaining silent, except to make yourself miserable. Besides, the other person might enjoy your silence!

Try to "cool down" before speaking with someone you are angry with. *Try* to keep a sense of humor and do not take someone else's anger personally. A fellow employee, for example, might be terribly upset or angry about an office situation—the new computer, perhaps—but this does not necessarily mean the anger is directed at you.

When in the midst of an angry exchange, try to stay calm and breathe evenly. Do not take the exchange personally or let it degrade your abilities in any way. Look for some small thing that is positive or even humorous.

After an angry exchange, it is important to "cool off" and relax. Try to forget everything about it except what might be constructive. Do not dwell on ugly exchanges and do not harbor ill feelings.

Dealing with Guilt

Guilt makes it impossible to act assertively. Have you ever accepted an engagement or appointment when you would rather not, just to avoid feeling guilty about saying "no"? Would you rather do a job yourself than to risk feeling guilty about asking someone else to do it? The person who cannot delegate responsibility because of fear of appearing bossy is overburdened, overworked, and frustrated. If this person has a managerial position, it shows poor leadership ability.

A guilt attitude will work against you in every situation and leaves no room for assertive behavior. Know your rights as an assertive individual and do not let guilt consume your feelings. One of your rights is to say "no" without feeling guilty. Another right is to make mistakes. (You are human after all.) You have the right to express your opinions and to assert yourself even though it inconveniences others. All these rights should be performed without guilt feelings.

Learn to shed your guilt and to handle an apology if it is your responsibility. Apologize with a direct, clear statement and no feelings of guilt.

Accepting and Giving Criticism

Giving and receiving criticism should be handled assertively so that the criticism can be used to good advantage to strengthen relationships. There are two kinds of criticism—constructive and destructive; be constructive both in giving and taking criticism.

Some negative ways to give criticism are:

1. "Why did you do that job this way?"
2. "You're *always* three or four minutes late." (This is usually an exaggeration.)
3. "If you don't straighten out . . ." (said in a threatening tone)
4. Criticizing in front of fellow employees or customers. (This is rude, inconsiderate, embarrassing, and poor timing.)

Some rules to remember when giving criticism are:

1. Never criticize while you are angry or when others can hear.
2. Never exaggerate—be sure you can back up your statements with facts or documentation.
3. Give clearcut criticism so that the receiver understands what behavior is being criticized.
4. Do not dwell on the subject. Once around the block is sufficient if you are clear and concise.

Be able to receive criticism in an assertive manner. Do not be hostile or unapproachable. Appreciate the fact that someone cares enough about you and what you are doing to want to help you. Also, be glad of the fact that you are receiving this information straightforwardly. Listen with an open mind and try to learn something. Make a genuine attempt to change whatever needs changing and allow yourself to grow and solidify relationships.

One of the most vital areas in business is the performance appraisal. Giving and accepting criticism in an assertive manner is essential at this point. Performance appraisals can be an effective management tool for increasing productivity, or they can be disasters.

People need to know what they are doing right, so that they can continue to do those things. They need to know what they are doing wrong so that they can change.

Though grossly over-simplified, this process is what takes place in the performance appraisal.

Can you picture the nonassertive or aggressive personality sitting in either the employee's or the employer's chair? First, assume the employer is the nonassertive type. The boss probably does not get particularly excited or enthusiastic about the strengths or weaknesses of the employee. This leaves the employee with the impression that it makes little difference whether things are being done correctly or incorrectly. When weaknesses are pointed out they sound something like this, "You really should be here on time and, well, if you can see your way clear to change your habit of being late, it would be appreciated."

Now assume the employer is aggressive. This boss would shout that the employee should be on time starting the next morning, adding emphasis by pounding a fist on the table and continuing, "or pick up your severance pay." The employee does not see this as an appraisal, but as a threat.

The nonassertive employee will sit through either of these situations without a word of reasonable explanation such as, "My spouse has been ill for the past month and it has been impossible for me to be on time."

Assertive Discipline

Assertiveness has been introduced into education and anywhere that discipline is a part of the learning program. Assertive discipline offers a positive approach to discipline. Assertiveness in this way is firm, consistent, and positive.

One instructor of an assertiveness seminar spoke about a statement often used by teachers at the beginning of a new school year, "Don't smile until Christmas!" In this way students get the idea they can't fool around. However, assertive discipline beginning on the first day of school is far more effective and enjoyable than not smiling until Christmas!

A truly effective teacher is usually referred to as a master teacher. A master teacher always is assertive in the classroom. This master teacher communicates clearly and firmly with the students. This teacher states what is expected in a concise, clear-cut manner. These teachers say what they mean and mean what they say. They leave no doubts in the minds of their students about what kinds of behaviors they expect in the classroom. They are prepared to back up every statement and commitment made. They don't give undue attention to the disruptive student, but give solid positive reinforcement to the student whose behavior is appropriate and acceptable.

A poor, ineffective instructor has either a nonassertive or an aggressive style. A nonassertive teacher says things like, "Why are you doing that?", or "What am I going to do with you?" The answer to that is most probably "nothing"! An instructor who is not respected by students and staff members is nonassertive, passive, and sometimes hostile. This instructor has no impact!

An assertive instructor gives no recognition to disruptive behavior. The behavior is not ignored, but the stated consequence for unacceptable behavior is carried out with no verbal or group recognition. A disruptive student is seeking attention and does not care if the attention is positive or negative—as long as it is *some* kind of attention.

An assertive instructor will, during the initial rule setting, state his or her expectations. Some of these things might be:

- "I do not tolerate anyone preventing me from teaching."
- "I do not tolerate disruptive behavior that prevents someone else from learning."
- "I expect you to follow directions."
- "I expect you to stay seated unless you have permission to leave your seats."
- "I do not tolerate talking without permission."
- "I expect appropriate language—no profanity."
- "I expect you to keep your hands to yourself."

Once these rules and expectations have been stated firmly and clearly, the assertive teacher backs them up, making no exceptions. Whatever consequence was predetermined for disruptive behavior must be stated clearly and adhered to without fail. Some teachers list their disciplinary actions like this:

1. First offense—name on the board—10 minutes after school
2. Second offense—check by name—20 minutes after school
3. Third offense—visit to the principal
4. Fourth offense—visit with the parents
5. Fifth offense—expulsion from class.

If it becomes necessary to take one or more of these actions the instructor will do it without any ado or attention to the offender. A nonassertive teacher might write the offender's name on the board and then say something like, "There, now you have your name on the board, are you happy?" This leaves wide open areas for a smart answer and more problems.

The next thing an assertive or master teacher does is to reinforce a student for doing what the instructor wants. The assertive teacher is positive and resorts to the negative approach only when the positive does not work. Positive almost always brings good results.

An assertive teacher motivates students through verbal praise, positive notes, or classwide recognition. Verbal praise is saying to the student, "I like what you are doing," or "You're doing a good job, keep it up!" Positive notes include similar remarks, but a written note is an added reinforcement. Classwide recognition gives the student attention through praise, rather than negative remarks. Progress reports are sent home periodically showing "up work." Assertiveness has a very important role in the classroom.

On the Lighter Side

How many of you have listened to Bill Cosby's comedy monologues? The man is a master of comedy and takes an everyday, common, ordinary happening and brings it alive with animation. His monologues exaggerate the truth about common happenings.

One of his most entertaining and amusing monologues involves a mother's role in trying to control the behavior of her child. He tries to point out how violent a mother's talk can be. Her talk can be aggressive, and full of fury and fire. At the same time, she may assume a nonassertive role.

Some children hear irrational statements from their mothers, who are angry and pushed to the limit. The statements are something like this:

- "If you *ever* do that again . . ."
- "I'll beat you black and blue!"
- "I'll knock your brains out!"
- "Your Dad will murder you when he comes home!"
- "I'll knock you into the middle of next week!"

After shouting one or all of the above, she says one or both of the following, enunciating very clearly:

"Do you hear me?"

"Do I make myself clear?"

These threats sound aggressive but are actually nonassertive disciplinary actions and get mother nowhere. On the other hand, Mr. Cosby ends this particular episode by reminding us that when father comes home, he states a fact in a very decisive, clear, monotone. His manner is unemotional; what he says, he means, and he means what he says. He says simply, "I brought you into this world—I can take you out!" Now that is *assertive!*

Conclusion

You will see many instances throughout this text where assertive behavior is important. It helps you with a job interview, with a promotion, and with day-to-day functioning at work, at school, or at home. It helps you as a parent raising a family or as a spouse. It improves your self-esteem, increases your personal power and helps you to develop leadership qualities.

Summary Checklist

A checklist has been provided to help you decide where your strengths and weaknesses lie. Be honest with yourself and use this checklist to discover where your assertiveness need improvement. Your mind, body, and behavior are all included.

1. Do I suggest solutions and elaborate on them when members of the opposite sex are present?

2. Do I speak in front of a group effectively?

3. Do I speak up and ask questions at a meeting?

4. Do I maintain eye contact, keep my head upright, and lean forward when engaged in a personal conversation?

5. Do I state my views to authority figures of the opposite sex?

6. Do I enter or exit a room comfortably when members of the opposite sex are present?

7. In a store do I request expected service when I haven't received it?

8. Do I request the return of borrowed items without apologizing for asking?

9. Do I label myself aggressive and impolite?

10. Do I apologize for something even if I feel I am right?

11. Am I comfortable with a group of friends when I am the only one without a "date"?

Take a look at yourself and your assertive powers. Remember—be honest.

1. Can I tell people that something they are doing is annoying to me?

2. Am I comfortable refusing to do a favor that I don't want to do?

3. Am I capable of telling people when I think they are manipulating me?

4. Can I accept a compliment by saying something assertive to acknowledge my agreement with the compliment?

5. Can I express my anger directly and honestly?

6. Am I flighty, emotional, or hysterical?

7. Am I comfortable openly discussing another person's criticism of me with that person?

8. Can I argue constructively with another person?

9. Can I accept rejection?

10. Can I refuse a request for a meeting or date without feeling the need to make several explanations?

11. Do I have the approval of the most significant male/female in my life?

CHAPTER **15**

Right-Brain, Left-Brain Dominance and NLP

The Brainstorm

Communication is not a simple topic. The more you find out about it, the more complicated you begin to realize it is. While the intent of this section is to make you aware, it is not unlikely also to confuse you somewhat. The concepts are complex.

Many of these ideas had not yet been identified when your seniors were receiving an education ten, fifteen, or twenty years ago. Who can tell what breakthroughs will be made in the next ten, fifteen, or twenty years or what your children and grandchildren will need to know to be better communicators. If you are confused at this point, congratulations! You are becoming aware of and concerned about the human beings you will communicate with. Take the time to find out more about the various concepts and become more in tune with yourself.

This chapter gives you a glimpse of how people see the world and accept information.

Did you see the movie "Psycho?" Perhaps you read the story "Sybil." These stories deal with split-personalities. The people whose stories of being more than one person were considered to be traveling life's road with their trains slightly off track, but here is some news for you. You discovered in Chapter 13 that you were housing three people within yourself. Now you are going to learn that you have two different people inhabiting your head as you discover that you are predominantly left-brained or right-brained. If your addition is correct, the count is now up to five people operating within that neat little compact body of yours. Before you drop your book to seek professional help, be assured that you are not abnormal—at least, no more abnormal than the rest of us. Everyone has these persons within.

The Need for Understanding

Why study transactional analysis, left/right brain dominance and similar theories? Here are four benefits of studying these ideas:

1. They provide a means of examining your life to see where you are deficient, where you are doing well, and what gives your life meaning or perhaps what gives it no meaning at all.
2. They give you ways to understand yourself better.
3. They provide ways to understand others and your relations with them.
4. They give you insight and make you more adaptable to change.

No matter what has happened to you in the past, whether planned or unplanned, the accumulation of knowledge about what makes you tick helps you to realize that you are responsible for what happens in your future.

You are responsible for *you.* You have choices to make. Information is available to help you make those choices. Do not blame others; do not blame circumstances. Take the responsibility for being what you want to be.

The student of transactional analysis views personality in terms of the Parent, Adult, and Child in order to deal with this personality structure within self and others.

Transactional analysis is one means of understanding yourself. Have you ever said to yourself, after doing something silly or speaking out of turn, "Did I say that?" or "I didn't *really* do that, did I?" It was you all right; however, it might have been the Child's ego state popping through in what should have been an Adult-ego-state situation.

Like transactional analysis, the information on the use and functions of left- and right-brain is scientifically based. The background is complex, but the results are presented in language that is understandable and usable.

Why bring psychology into the picture at all? is a perfectly legitimate question. First, remember that every thought, idea, or concept throughout this book is presented for consideration only. You must decide how much value each has for you. The more exposure to different ideas you have, the more choices you have in your personal development.

Second, your world will change more rapidly than that of any generation before you. You should become curious about current ideas and alert for what is to come. The next generations will have to sort through more information than do you.

Third, there is a magic word that cannot be ignored. That word is communication. The song tells us, "What the World Needs Now Is Love, Sweet Love." That may be true, but love must still be expressed by a sound, a movement, or a word. It does not matter if the tools for better communication are generated by psychologists or psychopaths. If the tools work or have potential, don't ignore them. Get acquainted with new ideas in these times of rapidly developing communication tools. Many tools are not even mentioned here. Begin your own search for additional and alternative knowledge—for your own sake.

Left Brain/Right Brain

You need to know that the brain is divided into a right hemisphere and a left hemisphere. Objects in the left visual field are perceived in the brain's right hemisphere and objects in the right visual field are perceived in the brain's left hemisphere. The two halves of your brain are connected by millions of nerve fibers that form a thick cable called the *corpus callosum.*

Just as you are predominantly left-handed or right-handed, you are also predominantly left-brained or right-brained. Neither dominance is better than the other.

There was a time when being left-handed was treated as less desirable. An elderly lady tells the story of how years ago her grade school teacher had tried to force her to write right-handed. Her parents intervened, informing the teacher that they were fully aware that their daughter was left-handed and if this was natural for her then she should be allowed to function as a left-handed person.

This story has no surprise ending. The little girl did not grow up to be a national figure. The story is true and the girl graduated as salutatorian of her high school class.

"Why shouldn't she be salutatorian?" you may ask. What is the big deal? You are right, there is no big deal. Left- or right-brain dominance is no big deal either.

The important thing is to know the characteristics of each brain hemisphere and to understand how you operate most comfortably and naturally. You should also be aware of what to do to make better use of both hemispheres of the brain so that you can come closer to utilizing the whole brain.

People with left-brain dominance tend to:

- Be goal setters
- Evaluate people, things, and situations
- Be critical
- Like competition (want to win)
- Do research before making decisions
- Like discipline and controls
- Like to get things done
- Like things in logical (sequential) order
- Like ritual
- Promote hard work

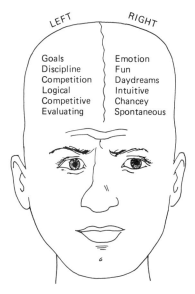

People with right-brain dominance tend to be:

- Good at visualizing
- Emotional
- Fun-loving
- Witty
- Dancers
- Daydreamers
- Good at solving unconventional problems
- Risk takers
- Resourceful
- Spontaneous
- Intuitive

The left side of the brain creates order through words, while the right side creates order through pictures. If, for example, you are putting a bicycle together, your left brain wants to read the instruction book while the right brain is looking to see if there are any pictures to follow. (The whole brain is probably looking for a way to duck out and avoid figuring it out at all!)

This book primarily encourages left-brain development by advocating goal setting, and an orderly approach to personal and career endeavors.

If you think about it, you will realize that the entire educational system is structured for left-brain-dominant learners. Special encouragement is needed for right-brain-dominant people. This is not—we repeat with emphasis—a criticism of the left-brain-dominant learner. There is absolutely nothing wrong with being left-brain dominant. As the world functions, it is a definite advantage. Being right-brain dominant is not a handicap either, for you are the creative element in this world. You may have trouble at report card time, but do not belittle yourself just because you have trouble in a left-brained environment. Do not use this concept as an excuse for bad grades, either. You work in a left-brained environment in school which forces you to develop that hemisphere and brings you closer to full functioning.

In addition to acquainting you with left- and right-brain functions, one of the objectives of this chapter is to allow you to begin developing that side of your brain that is not dominant so that you can perform with a full range of skills.

Since the educational system focuses on people with left-brain dominance and the acquisition of left-brain skills, this chapter dwells primarily on how to acquire right-brain characteristics.

Do not think that people are exclusively right- or left-brained. The key word is *predominantly*, which means that a person is more comfortable one way or the other. To describe someone as left-brained or right-brained is incorrect. Both hemispheres are at work. The objective is to work comfortably in both.

It's Not Mystical

Attempting to increase right-brain use can be quite uncomfortable, especially for left-brain-dominant people. The effort seems contrary to all the instruction and preaching you have heard most of your life. Nothing is mystical or unnatural, however, about letting your feelings *help* you make decisions. Few people will deny that in addition to the facts, a gut feeling enters into a final decision. This gut feeling is produced by the right side of the brain.

When you experience a feeling you cannot account for normally, stop for a minute and ask yourself why you feel as you do. Feelings and moods are the language of intuition, which is a right-brain function.

This whole thing is probably not as foreign to you as you first thought, is it?

One method of getting your right side to work is to recognize when and where you get your most innovative ideas. Some people say that their most innovative time is just after lying down in bed at the end of the day or when they are unable to sleep. Other people find their creative times come while driving, jogging, watching a T.V. program that isn't interesting, or while swimming, shaving, sitting under a hair dryer, or listening to symphony music. Maybe one of these samples applies to you. Recall when and where you were when an innovative thought hit you, then put yourself in that type of situation and relax. Don't force ideas; let them happen.

The Goal

The goal is to develop the side of the brain that is not dominant. Using both sides of your brain enables you to perform your job or live your life more efficiently, easily, and creatively.

People accomplish creative things when they are not confined by sequential thinking, controls, and discipline. Yet without the discipline, the creative answer to a problem has no direction for its implementation.

Strive to develop and use both sides of your brain. If you do not, you are limiting yourself, like having two hands and using only one. *Whole Brain Thinking: Working from Both Sides of the Brain to Achieve Peak Job Performance,* by Jacquelyn Wonder and Priscilla Donovan is a helpful reference.

Another stride in understanding human behavior and communication is a new concept called Neuro Linguistic Programming. Are you, by any chance, saying . . . Neuro who? Well, it isn't Nero Caesar, that's for sure! Neuro Linguistic Programming, or NLP, has been around for only a few years. It was developed by Richard Bandler, John Grinder, Leslie Cameron Bandler, and Judith De Lozier. The book *Frogs Into Princes,* authored by Richard Bandler and John Grinder, is probably the best resource available for gaining insight into this concept.

There are a couple of thoughts that come through loud and clear in Neuro Linguistic Programming that are not at all new to you. One is that NLP points out or reinforces the idea that human beings are complex creatures, individually and collectively. This is so obvious that it is surprising how often the reminder is necessary.

NLP also points out how unreliable words are. As you remember from Chapter 11, words are mere symbols. The word *car,* for example, can represent a different kind of vehicle to different people.

All words conjure up different recollections, based on different experiences. Since communication relies on using words, spoken or written, you hope that what they represent to you will be at least similar to what they represent to others.

This book is a perfect example. It is full of words, and for you to completely understand what the writers mean, each word or symbol must hold the same meaning for them and for you. The information you are receiving at this moment on the subject of Neuro Linguistic Programming is distorted, simply because it is second-hand. For first hand information, we refer you to the book written by Bandler and Grinder.

Different people think differently. That revelation is not amazing, is it? You must learn what the differences are and how to cope with them so you can adjust. You need to be in contact with others as you communicate. The skill to master is discovering how others think and changing your behavior patterns to coincide with theirs, to open clearer, cleaner communication channels.

You may find that NLP has some answers for you. You may find that NLP has some valid suggestions or some ideas worth considering. Regardless of how intensely you consider the information, you will certainly find it worth considering.

Before reading this section, you probably had never heard of NLP. Yet, you operated with some process or strategy of your own all your life. Your process, like most people's, is unconscious. Therefore, what Neuro Linguistic Programming has to offer is not really new; but it furnishes you with a frame of reference and a new vocabulary to make you aware of what has been going on all along.

NLP divides the ways people think into three principal categories, vision, hearing, and feeling. These categories are based on the senses. Internally, people generate visual images, experience feelings, or carry on mental conversations.

This information can help you know what is going on inside other people, and how to fit into their representational system to communicate more clearly. You must listen for clues in the ways other people choose to express themselves.

For example, consider the people who think visually. As they communicate, these people make statements like: I *see*, *Show* me, I'll *look* into the situation, Can we *focus* on the real problem? A person who uses the sense of feeling might say: I can *handle* that task, I certainly do have a *grip* on the problem I find it difficult to *grasp* what you are trying to tell me.

You must pay close attention to the person you are communicating with to determine what is being expressed and how it is being expressed. You use the same kind of references in your own speech. Adjust your behavior and choice of words to get on others people's wavelengths. Begin to talk their language, and communication improves.

Since human beings are so complex, be sure to remember that there is an exception to every rule. Whatever works with most people, does not necessarily work with everyone. The right-brain/left-brain concept, for example, is not accurate in every case. In some individuals, the functions might be reversed in terms of which side is the organization side and which is the creative side.

As you learn more about Neuro Linguistic Programming, you will discover that the originators of the concept are the first to say they have not examined all the possibilities for the use of their material.

Another way of looking at NLP is to think of it as a highly sophisticated, but subtle form of body language. An eye movement or the tightening of a muscle

can relate more than words, if you are alert and in tune with these indicators. This awareness is not reserved for psychologists alone. With understanding and practice, anyone who develops a discerning eye can use these clues.

Grinder and Bandler tell us, "You will always get answers to your questions insofar as you have the sensory apparatus to notice the responses." They are talking about the ability to pick up on the minute movement of the eyes, or the tension in a muscle.

Think about the different ways people think—through seeing, hearing, and feeling. People who think in pictures, raise their eyes. If the person is creating a picture from memory, the eyes go up and to the left. If the picture is of a constructed image, the eyes move upward and to the right. This is generally true for right-handed people; left-handed people move their eyes in the opposite directions.

An image recalled from memory is something you have seen before. What color are the shoes you are wearing—without looking? You simply remember. If you were asked how your shoes would look with hair growing out of them, you construct an image, because you have never seen hair growing out of your shoes.

To increase your awareness of the clues available as you communicate, notice others' eye movements when you converse with them. Eyes that are not focused and motionless also have a message. Eye movements will be different when you ask visual questions, auditory questions, or feeling questions. Different eye movements accompany each of these questions:

1. What color are your shoes? (visual)
2. How does rain hitting a skylight sound? (auditory)
3. How do you feel when you are sitting in a sauna? (feeling)

The eye movements are *visual accessing cues.*

The words you choose make you conscious of what portion of your complex internal process is brought into awareness. Words help you understand how to express yourself. The way you choose words to represent your experiences and understanding is termed your *representational system.*

When you use your experiences to interpret words, you are using your reference system. You use your reference system to decide if what you know is true.

Strategies, sequencing, processes, representational systems, accessing, referencing, eye-scanning patterns—all have a part to play in Neuro Linguistic

Programming. This strange concept is now less strange to you than it was a few minutes and a few pages ago.

The more you learn, the more responsible you feel for making the communication channels work. The better you understand what is happening, the more you must take responsibility for making it work. While information is an aid, it also complicates your life with new responsibilities.

The following example shows how people interfere with each other's reception of thoughts in everyday conversations. When you say something or ask a question, the other participants in the conversation go inside themselves to create visual images. People cannot pay attention to additional input from the outside while working on an internal visual image. You begin to feel ignored and throw out additional input, which is not received. Think about how this problem might affect a sales meeting, or any situation involving a speaker. Information pours forth like a waterfall. Sooner or later the listeners must access their internal understanding.

Listeners give all kinds of indicators as they look up and begin to visualize, or look down and engage in mental conversation. It makes no difference which internal state is taken. What is important at this point is what the sender of the information does.

The speaker should pause to give you, the listeners, time to process the information. If the speaker's tempo is too rapid, or if the speaker doesn't pause, you become confused and irritated.

Typically, what happens is that the speaker assumes you are uninterested, or have stopped paying attention, and counterattacks by talking faster and louder.

You feel attacked and confused and never really understand the content. Now a speaker who is an accomplished "rat" might ask you a question; thus ensuring that you feel totally inadequate in this communication situation.

To be fair, think how difficult it is for a speaker to assess every member of a group, and how many pauses it would take to allow each member of the group to process information. The whole point could be lost for lack of continuity.

The written word presents a similar problem, although it can be reviewed as often as necessary to get the meaning. The examples should help you understand the complexity of good communication, and alert you to what happens as you receive and deliver information.

When accessing smells, people give the direct sensory signal of flaring the nostrils. You can detect this signal, regardless of whether a person is using a visual or other primary access. Nostril flares, like the eye-scanning movements, help you read what is going on. Think of NLP as a more subtle and sophisticated form of body language. Eye scanning, changes in voice tones or tempo, changes in the skin color on the back of a hand, or the tightening and relaxing of muscles all provide information.

Summary

At this point you know a few terms and a smattering of the principles of NLP, but you have only a small sample of Neuro Linguistic Programming. You might say you have only a hand-shake acquaintance. Hopefully in the years to come, you will use NLP as a communication tool and be no stranger to the term.

T.A., Neuro Linguistic Programming, and left-brain/right-brain concepts are only representative of recent research. In addition, Alpha thinking, Beta communications, and many other ideas on human behavior also await you. Many other concepts exist and more are yet to be discovered through study, research, and refinement.

This excursion into the field of psychology was never meant to make you proficient in the use of any one of these techniques. We hope you will be alert to what is going on around you in the world today. You will be competing socially and on the job with people who understand these concepts. Ignorance of these ideas would handicap you. Whether you pursue additional information to increase your knowledge, or remain satisfied with this brief acquaintance is entirely up to you.

Summary Questions

1. List the functions or skills of the left side of the brain.

2. List the functions or skills of the right side of the brain.

3. Explain the statement, "The educational system has been structured for left-brain learners."

4. NLP divides the ways people think into three principal categories based on the senses. Name these categories.

5. In your own words, explain the value to you as a communicator of a knowledge of right-brain/left-brain dominance and NLP concepts.

CHAPTER 16

Listening

The Ear of the Beholder

Those kids never listen.

I've told you a hundred times; why don't you listen?

My parents just won't listen to me.

If those employees would listen to me just once-in-awhile, we wouldn't
have a discipline problem.

Nobody listens to me.

Does anybody out there know I'm here?

Does anybody out there care?

Have you ever heard any of these statements? Have you ever made any of
them? Why do you suppose most people answer yes to both questions? The reason
is simple. Because most people hear naturally, they take it for granted that they
are listening. Although hearing is a natural gift to most people, listening is a
skill that must be developed. Similarly, the ability to talk is different from the
ability to speak well—and ultimately to communicate.

By the way, has it ever occurred to you that you were given two ears and
one mouth? Could it be that this did not happen by chance, but because you

should be listening twice as much as you talk. If God had meant for you to talk twice as much, He would have given you two mouths!

There is an old saying that "Charity begins at home," and since this book deals with personal development, it seems only natural to start developing your listening skills with yourself.

Your conversations with yourself are your thoughts. Thoughts bombard you constantly, like a small radio inside your head that never stops broadcasting. The thoughts are produced by your Parent, your Adult, and your Child, as you discovered in Transactional Analysis. These thoughts come from your experiences; some are creative, some organizational. Thoughts enable you to respond to others during conversations. They come as suggestions when you are solving problems. They come as interruptions. They keep coming with such regularity that sometimes you are only half listening to yourself. Sometimes you have a totally unexpected thought. Have you ever said to yourself, "I haven't thought about this or that for a long time. I wonder what made me think of it now?"

Like other habits you develop in life, you have self-conversation habits or thought patterns. The habits you develop while holding these mental conversations can become attitudes. Review what you learned about positive and negative attitudes.

If you have become more aware of your attitude, then you are beginning to be in touch with your interpretations of and responses to life situations. This means that you are listening to yourself and becoming acquainted with that most important person—*you.*

If you have not made a decision to be positive then this chapter presents a second chance to get in touch with yourself. In addition, it will give more reasons why you should want to.

Understanding yourself begins as you listen closely to what you are thinking and become aware of your thought processes. To get started, you have to sort through all your random thoughts and isolate one subject. Then, concentrate on what you have to say to yourself.

When you first realize what is on your mind or how you talk to yourself you might be surprised. What you tell yourself may be totally negative. This internal dialogue may whisper depressing ideas and self-criticism.

Understanding other people is difficult unless you understand yourself. Have long talks with yourself and come to terms with yourself. Accomplish with yourself what you want to accomplish with others. Talk things over, argue, tell yourself what you want to accomplish and what kind of person you want to be. Question, negotiate, solve problems, make decisions. Understand what you want, why you want it, and where, when, and how to get it.

As you develop your ability to communicate with yourself you discover some important things about yourself—your beliefs, your values, and your attitudes. By understanding who you are and where you are coming from, you can change your behaviors if you want to.

By all means, be critical of yourself, but be careful not to be judgmental. You have good reasons for the way you are; use them as a starting point. Retain what you like and be critical of what you do not like. If you want to make some changes, talk them over with yourself. Then do anything you want to do, if you have a good reason and really want to do it.

You must take responsibility for yourself. If any one theme or objective is central to this entire study, it is that you must *make conscious choices for your direction in life.* You have ultimate control and power over your behavior. Many people go through life not realizing that they can and do have this control and that they themselves are the most powerful influence in their lives.

Take empathy, for example. Empathy is a wonderful trait. Empathy is being able to put yourself in another person's place, to see things as they do. It is a great help to communication. If you can understand another person's point of view, you can arrive at the answer to a problem with consideration for that person's feelings. However, with empathy, as with nearly everything, going too far can be detrimental. Suppose you were brought up to be considerate of others and to try to see how situations affect other people. (This book recommends that you do just that, but be moderate and consider the effects your decisions and actions have on yourself as well.)

As you exercise empathy, you may habitually relegate your own needs and desires to second place. In deciding where to spend an evening with friends, for example, you may consistently go where your friends suggest, even though the place is not your first choice.

Soon you begin to feel like the second-class friend. You ask yourself, "Why don't they ever listen to me?" or "Why don't we ever do what I want?" You may feel that "These aren't the good friends I thought after all," or "Maybe it is time to find new friends."

You have probably gone too far with empathy, and have become what is called a *door mat empathetic.*

What is happening to you socially is probably happening to you on the job as well. You go along with every idea your friends have; you accept every job your boss throws at you. You begin to resent them because they take advantage of you. You have set yourself up. What has happened is not their fault—it is *yours.* You are not bad, just making life difficult for yourself.

You should talk these things out with yourself. Changing course does not require a 180-degree turn; a few minor adjustments can make all the difference.

Empathy is a desirable attribute. Be happy you have it. Be aware of the other person's viewpoint and feelings, but be sensitive to your own. You probably do not need new friends. What you need is to give your friends the opportunity to be as good friends to you as you are to them. They need the chance to show it.

The next time your group is trying to plan an activity, be sure to express your preference. If the decision is to attend a movie, but your suggestion was to go to a ball game, be sure to extend the conversation something like this: "The movie sounds like a good idea, but I really do enjoy a ball game occasionally. Why not go to the movie this Saturday and a ball game next weekend?" Chances are you will get to your ball game. You don't dislike movies nor do your friends dislike ball games. The matter is one of degree of preference. You will probably enjoy each other more with some give and take.

On your job, the change can be made just as easily. You can still accept every job that the boss throws at you, with one adjustment—talk about it! Let the boss know what you are already working on and how much time it will take. Then ask the boss how the assignments should be prioritized. Your priorities and your employer's priorities might be totally different. You owe your employer this kind of feedback so that informed decisions on work loads and priorities can be made. The boss may split up the work or reassign some of your tasks to get you on the new assignment. In this case, you did not have to say no; you just informed the boss of the situation, to everyone's benefit. Recognize this as assertiveness— a combination of honesty, compromise, and communication, working for you because you listened to yourself.

You may be discouraged to find that some of your best traits can cause trouble and frustration. Take heart—your good qualities are really good!

People tend to put restrictive barriers and tight frameworks around themselves and their perceptions, and often do not allow themselves enough flexibility to adapt to varying circumstances. People squelch their own potential. We will discuss the development of your potential at length later. For now, let's center on some limitations you place on yourself. As you talk to yourself, you limit your abilities with phrases like these: "I could *never* do that," "I *can't* possibly do that," or "I *always* do that." Can't, never, always, are the most limiting words you can use.

Right now you might be telling yourself, "I'll *never* learn to listen to myself." Please do not say "never;" allow for circumstances. Tell yourself you can learn to listen to yourself, but you need better instruction than this book gives you.

As one means to help you begin to converse with yourself, try this exercise. Make a chart for yourself along the lines of the following example: Make three columns. In column one, write the limiting word you use when you use it. In column two, put the word with the whole thought you had at the time. In column three, write what you should be saying to yourself instead. Below is an example of what your chart should look like.

I	II	III
(The word you used: can't, never, always, etc.)	(The whole thought)	(What you should be saying to yourself instead.)
MONDAY	MONDAY	MONDAY
never	I'll *never* be able to draw.	I could draw if I wanted to take the time to learn. Drawing is simply not one of my priorities.

Make your chart as large as necessary and check yourself on a daily basis for one week. At the end of the week, discuss with yourself what is happening. Then discuss it with your instructor, a friend, or anyone you wish. By the end of the week, you probably will be using the third column only.

Now return to a familiar concept and apply it to your self-listening. Remember that words are only symbols. The words you use as you speak with yourself should be meaningful, since you know what they symbolize to you. Yet, you can be misled by stereotyping yourself. Just because you own a pinstripe suit, you can't label yourself a gangster. Just because you have trouble with this chapter you don't label yourself stupid—or do you?

Take care if you have this tendency to stereotype. You might believe yourself and develop a habit of negativism. When you say or hear the word "gangster," be sure to attach the actions of a gangster. Be sure that the actions you have in mind are universally accepted as those of gangsters. Carrying a gun is an example, but a gun alone is not enough evidence. You could be describing a duck hunter. When you gather enough evidence, you can arrive at a viable conclusion. The label "stupid" is just as easy to attach if you are prone to making rash judgments, but it is doubtful that you can gather enough information to make that label stick.

If you are sensitive enough to regard other people's feelings, why not have the same regard for your own?

Before moving on to other aspects of listening, review this bit of information from the chapter on positive attitudes, and apply it to listening to yourself. Remember to positively reinforce your desirable behaviors. Reflect on what you do well, give yourself a pat on the back for positive actions, and talk to yourself about positive improvements and changes. Do not dwell on past mistakes, do not tell yourself what you cannot do, but turn your mind to positive statements. A good way to begin is to reread the last sentence about what not to do. Change it to a positive statement.

Be supportive of yourself. Remember your successes. Deal with your accomplishments. After you have performed some task, step back and view it as someone else might. Then talk to yourself about the part of the task you did well and what you will do to improve the rest next time. Be your own best friend.

Listening is not a spectator sport. The listener is an active participant in the conversation game. In the course of a typical day, people spend 40% of their time listening, yet are only about 25% percent effective as listeners.

You do more listening than you do reading and writing put together. Stop and think of your typical day, and you will realize how true this is. Is it any wonder there is a need to develop listening habits to take advantage of this communication tool?

The example you are about to read is a good one because the entire communication is based on the idea that people listen attentively. If they do not concentrate, the communication is lost, with no opportunity for recovery. The example is not good, however, because it does not provide opportunities to practice the principles of active listening through participation. Nevertheless it gives you a good idea of what often happens in one-to-one communication. The example involves a familiar item—the radio.

Many people start their day listening to the radio—more accurately, *hearing* the radio. Perhaps you are one of these people; maybe your radio wakes you each morning. Some people want information on weather conditions to select proper clothing for the day. Some want the news; some tune in to have some company. In between conversations with family members, thoughts of upcoming activities of the day, getting breakfast, and performing the morning routine, something like this often happens. The weather conditions are broadcast and you say, "I missed that, what did they say?" If someone else is present, chances are good that the answer will be, "Gosh, I missed it too; I wasn't listening either."

Distractions and other thoughts trespass on the listener's concentration in one-to-one conversations as well.

Obviously the radio broadcast is a one-way communication and the listener cannot take an active part in giving feedback to the speaker, but listening to the radio is a great way to practice concentration.

Active listening puts the listener in the communication picture, making you, as a listener, a participant rather than a spectator.

The active listener does not interrupt, but encourages the speaker to continue talking. The first rule is to be open and accepting.

Listen attentively to what the speaker is saying and be alert to voice inflections and physical gestures that are telling you things that words alone cannot. Many people are too busy thinking of what they are going to say in reply, and their listening suffers from a lack of attention.

The listener invites the speaker to continue. You can let someone know you are receiving the message and following what is said with a nod of the head, a facial expression, a shrug, or other body language. The listener should provide feedback. This feedback should let the speaker know you have been listening. Make it brief to encourage the speaker to continue or elaborate. Do not swing the conversation to yourself as principal speaker.

This feedback could take the form of a brief summary of what was said, to let the speaker know that you listened and understood the message as it was intended. You could ask a question to get additional information or to clarify what was already said. In either event, the speaker knows you were paying attention.

Listening is no less important to one person or group than to another. It is as important in personal relationships as it is in all forms of business. The accountant needs well-developed listening skills, as does the journalist who acts as the eyes and ears of the general population.

We use a sales situation as an example to illustrate how quickly the conversational ball can be dropped because of inadequate listening skills. Listening is of paramount importance to salespeople, since conversations have immediate effects on profits.

Study this example: A woman and a man arrive together at an automotive dealership. They walk up to a salesperson and say, "We are interested in buying a car." Certainly the salesperson heard the statement, but if the salesperson was listening closely, it is obvious that no indication was given of the specific needs or wants of the potential customers. The salesperson must become a participant in the conversation at this point.

If nothing more was said, it would be only natural for the salesperson to show the couple the top of the line of new cars. Why not? The couple did not elaborate or offer any real information, nor did the salesperson bother to ask a question to get all of the parties thinking in similar terms.

What happens? Unless the salesperson happened to guess correctly, the couple acknowledge the fine features of the automobile they were shown, but add that they want to look around before making a decision.

Obviously, this salesperson needed more information. Did the couple want a new car or a used car? Was it to be their first car or a second car? Were they interested in big car comfort, or small car economy? Were they looking for a family car or a car for weekend camping trips? What price range did they have in mind?

Getting the right information through conversation and active listening would have put this salesperson in a position to assist the prospective buyers.

Listening Habits

Listening habits, like any other habits, take time to form. If they are bad habits, they take time to break and reform. Your habits constitute the way you behave.

The subject of behavior, what it is, and how it can be changed will be presented in a chapter of its own. It will be touched on here as it applies to listening behavior or habits.

Your listening behavior, like all habits, begins at birth. From childhood you receive information from people, events, and observation, and you shape that information. You behave as you do as a result of information you received that formed your:

Attitudes	Beliefs
Values	Priorities
Experience	Assumptions
Word Symbols	Images
Memories	Environment
Feelings	Stereotypes
Goals	Potential

The way you listen to what you hear as you accept and interpret messages permeates all these influences.

You are already familiar with transactional analysis and the "I'm OK, You're OK" positions. Whether or not you feel "OK" affects your listening habits. Let your exposure to transactional analysis and your knowledge about it serve you as you develop your listening skills.

Rarely can you talk to someone who doesn't give advice or make judgments. The luckiest people in the world are people who have someone they love or a good friend who will just listen, because they want to.

To give advice is easy. To say simply, "Can I help?" is more difficult, but more appropriate. Let the speaker decide. More often than not the answer will be, "No, but thanks for listening."

A Listening List

Where is there a checklist that presents all the factors connected with good listening? Who might have produced such a document to be used for reference? We searched books, periodicals, magazines, and other resources, and talked to people to discover the best reference to present to you. After all, how good can a chapter be without a checklist?

The result was unexpected. Not only one list, but list after list was found. Many were similar; none were identical. To use each would make this chapter excessively long, redundant, and boring. The following list includes only the titles of some of the lists you might encounter in your own research.

- Rules for Good Listening
- Stages of Listening
- Principles of Analytical Listening
- Kinds of Listeners
- Factors of Good Listening
- Bad Listening Habits
- Suggestions for Improving Listening
- Improving Listening Checklist
- Listening Style
- Attributes of an Effective Listener
- Methods to Improve Listening
- Barriers to Good Listening

While each of these lists is excellent, none are identical. Most of the concepts appear more than once, but not necessarily under similar titles.

To avoid repetition, we have combined the many ideas in circulation into one list. A few new thoughts will not be found in any other list to date.

A Comprehensive List of Helpful Hints to Improve Listening Habits

(This may be a record for the longest title, as well as the longest single list. Aren't you lucky?)

1. *Empathy*—The leader in the hit parade of good listening habits is empathy. This was the item most often found in the other lists mentioned. Empathy is putting yourself in the other person's place, seeing things from another's point of view. With empathy you become nonjudgmental as you receive information, and your nonevaluative responses make the speaker feel accepted. You pave the way for understanding. Empathy pays off in social relationships: Friends become more open because they feel accepted by you. In business empathy builds trust and relationships with long-term repeat customers. Empathy can work for you to alleviate a strained conversation during an interview. When both interviewer and applicant relax, a more meaningful exchange of information takes place.

One fact that needs emphasis is this: You do not have to agree with what the speaker is saying to empathize. Simply respect the speaker's right to a different viewpoint. The saying, "I may not agree with what you said, but I'll defend to the death your right to say it," is appropriate here.

2. *You Don't Say*—also referred to by some writers and lecturers as listening between-the-lines. What is actually said is only part, and often not the most important part, of the total message. Body movements, tone of voice, facial expressions, and gestures carry more of the real message than just the words.

How often have you heard someone say, "Maybe that's what I said, but it is not what I meant." When you detect that what is being said is not the real message, some judicious questioning or feedback could help the speaker get in touch with the intended message.

As a listener alert to the nonverbal messages coming from the speaker, you can send some nonverbal messages of your own. A smile, a shake of the head, and frequent eye contact to show interest are examples of how to use nonverbal skills to demonstrate that you are in tune as a listener.

3. *Feedback*—As a listener and student of listening, who is alert to all of the communication signals being sent, you know how difficult it is to be completely accurate in your reception of a message. Thus, feedback enters the picture. The speaker needs feedback to know that the message is being received—not just any message, but the intended message. The listener must check that what has been received is accurate. The question is one method of giving feedback. A question invites clarification of something said or elicits elaboration on a point, and furnishes you, the listener, with additional information or with evidence that what you hear is the message intended. Another way to give feedback is a short statement. "I agree with you," tells the speaker you are listening. If you disagree with what was said, your phrase might be, "Would you mind elaborating on that point?" Notice you do not have to agree, but do not disagree. If you listen carefully to the elaboration, you at least learn to appreciate another point of view, without necessarily agreeing on the point itself. Use feedback to clear any misunderstandings as they occur. Never let a point bother you, or you stop listening to dwell on your own thoughts about a point that you may have misunderstood.

4. *Use Titles*—Like a formal speech or a book with an outline, every speaker, even a friend conversing informally, has a central theme or topic. Try to zero in on that theme. From this central idea come other subtopics. Speakers in a formal or informal setting follow this same format. In the informal atmosphere it is up to you, the listener, to mentally sort through the information to isolate the main idea. Sometimes what the speaker wants to convey is evident, for example, "I want to talk to you about feedback as a technique for good listening." At other times a conversation begins with what seems to you an off-the-wall statement, and you wonder where the conversation is going. The question, "Have you ever had one of those days?" is an example of a vague opening. You can

logically suspect that the speaker's life has not been coming up roses recently, but you cannot be sure of the main topic of the conversation. The communication could be related to job, love-life, or money, or it could be a comment on the state of the world, or any one of an infinite number of other topics. You can put the conversation together if you listen for the central idea and then form subcategories in your mind. Then examples and elaborations the speaker makes on these points will fall into place.

5. *Attitude Alert*—Considering the earlier chapter on attitude, and the repeated references to it throughout the text, this discussion of attitude with regard to listening will be brief.

Listen for the attitude of the speaker. Be sure that your attitude as listener remains positive. Since you know attitudes are contagious, do not catch a negative one from your speaker or feed back a negative attitude.

Identify the speaker's attitude toward the subject so that you receive the correct message. Consider for a moment your knowledge of transactional analysis. Place yourself, as listener, in your Adult mode—not in your Parent or Child mode—in order to remain nonjudgmental and nonargumentative.

6. *Anticipate*—When you anticipate what a speaker will say next, one of two things will happen, you will be right or you will be wrong! In either case, you have to pay attention to find out.

7. *Take Inventory*—As you listen, review in your mind, what the speaker has been saying. Make sure that the points are consistent, not contradictory. The speaker may use an example that argues against what you thought was the speaker's position on the subject. At this point ask a question for clarification.

Periodically take inventory. Summarizing keeps you abreast of where the speaker has been so that you can discount repetition and devote your listening to new points. In formal situations speakers summarize to point out highlights. Why not convert this strategy to a basic tool for listening?

8. *Resist Distractions*—Probably the first comment that comes to mind is, "That's easy for you to write, but not so easy to do." You are so right. People can receive and process information at 300 to 500 words per minute. On the other hand, people speak at a rate of approximately 200 words per minute. By applying simple mathematics, you immediately see that there is a 100 to 300 word differential between the rate at which you take in information and the rate at which the speaker can deliver a message. No wonder Alvin and the Chipmunks sold so many records with their rapid-fire delivery!

Your mind has time to wander, but this gap makes it possible for you to use the techniques of Anticipation and Taking Inventory. Using these techniques keeps your concentration focused on the speaker.

Distractions come in all shapes sizes, and colors; most of all they come in abundance. A few examples will start you thinking of some of your own.

1. The good-looking gal or guy who just happens to walk by when you are trying to pay attention
2. The clock ticking toward quitting time
3. The deadlines you are missing
4. Someone who is trying to get your attention
5. The phone ringing
6. Competition from the radio or TV
7. A crooked picture on the wall
8. Passing traffic
9. A strange loud noise

10. An uninteresting subject or speaker

11. A fly on the speaker's jacket

12. Your stomach growling loudly

These examples merely scratch the surface. Distractions come at you from the outside and the inside. Distractions from within are the ones you allow when you let your mind wander. Combat these distractions by making a conscious decision to concentrate on the speaker and the message, and by channeling your mind to some of the suggested listening techniques.

To deal with outside competition for your concentration, use whatever resources are readily available. If you are standing in a lobby, position yourself so that you are facing a wall to cut yourself off from as many visual distractions as possible. If you are in a room where you can sit, pick a comfortable chair so you will not be squirming in agony from physical discomfort. Any small advantage you can give yourself will help you concentrate.

9. *Common Denominator*—This technique suggests that you search for something about the message or the speaker that you can use as a basis for agreement. This allows you to maintain a positive frame of mind. Tell yourself that despite the distasteful subject and the speaker's dreadful delivery and disheveled appearance, you appreciate the exposure to the perfect example of what *not* to say and do.

If you have come this far, you have a real grasp of positiveness. Share a secret smile with yourself.

10. *Be Critical of the Message, Not the Speaker*—If you must be critical, criticize the message for faulty facts, and unclear content. You can make this determination only if you are paying close attention to the total message. This kind of criticism means you are performing well as a listener.

If you are critical of the speaker because of your prejudices, however, you are letting your influence as a listener become inefficient and ineffective.

A speaker's appearance, gestures, or attitude should not cause you to become an inefficient listener. If the speaker has an accent, you should listen even more intently so you can bridge the gap in the situation. Certainly this is no time to throw in the towel and permit your mind to wander.

If you tune out, you will probably turn your speaker off too. Judge the message, if you must, but not the person. This example may help: If someone approached you and said, "Your child was just in a terrible accident and has been taken to the hospital in the emergency unit," would you care how the person was dressed, or whether that person had long hair or was bald? Would it make a difference if the person had an accent? Would it matter if the person was white, black, red, orange, or green? What is important is the message.

11. *The Sizzle*—In the world of selling there is a frequently used phrase that instructs salespeople to "sell with sizzle." The idea is that an appeal to the senses is a great motivator. For example, at one time or another you have probably walked by a restaurant and caught the aroma of food cooking. Suddenly you found it difficult or impossible to resist going inside and getting something to eat. The principle at work is the same.

Some words or ideas can stir immediate, almost involuntary responses in people. Just as a reflex causes your leg to jump when the doctor taps your knee with a hammer, some words and ideas can change an attitude instantly.

Some people have an extremely difficult time with the word "death," for example. These people find it distasteful to discuss making a will or buying life insurance. Related words such as "funeral" are also unwelcome in their vocabulary.

Political ideas also stir emotions. If you happen to be in conversation with a staunch supporter of your party, you show one type of emotion. If the speaker has the opposite affiliation, you will experience equal, but opposite emotions.

Senses and emotions are delicate and sometimes extremely touchy. To be in charge of your emotions takes a great deal of self control and constant awareness and vigilance. As a listener you must guard against letting your feelings run away with your mind and deterring you from your mission as a listener.

Do not allow your biases, beliefs, opinions, and frustrations to interfere with your concentration. Why not turn them into an opportunity? At difficult times, listen even more closely. In this way you collect all the information the speaker has before you make your rebuttal, if one is necessary.

If you turn the speaker off, you perform a double disservice. First you violate one of your good listening habits. Second, you rob yourself of the total learning experience.

12. *I Want to Solve Your Problems*—A grave mistake many listeners make is to try to solve the problem identified by the speaker. This kind of listening is not listening at all—it is interfering, and can destroy friendships and business relationships.

Earlier in this chapter you were exposed to a short segment wherein you read that people who have someone who will just listen are very lucky, indeed. Now, add the thought that not only are they lucky, but the good fortune extends to the listener as well.

Sadly, many listeners do not feel that people are qualified to solve their own problems, or they assume that merely voicing a problem is a call for help or a complaint. The result is often the same. The listener takes over as the speaker and offers advice or volunteers to do something about the situation.

The original speaker leaves the conversation thinking, "Don't you think I can handle this problem myself? You don't have much confidence in me," or

"Hey! That worked pretty well. I found someone who wants to solve my problems for me so I don't have to worry. You can bet I will dump more of them there."

These attitudes strain friendships or business relationships. When the listener volunteers to take the problem, the speaker is viewed as a complainer or an incompetent—or worse, an *incompetent complainer.*

The listener is responsible for turning the other person into the kind of friend or business associate people do not like. The next time a difficult situation presents itself, that person may return to dump another problem.

If the speaker asks for help, the circumstance is different. The best way to assist is to explore alternative solutions. Once alternatives have been listed, let the speaker choose the best course of action.

The one exception to this rule is the case of a husband and wife. In this relationship, sharing is the proper way to tackle successes and difficulties. *Sharing* is the key word—no dumping is allowed by either partner.

13. *Take Notes*—Note taking is familiar as a classroom technique. There is a *recommended* way to take notes—the right way is the way that works for you. The recommended ways to take more meaningful notes are as follows:

1. Notes are meant to be memory joggers, so limit your initial notes to key words and phrases. Review these notes soon after your initial encounter to complete the thoughts that you wrote in brief. Review helps set the material more firmly in your mind. Completing and adding to a brief note gives you a better reference for the future, when the original material becomes fuzzy.

2. Keep notes brief. While you make notes your attention is not fully focused on the speaker and listening suffers momentarily. Review notes as soon as possible, while you have the best recall, and expand on the brief thoughts you jotted down.

Applications for note taking as a listening technique stretch beyond the classroom, lecture hall, conference table, and seminar. Pocket notebooks and appointment calendars are handy items for taking notes. Business cards are nothing more than preprinted notes. Desks almost always have note pads standing by that can be grabbed simultaneously with the telephone receiver.

When people attend conferences, workshops, and seminars, they should carry a note pad and keep a record of new acquaintances with similar business interests. These people can be contacted later to discuss common business problems and situations.

Efficient note taking requires practice, but can be useful in your listening tool box.

14. *Active Listening*—This item appears on nearly everyone's list of listening tools. It is so comprehensive that it serves to summarize the other techniques listed.

Active listening includes refraining from judgments and evaluations of the speaker, and placing yourself, the listener, in the speaker's position (empathizing). The listener concentrates on main ideas, acknowledging and responding, but not interrupting or taking over the conversation. Active listening requires a conscious effort to ignore distractions, and to become aware of the full message by being alert to body language. The listener should probe, paraphrase, question, reflect feelings, and *work at listening*.

15. *Work at Listening*—Hearing may come naturally, but listening takes work. To develop good listening habits takes time and energy.

If you are determined to be a good listener, a good goal setter, or a good image dresser, do not give up on yourself. Practice is what is important and what enables you to achieve what you want. New habits are not formed overnight. Old habits are not discarded with a flick of the wrist. You must have a determination to change and stick to your plan. The change will happen.

Consistent practice works wonders. Active, efficient listening takes concerted effort but the rewards in terms of your ability to acquire ideas and information make the effort worthwhile.

Self-evaluation

On a scale of 1–10 (with 1 as the lowest score and 10 the highest) rate yourself on your listening skills with regard to the following items:

_____ Gives the speaker undivided attention.

_____ Asks the speaker to repeat something if necessary for understanding.

_____ Uses appropriate body language and other nonverbal cues to encourage the speaker.

_____ Takes steps to reduce outside interference and interruption.

_____ Takes steps to provide a comfortable setting conducive to listening.

_____ Lets the speaker complete a statement or topic before commenting or questioning.

_____ Concentrates on broad ideas rather than picking on an isolated fact or statement.

_____ Controls emotional bias and distractions (long hair, short hair, sex, accent, etc.)

_____ Makes use of questions and summarizing as feedback tools to gain understanding.

_____ Remains open and positive toward the speaker regardless of physical or emotional barriers.

_____ Takes short, meaningful notes.

_____ Reviews and expands on notes as soon as possible.

_____ Keeps alert to the speaker's voice tones, inflections, body language, and other nonverbal clues in order to receive and understand the total message.

_____ Separates fact from opinion.

_____ Avoids mental side trips.

_____ Refrains from interrupting the listening process by thinking of a response.

_____ Is committed to listening actively.

_____ Resolves to practice becoming a better listener.

Try to come as close to 10 as possible in each category. If you have rated yourself honestly you will discover that:

1. You are probably very efficient in some areas, but not so good in others.
2. You are already using the concepts to some degree. Congratulate yourself for that.
3. You can begin to improve your weak areas because you know where to concentrate your efforts.

Listening in a Hostile Situation

Few experiences are more traumatic, unpleasant, and undesirable than confrontations. When someone pushes you either physically or verbally, the automatic response is to push back.

Confrontation situations occur on the job between supervisors and workers, in social circumstances between friends, and among members of a family. The best approach is to stay cool, calm, and collected, and listen. To adopt this stance is more easily said than done, as you must control every natural inclination you have to fight back.

A problem exists in a confrontation situation, whether it is real or imagined. The first order of business is to identify the problem. Then proceed to resolve it.

A good listener knows that all of the messages tossed out have to be sorted to find the main idea or problem. The listener takes into account the intonations, body language, and other verbal and nonverbal cues.

The response must be constructive and tension-reducing to set the stage for a positive and constructive conversation. A technique that works surprisingly often is the use of the familiar "Thank you."

"Thank you," spoken sincerely by the person under attack, is the last response the aggressor expects to hear. The hesitation which normally follows gives you the opportunity to explain why you are thankful for the complaint and sets up the positive atmosphere.

The explanation follows these lines. "I am grateful that you came to me with your complaint rather than harboring bad feeling about me (or my company or my product). You might have talked behind my back, or never spoken to me again. I appreciate that you are giving me a chance to explain.

Next, attempt to find some point of agreement on any part of the main idea of the speaker's conversation. If you can reach agreement on even the smallest item, you have taken a positive step toward diminishing hostility.

Let the complainer or aggressor do most of the initial talking, to release the aggressive energy. When the energy is spent it will be easier to carry on a two-way conversation.

Avoid getting caught in the game of overreacting to someone else's over-reaction.

Listening and Time

To be good at listening means that you devote time and effort to the commitment. Managing your time is an important skill. Since good listening habits require that you give the speaker your undivided attention and concentration, you must give up some time to permit that individual to communicate fully. When you make the commitment to be a good listener, you must also decide to give listening a priority in your time budget.

Failing to make the time commitment can interfere with your performance as a listener. Consider all of the competitors for your time. All the people and things—including yourself—that whisper to you constantly, "Take care of me *first.*"

Who and what are these interrupters? On the job, those responsible to you want you to listen to them. Those to whom you are responsible also want you to listen. Work itself is awaiting you, screaming, "Take care of me!" Your loved ones expect to have a slice of your time, interest, and attention. Your bank account yells for help; your monthly bills insist that you take care of them. Your car is waiting for you and informs you with rattles and bangs that it grows impatient. The IRS gently whispers, "It's tax time—don't forget us." On and on, the list could continue.

With these and thousands of other thoughts bringing worry and tension, is it any wonder that people are preoccupied and find concentrated listening difficult?

Taking time to listen to the first communicator can save time in the long run. What you do not listen to the first time will probably have to be repeated, costing more time. A minor problem that may have been solved by listening in the early stages, can turn into a larger and more difficult problem that will take more time to solve.

Consider this example: You are listening to someone, but in a preoccupied state of mind. The conversation is finished, and you go on about your business, but your mind wanders back to the recent communication you only partially heard and understood. These thoughts interrupt and interfere with your concentration on the task at hand. This halfway listening and loss of concentration can begin to snowball, until your perception becomes foggy. Now you have to start from the beginning and get a grip on situations you should have understood the first time around. Many people admit this happens quite frequently, so do not feel lonely if it has happened to you. You can do something about it, however, if you improve your listening habits.

Parting Shots

A little review and something new will close this chapter. Think about this: If you really begin to listen, you become involved, and when you become involved you want to participate. When you find yourself at the participation stage you know you are on the way to becoming a professional listener. Remember you may *hear* with your ears, but you *listen* with your mind and all your senses.

As you refine your listening skills you will discover many conflicting ideas. "Absence makes the heart grow fonder," contradicts, "Out of sight, out of mind." A seasoned listener knows that either statement could be appropriate, depending on the circumstances. This example shows that two points of view can be valid, even though they contradict each other. Another factor to consider is the disposition of the speaker and whether that individual is a positive or negative person.

There is another kind of conflict in thinking that may present itself. You should be aware that, "The wheel that squeaks gets the grease," meaning you have to speak out loudly and often to get your way. If you do not speak up, people will walk all over you.

Remember that there is a time and place for everything. Being a good communicator requires both speaking and listening. Being a good listener does not mean you give up your right to speak. Listening prepares you to speak when it is your turn with knowledge, clarity, certainty, and authority.

When you are *speaking,* you hear only what you already know. When you *listen,* you learn what others know. In the first instance you are educating; in the second, you are being educated. The more you know, the more advantage you have.

The following game can aid you in developing your listening skills. Take an object, like a tennis ball, or simply a wad of paper. What the object is does not matter, but it must have some symbolic meaning for the speaker. The individual holding the object is the only person in the group who is allowed to speak. Other participants may not ask verbally for the object, but they may indicate through body language that they want it and they have the opportunity to add to the conversation.

The original holder of the object begins the conversation. To be heard, a new speaker must indicate a desire to speak by holding the object before beginning to talk. The second speaker, and each succeeding speaker, must briefly summarize what the speaker or speakers before have said before adding new thoughts of their own. This rule ensures that the message received is what the preceding speakers intended to send. The game continues until every person in the group has had an opportunity to practice listening techniques.

The subject of listening is probably one of the more thoroughly covered topics in this text. Yet we remind you that you still have a great deal to learn about the skill of listening. Never take for granted that you know all there is to know about a subject. If you do, you will be disappointed. Promise yourself that you will never stop learning and growing. Add constantly to what you learn here. Hold tightly to the thought that learning is a lifelong endeavor. No one ever knows all there is to know about anything.

Believe it or not, and like it or not, *listening* figures in the profit and loss statement of every small business, large company, and conglomerate in the world. Poor listening causes mistakes—costly mistakes. Gathering information for decisions is imperative and much of the information pours in orally. The concept of listening as a skill has just begun to be recognized. Businesses large and small, are beginning to realize how much impact good listening has on the human relations aspect of doing business. Listening is reflected in the attitudes of employees and customers, in production and turnover, and in sales.

Perhaps because hearing is such a natural part of life, learning to listen seems redundant, foolishly simple, like child's play. Few take it seriously or see a need for special training in this skill.

Summary Questions

1. When in life does listening begin?

2. How much of your time is spent listening? State your answer as a percentage.

3. At what percent efficiency do people listen?

4. List 10 interruptions that make listening difficult. (such as bills to be paid, IRS, etc.).

5. Why does listening require that you set a time priority for it?

6. Review the section on distractions. Make your own list and include at least ten new items of your own.

7. Try the listening exercise using a tennis ball or wad of paper as described in this chapter. Groups of 5 or 6 are the most productive. Appoint an observer for each group to take notes during the exercise. Perform the exercise in 15- or 20-minute time frames. Have the observer report on the exercise after each session.

Author's Note

The next section is composed of three chapters: a chapter on careers, a chapter on interviewing, and a chapter on careers. You are not seeing double; there are two chapters on careers.

Much discussion took place before aligning the chapters in this manner. The first chapter concerning careers contains information that is aimed primarily at people who have never been in the work force. Its emphasis is on preparation for your first job.

What is the value of this chapter to the already employed person? First of all, it provides a review of how to plan to get a position. Second, you may find a few new ideas to help make the job search easier. Third, even an employed person may have missed the opportunity to be exposed to this kind of material.

The second chapter on careers deals with the employed person who is interested in career change or career advancement.

The value to the never before employed individual is the realization that an early career choice is not necessarily the only career choice that will ever be made.

The decision to include both chapters was made in the belief that both sides of the career picture could be of value to each individual reading this book.

Thank you.

CHAPTER **17**

Seeking a Career

Get Ready to Go for It!

Careers is the topic. Your plans for your career are the focal points. Before striking a serious note, however, it is as good a time as any to get the typical jokes out of the way. This chapter is not devoted to car-ears, nor does it concern car-rears, but *careers*.

Often you hear about the good ol' days, and maybe they were. Sometimes you hear about the bad ol' days, and perhaps they were that, too. One thing about the old days is that they were simpler ol' days when it came to career pursuit, selection, and preparation.

Filling Dad's shoes, even if those shoes pinched, was the typical career choice, if any choice existed. The assumption was that the son would take over Dad's business, pursue the same profession, or learn Dad's trade.

Women also had a career choice: to be wives and mothers or to remain at home to take care of their parents. Although these careers were worthy, they were confining. Careers in the world of business and industry were all but closed to women.

Boys were allowed some choice, albeit limited. The lawyer's son might become a doctor or the baker's son, a butcher, but no one strayed too far in the social order.

Much potential was wasted. The choices available to members of minority groups were even more limited. Although the good old days or bad old days are not entirely gone, considerable changes have taken place.

The waste of our potential because of self-imposed limitations is the biggest crime of all. You have studied some of the causes of these limitations, for example, your inability to release all the power you possess in both hemispheres of the brain, and the Adult, Parent, and Child ego states that you have built. The traditions you observed while growing up—even your schooling, which is intended to expand your mind and horizons—can hamper the release of your potential. From the day you were taught to color pictures by staying within the lines, you learned to limit yourself. Certainly you must stay within limits and boundaries sometimes, but at other times you must go beyond ordinary limits to be open to new ideas, discoveries, and improvements.

The subject of realizing and releasing your potential deserves a chapter of its own. We include it here so that you realize that any career you choose is within your reach if you are willing to do what is necessary to attain it.

As times change, circumstances change, and the difficulties encountered in making a career choice change as well. The setting has shifted from one of limited choices to one of almost unlimited choices. Many of today's occupations did not even exist in the old days. This increase in the range of choices is partly due to the rapid increase in technology. Today the difficulty is to find out what all of the possibilities are, to sort through this mountain of information, and to zero in on the most appropriate and appealing opportunity.

The number of occupational options is in the thousands, and as research and technology increase more and more options appear daily. Just deciding on a career path is an exhausting task. You could almost make a career out of choosing a career. In other words, you must realize at the outset that it takes work on your part and some in-depth research to determine the direction you want your working life to take.

If you are easily discouraged, you might fall into one of several traps that await you. One of these traps you have already encountered: the amount of work necessary to make an informed decision. Another trap is the economic climate. If your positive attitude slips, you may become discouraged in a period of high unemployment.

The economy influences available opportunities. However, don't let pessimism and depression govern your outlook; it is a time to realize that more than ever you need a solid career plan.

Competition is tougher—no argument—so you must become a tough competitor. Do this by accumulating the best qualifications you can. Know where and how to look for opportunities.

Plan Carefully

Every bit of technique you picked up from the chapter on setting goals will be useful to you as you set career goals. Laying out a well considered plan for your career is crucial. You journey down a road that typically takes forty years to travel—a long time to wander aimlessly, trusting luck to provide your primary source of income.

Money, money, money! Is it a major concern? A concern, certainly, but major? Be cautious—never make money your *only* consideration. Where monetary rewards fit in your list of priorities is up to you, but if it is your one and only motivator as you begin working, you may regret limiting yourself so narrowly.

As time passes, you can be certain that personal circumstances will change. People find that work takes on different personal proportions as changes occur in family status, physical abilities, feelings toward accomplishment and satisfaction, and pure enjoyment of a job that stimulates you to get up and look forward to each day.

Many Choices

Remember when you were young and someone asked, "What do you want to be when you grow up?" (In the case of Dennis the Menace, the neighbors asked, "What do you want to be *if* we *let* you grow up?") Typical answers included a cowboy, a nurse, a fireman, and similar occupations. These are worthy occupations; if you aspire to any one of them, you could be making a wise decision— as long as it is an informed decision.

Now that you are older and faced with the decision, you realize that the great number of career possibilities complicates the decision. The possibilities number over 20,000, and the job of making a choice is complex.

The United States Office of Education has grouped jobs into fifteen clusters. The following is a list of those clusters with a few samples of possible occupations under each.

Agriculture

Farmer
Agronomist
Horse Breeder
Agricultural Engineer
Wildlife and Conservation Technician
Entomologist
County Agent

Business and Office

Accountant
Computer Programmer
Banker
Secretary
C.P.A.
Realtor

Communications and Media

T.V. Producer
Cameraperson
Newscaster
Stage Hand
Disc Jockey
Journalist

Construction

Draftsman
Carpenter
Stonemason
Architectural Engineer
Surveyor

Consumer Education and Home Economics

Homemaker
Dietician
Home Economist
Nutritionist
Credit Manager
Consumer Affairs Manager

Fine Arts and Humanities

Playwright
Entertainer
Historian
Designer
Cartoonist
Astronomer

Health

Dentist
Dental Hygienist
Doctor
Veterinarian
Medical Technician
Physical Therapist

Hospitality and Recreation

Professional Athlete
Hotel Manager
Ski Instructor
Hostess
Waitress
Stunt Person

Manufacturing

Millwright
Electrical Engineer
Machinist
Foreman
Sheet Metal Worker
Tool Designer

Marine Science

Hatchery Manager
Aquanaut
Oceanographer
Commercial fisherman
Hydrologist
Marine Biologist

Marketing and Distribution

Salesperson
Retailer
Advertising Manager
Marketing Manager
Merchandiser
Wholesaler

Natural Resources and Environment

Conservationist
Environmentalist
Sociologist
Forest Ranger
Urban Planner
Forester

Personal Services

Barber
Travel Guide
Tailor
Gardener
Marriage Counselor
Manicurist

Public Service

Teacher
Lawyer

Fire Fighter
Emergency Unit Operator
Census Taker
Member of Armed Services

Transportation

Pilot
Cab Driver
Bus Driver
Air Traffic Controller
Ship Captain
Railroader

To say that this list is merely a sample would be an understatement. Yet it serves as a place to start your thought processes. Your next stop is the library, where you can study some of the following references.

The *Occupational Outlook Handbook* and the *Dictionary of Occupational Titles* define the career. Find out what education and experience the career requires in the *Occupational Outlook Handbook,* trade magazines, and want ads in your local newspaper. You can find out what businesses hire people in the career that interests you in the *Occupational Outlook Handbook,* in want ads, and by looking

in the yellow pages. These references also give you some idea of salary ranges and prospects for the future.

Armed with this research you can begin. Get some professional advice from a career counselor. These people can supply you with testing mechanisms and additional references and can put you in touch with other individuals who can assist you.

Specifically, the counselor can acquaint you with your strengths, weaknesses, and aptitudes. While you familiarize yourself with your aptitudes, values, beliefs, priorities, and abilities, the counselor gives you general career directions. Counselors help in a general way with suggestions and recommendations based on test results and on information supplied by you in an interview. They allow you to make up your own mind. Should you decide to pursue a career choice that the tests show you not particularly suited for, do not be discouraged. Tests overlook desire and determination. Pursue that career vigorously! However, keep your eyes open to the fact that you may have to work a great deal harder to reach your goal than others who have a more obvious aptitude for that line of work.

Vast Numbers

Books such as *The Third Wave* or *Megatrends,* and publications that deal with future trends give some idea of what lies ahead. Many economic development programs are in progress throughout the nation, as cities large and small try to equip themselves to be economically strong through the year 2,000. One item of great consequence to you is population demographics—in particular, the "baby boom."

If you were born in the mid-forties to mid-sixties, known as the "baby boom" years, you are in competition with the largest number of career planners ever. Many of your competitors are aware of this fact and know how hard they must work on a career plan to be competitive. You need the same knowledge and hard work to compete with them.

Because education gives career seekers an edge, you can rest assured that you will be competing with more college students and more college graduates than ever before, as you *choose* and *enter* your first career, and when you change careers or plan for advancement. These words may sound discouraging. They are not intended to discourage, but to caution you. The message is "Know all you can." Realize the importance of thinking things through and being informed and thorough. Lay out a plan for yourself and do not take shortcuts that you will be sorry for later. Forewarned should be forearmed as you wage your battle for a career.

Career/Life Planning

In recent years the topic of career planning has attracted an additional word, becoming *career/life planning.* Career/life planning deals with your whole day— all 24 hours of it, and all seven days of every week.

Your activities outside your working life have an effect on what you do at work. Your occupation has a bearing on your at-home hours. You do not turn your work or your private life on and off at the touch of a switch; each overlaps the other. The nine-to-five job is a myth. If you do not occasionally take home a briefcase full of work, you regularly take home a mind full of it. You talk about your job at social gatherings. At work you talk about your time off.

One of the most difficult problems companies must cope with is the alcoholic employee. This social, private-life problem invades the work place. This problem may not be a problem contracted in the work surroundings, but it certainly affects them. Similarly, the frustrated employee who gets chewed out by the boss is not likely to be all smiles upon arriving at home, and may kick the dog or yell at the spouse! Neither of these examples is part of anyone's career plan, but both could result from failure to plan.

Get With It

So far, this chapter has tried to convince you to make a career/life plan for yourself. If it has succeeded, you should be restless enough to ask this question: "Why not get down to cases—can you get me a job or can't you?" The plain truth is, only *you* can get you a job or plan your successful career and life.

The chapter includes some specific exercises to get you started. Remember that this is not a career planning book, but only a chapter in a professional resource development book. The exposure to concepts may motivate you to take a course in career/life planning, or pursue the information you feel is vital for your success.

At this stage you must become better acquainted with yourself. If you have listened to yourself and have considered your Adult, Parent, and Child ego states, and your dominant brain hemisphere, you have been using your time wisely. The better you know yourself, the better you will be able to plan your career. By now you may be chomping at the bit to do something, and so you shall.

A Self Status Evaluation is the beginning point for any career/life plan. You will make this evaluation many times if you are serious about having a plan. Each time you receive additional infomation you should begin again, or at least review, to be sure you have not changed your mind about your previous plan.

Take a sheet of paper and answer the following questions:

1. What is presently happening in my life?
2. What things do I have that contribute to my financial survival?
3. What things do I need for my financial survival?
4. What things do I have that would contribute to my emotional survival?
5. What things do I need for my emotional survival?
6. What things do I have that contribute to my sense of accomplishment?
7. What things do I want that would contribute to my sense of accomplishment?
8. How effective is my current situation in meeting my needs?
9. What options are available to me to alter my situation?
10. Which can I do first?
11. When will I start?
12. When will I have accomplished it?

Career planning is something you do with or without reading about it. It is a natural thing that is necessary for everyone who needs or wants to work. You think about what you want to do and how much money you need to pay your bills and survive. You know what you want to do for your life's occupation, and how many dollars it takes to give you the freedom you want.

Career planning and life planning help you concentrate on a logical, systematic approach, defining some of the processes that you might otherwise approach in a haphazard fashion.

Backward Glance

If you have a past, use it. Because of your past, you are what you are today. Reviewing where you have been helps you decide where you are going. If you are building your first career plan, you do not have much work experience. People building a second or third plan have the advantage of being able to draw on previous successes to avoid mistakes.

Planning, includes both career and life aspects—feelings and opinions, likes and dislikes. Be "up front" with yourself and admit your preferences.

Analyze yourself by answering the following questions, and let yourself go. State the facts and elaborate on your feelings about the facts.

1. Who has been instrumental in forming your attitudes?
2. What are your attitudes toward work, family, friends, education, career planning, etc.? (Include in this list other topics you feel strongly about.)

3. What are your interests?
4. Are your attitudes predominantly positive or negative? Why?
5. What are your strengths?
6. What are your weaknesses?
7. Have you ever had to make decisions?
8. What decisions have you made?
9. How would you rate the importance of those decisions?
10. What jobs have you held?
11. What did you like/dislike about those jobs?
12. What experiences did you have at work?

Geography

Some people know a little bit about a lot of things. When it comes to career and life planning, the more you know about a lot of things, the better plan you can make.

Geography is a topic you should know more about. This advice may seem to come from left field, but should make good sense to you shortly. Geography can be an important ingredient in your job selection recipe and career plan.

Some occupations exist only in certain locations in the country, while others require you to relocate to move up the promotional ladder. Relocation could be necessary repeatedly, and some of those relocations could be outside the United States. Decide on the size community you find desirable. Climate has an influence on some people. Adjustments to cultural differences are necessary in different localities. School systems and state and local governments present important considerations.

Perhaps this brief glance at location differences encourages you to get out that old geography book for a review. At least you can see why geographical preferences in your job search and career plan are important. Do not overlook this topic if any of the items mentioned above hold significance for you.

Economics

You need a knowledge of economics in your career plan and job search. Economics is not normally a subject that makes you want to stand up and cheer. On a scale of fun things to do, studying economics typically falls somewhere between having an appendectomy and a dental check-up.

Nevertheless, you live with economic conditions. They influence the job market, and affect your career selection, your job security, and the competition you face in your job search. You need to have a grip on basic economic principles and to keep in touch through various news sources with what is happening each day. Economic principles such as the laws of *supply and demand* and *diminishing returns* can be important. As you read about the baby boom, you were alerted to the fact that the supply of job seekers is going to be large. Therefore, you should review your career plan with these questions in mind:

1. How many people are interested in the same occupation that I am?
2. How many want to live in the same part of the country that I do?
3. How many have less, as much, or more education than I have?
4. What will happen to the salary range in that occupation if the supply of people for that occupation is great, and the number of positions is small?

These questions and more should occur to you, and each should be researched and answered for a knowledgeable career selection.

Marketing

Many areas of awareness and study are important in your career plan. Some are incorporated in this chapter; others appear throughout the book; still others you should search out. An obvious place for your search is a specifically designed career/life planning course. Other available options are workshops, seminars, and conferences, with sessions specifically addressing themselves to career-related topics. Books and articles are also helpful.

Two valuable subjects to consider are advertising and sales. After you have completed the self-evaluation exercises and you have a list of facts to consider in making a career selection, you must take your product and market it. Here sales and advertising enter the picture.

Why are these skills important? Think of it this way: The information you collect, sort through, and have on hand constitutes the facts you need for your resumé and interview preparation. You must present those facts in an attractive package. The presentation requires marketing skills. Your resumé is the advertising message you send out; the interview presents you the opportunity to display your selling skills.

Advertising makes people aware that a product is on the market and gives good reasons to buy it. A good advertisement gets to the point, hits the highlights, and is attractive to catch the eye. On radio and T.V., the message is delivered in 30 or 60 seconds, so it is short and forceful. One major objective is to get the reader or listener to act on the message. Isn't action what you want when you deliver a resumé? You want to know as soon as possible whether or not you will have the opportunity to sell yourself in an interview.

The heart of selling is the ability to convert features into highlights and benefits. The sequence of events that takes place in a selling situation consists of five distinct steps.

A short lesson in selling is appropriate here, but remember that this is a short course. You should know much more about selling to consider yourself proficient.

Every sale is composed of these steps:

1. Gaining *attention*
2. Holding *interest*
3. Building *desire*
4. Winning *conviction*
5. Getting *action*

First, you will learn how each step in the sequence works. Then a sample application of each step, showing how it might be used in a resumé or interview, will be presented.

Gaining attention—One way to look at this step is to think about the headline of a newspaper story. The headline should make the reader want to know more. As the headline catches the reader, so you must catch the attention of the reader of your resumé or of your interviewer. The first thirty seconds are the most important of the entire sales presentation. This thirty-second opener is your sales headline.

Recall from the earlier chapters on communication and listening that attention is a must for good communication. Helping your reader or listener to focus on you gives you an advantage. The chances of being remembered are in your favor.

Holding interest—Now that you have captured your reader's or listener's undivided attention, hold it through the use of the interest link in the chain. The interest link is like the rest of the newspaper story. Here you explain and elaborate on the statement or claim that you made in your opening. If you hold interest, the person is encouraged to participate by asking questions. Questions are a clue that you are being listened to, and they can be used in the building desire phase, which is next in the sequence.

Building desire—Before prospects can make a positive buying decision, they must see themselves owning and enjoying the product or service. Prospective employers need to visualize you within the organization and to see how you will enhance the operation. You tell your story, stressing your abilities and qualities (features), and relate how these abilities and qualities will contribute to (benefit) the employer and the organization. The more you know about the employer's business and operation, the more your presentation can be tailored to the specific situation.

Winning conviction—The time has come for you to convince the people you have been addressing that everything you have said and done is true. Until now, your written or spoken words have been telling your prospect about the product or service you are offering, but it has been your word alone. Now you provide proof. Naturally you are biased about yourself—as you should be. To substantiate what you have been saying, bring forth third party testimonials. In the case of a job application, these testimonials would include your references, both personal and employer recommendations. If you are applying for a selling position, records substantiating whatever claims you have made or documentation that you were salesperson of the month or year on several occasions, would be appropriate.

Getting action—In sales, this step is called the close. You want the person you have been addressing to do something—preferably to hire you. A full-fledged sales and advertising course will acquaint you with many types of closes.

Before showing how the sales sequence can be applied to the interview or resumé, the concepts of features and benefits will be discussed.

The basic objective in career/life planning is to examine every facet of yourself and to understand who you are and what you want. When you have finished, you have a collection of facts that you can draw on to make informed choices. In sales, this collection of facts and understanding is called product knowledge.

Knowing your product is not enough, however. You must take the facts and make them attractive to a buyer. The facts are the features. Make the features attractive to the buyer, by finding out how the feature will benefit the user.

Each feature must have a corresponding benefit that suits it to the customer's needs. Unless you uncover that benefit, the prospective buyer, (employer) may not see the use of the feature. Employers choose one applicant over another, because of one or more features that particularly benefit the employer or the operation. Therefore, the applicants capable of translating their features into benefits for the employer, have the most job opportunities.

In the sales fraternity, benefits are referred to as "hot buttons." Hot buttons trigger buying motives or, in this instance, hiring motives. These motives or reasons fall into two categories, rational or emotional, or some combination of the two. On the rational side (well thought out and planned), hot buttons are sparked by practicality, utility, dependability, and economy. The emotional side (satisfying an inner need or impulse), is spurred by curiosity, desire for pleasure and amusement, desire for social status, and feelings of love, hate, fear, or vanity.

What's the Difference?

When you have collected all the facts and you know your strengths and weaknesses, needs and desires, you will discover that you are not so terribly different from thousands of other job seekers and career planners.

You are not the only person with a college education; you are not the only person your age; you are not alone in preferring to live on the West Coast. Whatever single fact about yourself you choose, you can be sure that you are not the only person with that feature. The combination of features you possess is what differentiates you from all others. Learn how to show off the specific unique package that is you. State your case in terms of how this unique combination will benefit an employer.

Take particular care to avoid generalities. As a customer, you tire of hearing salespeople say, "This product is the best on the market." You want to hear why it is the best, and especially why it is best for you. Interviewers think this way, too. An interviewer wants to know why the applicant should be hired. "What can the applicant do for me? Why is this applicant better than the rest of the people I have interviewed this past week?" These are two examples of an interviewer's train of thought. If you are talking benefits to the prospective employer, you answer these kinds of questions.

Most employers are willing to pay a fair price for something of value. The employer determines the value of an employee in terms of benefits to the business, derived from the features (abilities and knowledge) possessed by the employee. Applicants who can see an employer's needs and sell the benefits of their talents are successful in applying sales techniques to a career/life plan.

The Sequence in Action

The following shows how to use the sales sequence in an interview. You could repeat the sequence many times in each interview. Each time you introduce a new benefit you begin again. The following monologue is relatively short to keep the concepts obvious. Assume the applicant is searching for a teaching position and has been in teaching before.

Gaining attention	"I can help you in two special ways: I can save you both time and worry."
Holding interest	"I can promise you this because I have taught before so I am familiar with teaching methods. I have handled dif-

Building desire

Winning conviction

Getting action

ficult students without involving superiors every time a difficulty arose. You will not have to explain procedures as you would to a person just beginning in the profession."

"Can you picture yourself hurrying to prepare for a meeting or gathering information for a report when suddenly you have to drop everything to handle a disciplinary problem? Because I have had experience in this line, I can cut down such interruptions for you."

"Here is a list of my references. I am sure they will substantiate what I have been telling you."

"Do you want me to start next Monday?"

Perhaps the career planning concept took what you think were a couple of unexpected twists in the preceding pages. Unexpected, maybe, but a necessary digression for you to consider for thorough career search preparation.

Education Plus Experience

Traditionally, a young person looking for work has education or experience, rarely both. Consider the example of two classmates who graduate from high school. One has a job lined up and goes right into the working world. The other elects to go to college for an additional four years of education.

Assume that four years later both are looking for jobs. The one who went to work has experience, but less education than the friend. The college graduate has the education, but lacks experience. Neither gets the job; both feel cheated in different ways.

The times have finally caught up with the needs. Opportunities to combine education and experience are now available to both people in the above example.

A variety of educational opportunities are available for people who take a job immediately after leaving high school. Night classes offered by colleges, universities, community colleges, business schools, trade schools, and community education classes are a few of the more obvious avenues. Workshops, seminars, and conferences are sponsored by these institutions and by professional organizations, private industry, and chambers of commerce. These organizations invite citizen input as to what is of interest so that they can try to produce materials to meet the needs. Some employers help with or entirely finance education for their employees.

For the person who selects the college education option, cooperative education and internship programs enable students to work at career-related jobs and receive college credits as well. Students acquire some experience to fill in that section on a job application.

Education has taken on elements that provide economic understanding and marketable skills relevant to a student's career plans. Course design responds to the need for reality in learning, instead of simply presenting theory about how things should happen. Courses and instructors must keep pace with a rapidly changing technology in a rapidly changing world in order to be relevant.

Career-directed studies do not replace the basic and typical courses; in fact, this new direction shows the dire need for the study of reading, writing, and arithmetic—the backbone of any education. Career-directed studies point out the need for basic studies.

The person who elects to follow the path of formal education after high school should never become complacent after gaining a degree. Education is a never-ending process. In a changing society, education must be a continuing pursuit throughout life.

This approach to education makes more informed career choices possible. You have more opportunities than ever before to identify strengths, weaknesses, interests, and aversions in an atmosphere of application to the job. The opportunity to relate the requirements of the working world to the educational experience is extremely valuable for a full and useful life.

Career decisions may be required of you several times. Decisions about promotions and assignment changes confront you constantly. Decision-making skills are necessary for career selection and satisfaction regardless of job market changes.

Career-oriented education recognizes that many technical skills are just as useful and valuable as professional and managerial skills. Discipline, attitude, and personal traits are emphasized not so much for their own sakes as for their applications on the job. Lack of discipline is a major problem in business and industry that can be dealt with on the job, but is best handled through a student's realization that discipline is a necessary skill for success in a career. Career-directed education teaches people the values of a work-oriented society. Practicing those values makes them become personal values and work becomes meaningful and satisfying.

Your First Job

When you learn to drive a car, you get behind the wheel, start the engine, and move into traffic. That is how you find out if you can do it, or if you even like to do it. The preparations—studying the driver's manual, taking the driver's education course, and driving in a simulator—are all worthwhile. The preparation enables you to perform well quickly and to evaluate the experience readily.

The time and effort you expend preparing for a career choice (and you will expend a great deal of both), are insignificant compared to the time you lose floundering and guessing your way along. Yet, all the preparation in the world cannot guarantee that you will like your chosen career or perform well. Preparation only puts the odds in your favor and shortens the experimentation phase of career selection.

Face the fact that when you embark on your first job it will be much the same as when you first moved out into traffic as a new driver.

In a real sense, your first job is a continuation of the preparation and learning stage of your career plan. One obvious difference is that you are an integral part of the setting and can learn from others through first-hand, daily observation. This gives you insight to other careers you may find appealing, that you had not thought about before.

Get Ready

The next phase of your career plan is to convince someone to give you an opportunity to get started. The next chapter concerns itself with resumé preparation and interviews.

If you have done your homework well, you have all the facts on hand that you need. Simply pluck from your career plan the information you need to prepare a resumé, or to fill out a company application form. You can interview comfortably with the knowledge you have provided yourself.

Sample

This book provides only samples and options. You may explore many useful areas if you decide to take the time and expend the effort to develop yourself. Each topic covered could fill a complete book or course. You have an obligation to yourself to gather more information in those areas that interest you most, or where you have the most need.

A course in career/life planning is highly recommended. Such a course gives you the opportunity to explore yourself in many areas, to scrutinize your personal and work values, to prioritize your interpersonal relationships, to take inventory of the transferable skills you possess, and to reflect at length on your personal qualities.

One course activity is making a complete list of every item that could be included on an application form, so that it will become a simple matter to transfer the information to a resumé or application. You receive the tools that enable you to focus on your future as well as your present, and to make a plan for meshing the two.

As you research, choose, study, and implement, you need to practice your listening skills. Especially important is listening to yourself in conversations like this:

Now that I know my strengths and weaknesses, my preferences and abilities, I must choose a career consistent with my life plans. Where I work, whom I work with, and whom I spend time with in social activities influences who I become, and affects my family.

This kind of conversation occurs repeatedly, getting more specific as you consider each like and dislike, each trade-off, and each factor that calls for a decision.

The kind of thorough preparation you need takes a great deal of time and effort. However, the better the preparation, the more time you gain when you are ready to move into your career. You will find it was time well spent.

Summary Questions

1. Why is it so difficult to choose a career?

2. Make a list of occupation clusters. Which three interest you most?

3. List three library references that can help you with your career selection.

4. Why is it important to combine career planning with life planning?

5. This chapter is designed for the first-time career planner, as well as for those who are planning a career change. Those seeking a first career, should at this point establish a career plan in order to apply the information to the interview chapter. Then read the chapter on changing careers. Those anticipating a career change should read the chapter on changing careers and then go back to the interview chapter to apply your career plan. Build your plan around the Self Status Evaluation and the self-analysis questions appearing in the chapter on pages 000 and 000. Also build a marketing plan to use in the resumé and interview phases of your career search.

CHAPTER 18

The Interview

Go for It!

Except for the first day on a new job, or having a tooth extracted without novocaine, a job interview probably ranks highest on a list of things guaranteed to make you shake in your boots! Even the most seasoned job seeker becomes a trifle unstrung over an interview. To overcome some of this anxiety prepare yourself in the best way possible.

Consider your packaging (appearance), your features (skills), and your benefits (experience and knowledge).

Most lasting impressions are formed in the first 30 seconds of meeting. This fact applies to social meetings, business contacts, salespeople, interviews, and casual acquaintances. If you have only 30 seconds to give a favorable and lasting impression, you must be well prepared for an interview. Being prepared, as in the scout motto, relieves much apprehension and fear and allows you to present yourself as a well-qualified individual. *You* may feel as if your stomach is a cocoon bursting with a thousand butterflies, but no one else needs to know that!

Most interviews are relatively short—especially when you consider the time spent preparing for them. Yet, the entire course of your future hangs in that half hour or so. Your boat will pull out of the harbor without you if you don't prepare. Determine that the interview will climax many hours of careful work and study.

More unemployment, layoffs, job eliminations, and closings of companies are happening than have been seen in many decades. Therefore, it is increasingly important that you interview well. You face an employers' world; the employer can *and does* hire the cream of the crop. An employer can afford to be choosy because so many applicants are competing for each job. Therefore, the urgency and need to prepare yourself for a favorable interview is greater.

Usually the first requirement is a written application or a resumé. Often the interview is the last step and is considered a favorable and encouraging sign. This practice is not followed in all cases, however. Employers follow no set pattern. Some firms ask for an interview first and then a written application. Some companies *never* interview and some request all three—an application form, a resumé and an interview. Each company decides its own hiring policy.

Your attitude about yourself, your employment, and your capabilities for the specific job are all-important. Your self-image shows. You need a positive attitude to accentuate your positive traits. Let your interviewer know what jobs you do especially well; if you are a skilled and competent typist, for example, make that fact known. If typing is *not* one of your specialties, do *not* point that out—the interviewer will find out soon enough! If you are asked a direct question about typing skills, however, you are obligated to be truthful. If it is a weakness—tell it like it is—but do not dwell on it!

Sometimes having a positive attitude is difficult if you have:

1. Applied and been rejected for a number of jobs
2. Been laid off or fired
3. Quit because of uncomfortable working conditions or situations

Consider case number one first—you have applied for numerous jobs and not been accepted. You will have to "get your dobber up." Hundreds of people are applying for the same job openings—you simply have not been chosen yet. Consider the fact that you were not chosen as poor judgment on the part of the interviewers. The companies lose—they will never know what they missed!

Imagine yourself in an interview across from your prospective employer. Questions have been fired in rapid succession for several minutes. Now silence falls—a time for both of you to regroup and move on. In the anxiety of the moment and the prevailing silence, your stomach growls, snarls and squeals. Its woofer and tweeter are definitely in working order. It sounds in your ears like 20 motorcyclists starting their cycles, or the bellowing of two hundred head of cattle in a sale barn on a busy day.

The choice is yours—you can shuffle your feet, change positions several times, fold your arms tightly across the stomach area, hold your breath for fifteen minutes, or scoot your chair the full length of the room. Your other choice is to look placidly at your interviewer, smile and say to yourself, "Hey look, I'm human! Kings and queens have stomachs that growl, the President of the United States has a growling stomach and the interviewer's stomach probably growls too!"

Case number two requires that you rebuild your image. If you were fired or lost your job, your self-esteem may have taken a nose dive. You are probably uncertain and have lost confidence in yourself and your abilities. You feel apprehensive about looking for another job. Unless you talk positively to yourself, your self-doubt will show and hinder your chances of employment. Work hard to get rid of stress and to rebuild your self-image.

The third example assumes you chose to leave your job because of uncomfortable or undesirable working conditions. This presents another situation for rebuilding self-esteem. For example, imagine that you work for a boss who:

1. Makes undesirable advances
2. Gives only negative criticism
3. Intimidates
4. Claims to be always right—no questions asked
5. Makes unrealistic demands for perfection
6. Values professionalism but does not see *you* as a professional.

If your boss does any or all of these things, your decision to seek employment elsewhere is apropos—the sooner, the better! You need to shed the boss' shackles and regain your pride, improve your abilities, and rebuild your confidence. In an interview, however, do not compare, run down, or repudiate the reputation or personality of a former employer. You gain nothing and might lose face in the sight of your prospective employer.

Consider your goals when interviewing. If you want the job you are being interviewed for, you already have ideas on how you will keep that position. If you want to advance in that company, you probably have ideas on how to advance.

Consider packaging—what you do to make a favorable and lasting first impression, including personal hygiene, posture, makeup, hair, and wardrobe.

Your hygiene is important when applying for a job. The interviewer notices your hands more than any other single thing. Be sure your nails are immaculately clean with no ragged edges and your cuticles are pushed back. Trim your nails so that they are approximately the same length. Women who polish their nails should use colorless polish or a subdued shade. Be sure the hands are well scrubbed and apply lotion so they do not appear rough, chapped, or dry.

Your hair should be styled and cut appropriately. Hair should be squeaky clean and combed or brushed to a high lustre. Wild hair cuts or way-out styles are not acceptable. The important thing is to be well-groomed. Whether your hair is long or short, shoulder length or crew cut, wavy or straight, be sure it looks neat. Go to a reputable hair stylist before your interview.

Be sure your shoes are not scuffed or noticeably worn, have no run-down heels, and are color-coordinated with your clothing. You might want to avoid crepe-soled shoes on interview days because it is easy to stub your toes on a carpeted area, giving a clumsy appearance. Avoid squeaky shoes or ones that click or make a lot of noise.

Your body must be clean and sweet-smelling. A shower or bath, body lotion, deodorant, and lightly scented cologne achieve the desired results.

Men should be clean-shaven with moustaches and sideburns trimmed appropriately.

Your breath should be fresh too. Chewing gum does not achieve this—only thorough, constant, faithful brushing and a good mouthwash give desirable results. Never chew gum during an interview; and avoid even breath mints. A mint can be heard clicking against your teeth, and in a nervous state you might choke on it. Consider the impression choking on a breath mint would make when you are answering a question about monetary integrity. After choking and sputtering with your eyes watering, try to convince the interviewer you would not consider embezzlement!

When preparing for an interview, think of how you want to look. Be sure you are in tune with the employer and the times. What is or is not acceptable depends on where you are, the job you are seeking, the kind of firm you will represent, the kinds of customers you will be dealing with. Modes of appearance change—some very rapidly. Remind yourself that you are going to neither a funeral, nor a gala fashion affair. Be moderate and conservative, but not so conservative that you are about as interesting as a jar of mayonnaise. Be attractive, not distracting.

Always dress tastefully, ignoring fads or outrageous fashion trends. Do not dress too casually or too formally and avoid bright colors, plaids or stripes. Reread the image dressing chapter to refresh your memory on how to dress to create a successful image. In the long run it might be wise to spend a little more for an interview suit than you otherwise pay for a suit. Keep in mind that black indicates power and the desire to succeed.

Keep in mind, too, that some professions dress conservatively, a few wear designer fashions, and some wear blue jeans. Industry, education, banking, and many others fall into the conservative class, while designer clothes are worn strictly in modeling or fashion design. Construction workers, plumbers, and electricians fall into the blue jean group. Dress appropriately for the position for which you are applying.

Men should wear knee-length dark socks. Never wear white socks and be branded a greaser! Knee-length hose assures you that your bare leg does not show when you cross your legs or bend the wrong way. Bony knees and hairy legs immediately strip a man of his authoritativeness! Ladies—absolutely no runs in the stockings, and gents—no holes in your toes or heels.

Take a last good look in the mirror before going for an interview. Start at the top and work your way to the bottom, scrutinizing each inch. Smile at yourself, checking for food particles on the teeth. There's no need to look like a jack-o-lantern before Halloween!

What about smoking? Three little words say it—*don't do it!* Never smoke in the presence of an interviewer. Refuse the offer of a cigarette by saying, "Thank you, but I just put one out." Should the interview be long, and the interviewer offers a second time, it may be all right to accept. Rely on common sense to judge the circumstances. If you are a non-smoker, never be critical by saying, "No thanks, I don't believe in smoking." Your attitude may please some interviewers, but might condemn or offend an interviewer who smokes. You are out to gain points—not lose them!

When you have been requested to come in for an interview, you might consider taking a potent tranquilizer, applying denture paste to your teeth to keep the chattering down, tying your knees together to prevent them from knocking, or dragging your teddy bear along for security. If you seriously study ahead of time and prepare yourself well for an interview, however, you will not need any false supports or props. The importance of preparing to the best of your ability cannot be stressed enough. Study this chapter long and hard and read and reread if necessary.

When you arrive for a job interview, expect to wait in a reception room before your interviewer is ready. Be a little early for an interview—ten minutes is a good amount of time. Being late may be fashionable in social gatherings, but being late for an interview is an unforgivable sin and a sure way to lose the job!

While waiting in the reception room, be pleasant to everyone especially the receptionist. Remember that you are trying to make a favorable first impression. You may not have much time with the receptionist, so make every minute count. A receptionist may carry considerable weight with the boss, sometimes helping to make the decision when asked the impression of a waiting applicant. Make *your* impression a good one!

If you know your interviewer's name, be sure you pronounce it correctly. You might have to introduce yourself to your interviewer. If you are not nervous, make points by pronouncing your *own* name correctly too!

Never take anyone with you to an interview. Doing so indicates to the employer that you need moral support or that you are unable to function alone. Some things you *have* to do by yourself—thinking is one, dying is another, and going to an interview is another!

Being interviewed is a matter of selling yourself. You have to sell the interviewer on the idea that you would be good for the business, that you are needed for the particular job opening, that you like people, and that people generally like you. You must convince your interviewer that you take your business and job very seriously and yet, you do not lack a sense of humor. If you lose your sense of humor, you have lost more than a job!

When you enter the office, the interviewer usually extends a hand and you shake it. Shake hands firmly. The feeling of sincerity in the clasp makes the impression. Limpness indicates a cold fish, and introduces doubt about whether you are glad to meet someone.

The handshake is not a muscle contest, either. Convey warmth and sincerity with a firm handshake, but don't crack knuckles. During the interview, be careful not to betray nervousness by wiping sweaty palms on your trousers or skirt, tapping fingers on the desk top, rattling keys or change in your pockets, fingering beads on a necklace or bracelet, twisting a lock of hair, pulling on imaginary hangnails, or twiddling thumbs.

Do only what you are invited to do—stand until you are advised to sit. If given a choice of seats take a straight chair as close to the interviewer as possible. If a sofa is available, avoid sitting on it unless you have no other choice. Your physical being is dwarfed in a large piece of furniture; thus your power is dimin-

ished. After easing your body into a chair, be conscious of what you learned in the chapter on posture. Sit forward in the chair with good posture and both feet flat on the floor. Sitting forward indicates you are interested and you will appear in command of yourself, resulting in a more comfortable interview.

Needless to say, rely on your social graces. Be courteous and respectful in every way. Be a good listener, and speak only when given the opportunity. Do not interrupt your interviewer at any time. Be interested in everything you are told, and always let the interviewer take the lead. Smile often—but be sure it is genuine. Avoid any confrontation that might lead to an argument or disagreement. An interview is not a good time to display an argumentative mood.

Use your interviewer's name often, and answer yes or no, rather than yup or nope. Do not answer a question with a mere yes or no—elaborate for the sake of clarity or explanation. Tailor your answers so as not to be boring and windy. Hit a happy medium when presenting your abilities. Neither overrate nor underrate yourself; either extreme will be harmful to you. A good interview is conducted with common logic. Stage a mock interview with a friend and ask for constructive criticism and advice.

Never mumble and do not shout. Find a pleasing pitch for your voice so that you can be heard and enunciate your words distinctly. Be expressive.

Body language is important in the interview setting. You must maintain eye contact with your interviewer at least 85% of the time. Avoiding eye contact indicates you lack interest or confidence. Look away briefly, to avoid feeling intimidated. Never stare at your interviewer—or anywhere else, for that matter!

Watch your facial expressions. Rolling your eyes, biting or twisting your lips, or twitching your nose gives an impression of lack of self-control and uneasiness. Keep your hands in your lap, extended toward your interviewer. Your legs should be crossed at the ankles or kept flat on the floor. Scuffing your feet implies tension.

Be sure to pack a large briefcase of assertiveness to take along on your interview. Remember these all-important words: Be assertive, not aggressive, and heaven forbid don't be passive at a job interview! Your assertiveness, used appropriately and strategically, may land you the job.

Answer questions as logically, persuasively, honestly, and smoothly as possible. This is no time to be modest about an ability you possess. If you type accurately, for example, or if you have exceptional selling tactics, or rate high in personal relations, or have any other skills that would be of value in that job, let your assertiveness hang out—tell the world you can do it. However, draw a line between being honest and frank and being boastful and cocky. Neither of the last two traits will win you any points.

Some general tips are listed below. Etch them in your memory for a successful interview.

Tips for a Successful Interview

- Be alert, not tense.
- Be relaxed; do not slouch.
- Meet the interviewer's eye, but do not stare.
- Smile frequently, but do not be a toothpaste commercial.
- Be truthful and avoid getting caught in contradictions.
- Stick to the subject; do not ramble.
- Take notes, but do not write a book.
- Be confident, not egotistical.
- Be thorough, but not long-winded.
- Be thoughtful, but not slow.
- Be courteous, but do not be an apple polisher.
- Be honest about your politics and religion, but do not be fanatical.
- Be positive, not negative.
- If the interviewer is a talker, be a good listener.
- If the interviewer is a listener, be a good talker. Draw the interviewer out with appropriate questions.

Many different techniques are used in interviews. You might be interviewed for three different jobs, with three different companies, and experience a different style of interview for each.

Sometimes an interview begins with small talk about the weather, the new movie in town, a trip, traffic jams, or something of local interest. During this time, the interviewer is forming a first impression, so do not lose competence or credibility by being careless. During this time, you both feel each other out and become relaxed and comfortable with the task at hand. Small talk is not always used at the beginning of the interview; some interviewers may use it in the middle or at the end and some do not use it at all.

In some interviews, the interviewer acts mostly as a listener, and encourages you to talk about yourself—to express your feelings, your beliefs, your outlook, and your intentions. The purpose of this type of interview is to observe your behavior and emotions. You will be making that all-important impression while expressing yourself.

A more formal style of interview utilizes preplanned questions and is delivered rapidly. This interviewer is concerned more with facts and explanations than with personalities, mannerisms, and behaviors.

An empathy interview is another style that is implemented extensively in education for interviewing teacher applicants. In this interview, the applicant is given a tape-recorded set of circumstances or a crisis in a classroom setting and then asked how to handle it. Empathy is associated with sympathy, warmth, or a fellow feeling, and the empathy interview tests your ability to put yourself in another's shoes.

A type of interview that fortunately is seldom used, is the stress interview. This interview deliberately creates stress to observe how you react under pressure. Few interviewers resort to this technique of purposely using stress techniques. Some of the means of creating stress are listed below:

1. Putting you on the defensive
2. Interrupting while you are speaking
3. Firing questions at you rapidly
4. Not commenting after you have spoken (horrible silence!)
5. Criticizing what you say

The interviewer using stress techniques is watching for your emotional control—whether or not you can remain calm and pleasant and keep from blowing billows of smoke from your nostrils. If you remain stable and amiable during this time of stress, the impression you give is undoubtedly a favorable one.

Your personality carries you through an interview. If you feel good about yourself, if you like people, if you have a sense of humor, respect for others, and a wish to succeed, you have a distinct advantage. Let your light shine during an interview.

The do's and don'ts of an interview that are listed below can prove invaluable in presenting desirable employment traits.

Do Be	*Don't Be*
Optimistic	Unprepared
An interested listener	Negative
Logical	Deceitful
Courteous	Discourteous
Amiable	Overconfident
Enthusiastic	Arrogant
Honest	Aggressive
Personable	Argumentative
Neat in appearance	Indifferent
Well prepared	Emotional

When the interview takes place you are center stage. Each interviewer has a slightly different approach and emphasizes different traits. Each interview will be different from all the others.

Interviewers work into questions in an infinite number of ways, but the questions themselves fall into seven basic categories. Examine these categories and the sample questions in each; some questions fit into several categories. This questioning process gives an interviewer a complete picture of you—your likes and dislikes, your habits, your skills, and your areas of greatest interest and knowledge.

These questions represent those most frequently asked by interviewers. No single interview includes all these questions, but you should study the questions and prepare answers in your mind for all of them. Your interview should not sound rehearsed, but should flow smoothly, without long pauses and stumbling half-answers.

By answering all of these questions, you prepare to answer the ten or fifteen questions you will encounter in an interview. You can give a coherent, well-thought-out picture of yourself. Some of the questions you may consider irrelevant or too personal—plainly no one's business. You must judge whether or not to answer, but either way you take a risk. If you decide to refuse, be tactful and unabrasive in your refusal. The seven categories include: personal information, educational background, work history, questions about the job you are applying for, about the company, about your goals or ambitions, and general questions. Here these questions are neatly categorized, but an interviewer gives them at random, and you have little time to collect your thoughts and shift to another frame of mind. Questions about your family will be mixed with questions about your part-time jobs. Your future plans might come up with questions about your interest in sports. The interview is not intended to put you totally at ease, but to test how well you think on your feet. Study the questions in the following categories:

Personal Questions

1. Why did you choose this particular field of work?
2. How did you spend your summer vacation?
3. How do you use your spare time?
4. How old were you when you began working at part-time jobs?
5. Do you have any hobbies?
6. Are you interested in sports? As a participant? As an observer? What is your favorite sport?
7. Do you enjoy solving puzzles?
8. What do you do to keep in good physical condition?
9. What type of literature do you enjoy most?
10. Do you subscribe to any magazines?
11. Do you attend church regularly?

12. Do you drink? What are your drinking habits?
13. Have you ever used drugs? Do you use them now? What kind?
14. What size city do you consider ideal?
15. What geographical location do you prefer? Would you consider any others?
16. What is your father's occupation? Your mother's?
17. Do you live with your parents?
18. Do you own any insurance?
19. Do you have a savings account? Any other investments?
20. What is the approximate total of your debts?
21. Do you like to travel?
22. Are you engaged or going steady?
23. What types of people annoy you the most?
24. Is it an effort for you to tolerate persons with different backgrounds or interests from your own?
25. Are you eager to please?
26. Have you ever had any serious illness or injury?
27. Have you ever tutored an underclassman? In what subjects?
28. What are your special abilities?
29. What would you do to get ahead?
30. Do you think grades should be considered by an employer? How much emphasis do you think they should receive in your evaluation?
31. What are the disadvantages of your chosen career field?

Questions About Your Education

1. How did you rank in your graduation class in high school? In college?
2. Why did you go to college?
3. Why did you choose that particular college?
4. Why did you choose *not* to go to college?
5. What courses did you like best? Least?
6. Which of your college years was the most difficult?
7. Have you ever had any difficulty getting along with students and faculty?
8. Do you feel you have done your best scholastically?
9. When did you choose your major? Did you change your major at anytime?
10. In what extra-curricular activities did you participate? Which did you enjoy the most?
11. What extra-curricular offices have you held?

12. Do you think the time devoted to these activities was well spent? Why?
13. Have you any plans for graduate work?
14. If you were starting college all over again, what courses would you take?
15. Did you change colleges at any time in your school career? Why?

Questions About Your Work History

1. What jobs have you held?
2. Which job did you enjoy the most? The least?
3. What have you learned from the jobs you held?
4. How did you get these jobs?
5. Why did you leave?
6. What percentage of your school expenses did you earn?
7. How did your employers treat you?
8. Can you get recommendations from your previous employers?

Questions About the Job You Are Applying For

1. Are you looking for a permanent or temporary job?
2. What type of position are you most interested in?
3. Why do you think you would like this particular job?
4. Are you willing to locate wherever the company sends you?
5. Do you prefer to work with other people or by yourself?
6. Are you interested in research?
7. If you were entirely free to choose, what job in our company would you like?
8. What are your starting salary requirements?
9. Why do you think we should hire you?

Questions About the Company

1. What do you know about our company?
2. Have you ever used our product or service?
3. What interests you most about our product or service?
4. Why did you apply to us?
5. Do you know anyone who works for our company?
6. What are your ideas of how business operates today?
7. Would you rather work with a large or small company? Why?
8. How do you feel about overtime work?

Questions About Your Ambitions

1. How long do you expect to work?
2. What type of work interests you most?
3. What do you expect to be earning annually by age thirty? At age forty?
4. What position in our company do you want to work toward?
5. What opportunities are available in the career in which you are interested?
6. What are the special qualifications you have that will make you successful in this career?
7. How have you already demonstrated your initiative and willingness to work?
8. What plans have you made for your career future?

General Questions

1. What do you think you have to do to get ahead?
2. Define cooperation.
3. Are you more interested in making money or in giving service to others?
4. What type of supervisor do you prefer?
5. How many brothers and sisters do you have? How do you feel about your family?
6. Which of your parents has had the most profound influence on you?
7. Who are your best friends?
8. What personal characteristics do you feel are most necessary for success in business?
9. Can you take instruction and criticism without getting upset?
10. Do you like routine work?
11. Do you like regular hours?
12. What is your major weakness?
13. Tell me a story!

How Do You Do?

At this point, take a break for humor. Consider a young applicant who is in every way ill-prepared for an interview. This applicant first contemplates whether the correct way to greet the interviewer is with "Hello" or "How do you do." The second question in mind is how to describe a previous job as a gas station attendant. The decision to say, "I was in the gas business or the oil business," is a mind boggler. In this confused, ill-prepared, and tense state of mind, the applicant meets the interviewer, jumps up and shouts, "Hell—do—I used to have gas!" End of interview!

Review

Give the following tips your undivided attention.

Don't get carried away—After you have made your point, let it go. Do not elaborate, causing your interviewer to lose interest.

Leave bad habits at home—Concentrate on not being nervous so that you will not be tempted to pick at imaginary lint, scratch a non-existent itch, or fiddle with the buttons on your blouse or shirt.

Keep your eyes on the target—the eyeballs of your interviewer. Stare out the window or look at the wall hangings at a later time.

Be aware of your body language and that of the interviewer—Watch your body movements so that you do not give the impression you are nervous, insincere, or bored. Also observe your interviewer's body signals to pick up signs of disinterest or boredom.

Do not blow yourself out of proportion—Eliminate boasting about past accomplishments or innovations. Soften your greatest achievements with humility. Bragging gives the impression of having to convince yourself you are good, and interviewers are turned off by conceit. Be convincing and believable at the same time.

Slang expressions are taboo—Not only are slang words unnecessary, but expressions such as, "It's the most, It was the greatest, you betcha, like I say, ya know," or "neat," should be reserved for weiner roasts. Employ correct grammar and usage and make your sentences crystal-clear.

Some useful tips on how to respond to your interviewer's questions to give an impression of positive thinking are described below.

Draw on the word *responsible* and its derivatives. Instead of saying, "My job was to . . ." say something like, "I was responsible for . . ." or "My responsibilities were . . ." *Responsible* is a more impressive word than duty or job.

If asked what kind of job you are interested in, avoid answering, "Just anything!" Be specific about naming the job title you prefer. When asked to tell about yourself, do not ask, "What do you want to know?" Instead, expect that they are interested in some of your background and a few statistics about birthplace, family interests, or hobbies.

Be tactful, courteous, sincere, and natural. Be yourself, but be sure you are your best self!

Become familiar with the company and its policies before you apply to that company. Investigate the line of services the company offers, and learn as much about the product and the company's future plans as possible. Gain as much knowledge as you can before your interview and use this knowledge to your advantage. Impress your interviewer with your interest.

Information about companies is available through annual reports that you may obtain by calling or writing the specific companies. Company publications or magazines are another source. Sometimes the most reliable and down-to-earth information can come from people in the field or from employees you know personally. Be careful that the information you gather is accurate.

Types of information you might use to fortify yourself are listed below:

1. Company reputation
2. Company growth potential
3. Number of employees on staff
4. Major company services
5. Company product
6. Company methods
7. Company problems

Armed with the tips, rules, and do's and don'ts of an interview from the preceding pages, examine a simulated interview. Before you read each answer the applicant gives the interviewer, form your own answer in your mind. Make an analysis of your own before reading our analysis that follows each answer. Observe how positive attitudes are used, goals are stated, honesty is displayed, and enthusiasm is apparent.

An interview for a sales position could go something like the one described below. Picture the interviewer as a man, about fifty years of age, the personnel manager of a large corporation. The applicant is a young man just out of school. The job is selling large appliances in a department store.

The interviewer invites the applicant into his office. He holds the application in his hand and puts it on his desk where he can easily use it while asking questions. In an attempt to put the applicant at ease, he discusses the hobbies and outside interests noted on the young applicant's resumé.

Interviewer: "I see you are interested in golf and water skiing and that you played basketball while you were in college. What do you usually shoot for 18 holes of golf?

Applicant: "Well, it has been debated whether I play the game or not, but I usually shoot around a 94."

(Now analyze in your own mind what has just taken place.) Analysis: This general type of question could be asked about what kind of literature you read, what your favorite pro football team is, or any line of extra-curricular activity the interviewer settles upon. The applicant should not give a one-word, one-phrase, nervous answer. The interviewer is making small talk to bring out the applicant and help break the ice before getting down to something more serious. If you happen to be the club champion, say so; this is your chance to boast without bragging—just do not replay the entire tournament!

Interviewer: (using the applicant's name) "I'm happy you chose to apply to our company. Why do you think you would like working here?"

Applicant: "Your product has a fine reputation, your company has a high standing within the industry, and its growth and progressive outlook impress me. I have spoken with several of your employees, and their high regard for the firm influenced my decision to submit my application."

Analysis: This answer tells the interviewer several things. The applicant did not apply blindly—he took the time and trouble to research the industry and its policies. If the applicant has used the product, he should say so at this point in the interview. A knowledgeable answer shows interest in this company and the particular job. The applicant has also complimented the firm's reputation.

Interviewer: "Do you feel you have received the education you wanted?"

Applicant: "I felt the school's approach in this area was excellent. I had the opportunity to study the theory of sales, and the chance to perform in numerous business-simulated situations so that I could relate my knowledge to practical situations."

Analysis: Emphasis is placed on the *positive*, not the negative. Even if you hated the school you attended, find something good to say about it. If you speak well of what you have done in the past, the interviewer gets the feeling you will speak well of the company you will be working for. If you disliked your school, he may question how well educated you are.

Interviewer: "While you were in school, were there any courses you did not like, or any instructors with whom you did not get along?"

Applicant: "I prefer to work for the kind of person who will point out my mistakes early, before they become habits. Someone who recognizes a job well done, as well as gives criticism, helps me know when I am doing something right. I like a supervisor who is approachable, one I feel I can talk to."

Interviewer: "What do you consider your greatest weakness?"

Applicant: "I find my greatest weakness is that I get so concerned with my customer's problems that I am unable to forget them after business hours. If I find out something personal about them, I find myself worrying even though I cannot help or interfere."

Analysis: In answering this question, remember not to give a negative picture of yourself by saying, "I find it difficult to get up in the morning," or "My mind wanders while I am talking to a customer." Instead, try to think of some strengths you have.

Interviewer: "What do you consider your greatest strength to be?"

Applicant: "I believe I have determination. If, for some reason I have been unable to sell to a customer, I try to figure out why, and approach that customer again."

Analysis: This applicant has chosen a trait which will stand him in good stead in the position he is seeking. Try to choose one of your strengths that will serve you in the particular position for which you are applying.

Interviewer: "What do you hope to be doing and earning ten years from now?"

Applicant: "I would like to be moving up to supervisory positions, and earning a salary commensurate with management positions."

Analysis: This answer is vague and unspecific, but it shows ambition, which is what the question intended to bring out. A specific answer is hard to pinpoint, because fluctuations in the economy affect your monetary goals. The main idea you wish to convey is that you do not want to remain in your first position for the rest of your working life.

After this initial interview, you may be asked to take tests. These may include tests of typing, aptitude, or attitude—skills or qualities required of all applicants for the position.

When you have finished any tests, the interviewer may ask you if you have any questions. Sometimes it is best to ask very few or perhaps no questions at all. Be cautious how you phrase a question, and what you ask about.

Nothing will turn an interviewer off as much as a question like "How much vacation time would I get?" or "How many fringe benefits do you offer?" Ask about benefits one at a time, giving the interviewer a chance to open up with you. Some of your questions will be answered by the interviewer without your having to ask.

Not all the questions you studied earlier were asked in this interview, but something pertaining to each of several categories was asked. The answers given by the applicant in the sample interview have certain characteristics of all good answers. They stressed the positive, they gave the interviewer a total picture of the applicant and his personality, and they left the interviewer with the impression that this applicant would be an asset to the firm.

Before parting, the interviewer may indicate when you can expect to hear the results of the interview. If not, ask when you may expect a decision to be made on your application. As soon as you return home, or even before, make a note of the interviewer's name, the date of the interview, and when you expect to hear the decision. If you have not heard from the interviewer within a week after the date given, call. If you are sincerely interested in obtaining this position, remind the interviewer of your application and interview. Doing so may tip the scales in your favor. Be prepared for one of two results from your interview:

1. a job offer on the spot
2. no definite job offer

If you are overwhelmed with a job offer and would like time to think it over, be diplomatic in your postponement of acceptance. Be frank. Perhaps you are tempted to say yes immediately, but you would like forty-eight hours to digest all the information you have just received. Tell the interviewer you will call at a specific hour and day (about forty-eight hours should be maximum). Be definite; make it obvious you are interested and did not just waste the interviewer's time. Do not embarrass the interviewer for having confidence in you.

If the interview does not culminate in a job offer, try not to be too disappointed. The interviewer may have to check with a department supervisor before making a commitment. Perhaps your interview was not the only one scheduled. The interviewer may want to check your references, or may be unsure that you are the person to fill the position.

As you leave, smile. You may be pitted out, but be sure you show as much confidence at the end of the interview as you did at the beginning. You might remind the interviewer that your address and phone number are in the resumé, and that you would welcome further contact if there are any questions. Thank the interviewer for the time and interest shown you, and leave. Do not dawdle. You will be stopped if the interviewer has anything to add.

If you do not get the first job you apply for, do not be discouraged. Jobs and companies differ a great deal. The next interviewer may find you are just who the company has been searching for. With each interview, and your self-analysis afterwards, you learn and improve, making the next interview better. You are gaining experience and learning from that experience. The important point is that you keep trying.

Review Questions

1. Name at least three sources of information available to you when you wish to find out about job openings.
2. Name at least three sources of information about companies you are interested in.
3. Do you think extracurricular activities should carry weight in a job interview? Why or why not?
4. You, the student, are applying for a job and the interviewer has asked several questions. Answer them carefully.
5. Prepare a resumé of your education and job experience. Have your instructor or someone else interview you for a position as an advertising/sales promotion representative with a local ad agency.

6. Select three classified ads from a newspaper or trade magazine. Write a letter of application to answer each advertisement. The letters will be evaluated on neatness, good use of English, proper set-up, sensible content, and flow of ideas.

Thank You

From childhood your parents pounded into your head, "What do you say when someone gives you something?" Of course you remember—say, "Thank you." By offering you an interview, the interviewer has given you something: an opportunity to sell yourself. You have benefited from time and money spent on your behalf. In return for this opportunity, express your appreciation. A verbal thank you is a natural response at the conclusion of an interview, but a letter of appreciation should be written immediately afterward.

Begin your letter by saying, "Thank you for the opportunity to interview for the position of . . ." or "I would like to express my appreciation for the time you took to interview me." You might say that you are still interested in the position and briefly mention anything of importance that you may have neglected during the interview. This letter should be brief, well written, and grammatically correct, with no spelling errors. It should be neat and not overly gushy—remember it represents you in absence. A note of appreciation, especially an unexpected one, may be just the prod the interviewer needed to offer you the job. You have nothing to lose and everything to gain from a timely thank you letter.

A sample thank you letter might look like this:

121 Yorkshire Blvd.
Apartment 102
Oberlin, KA 67849

Mr. Roger Jones
Personnel Manager
St. Luke's Hospital
Oberlin, KA 67849

Dear Mr. Jones:

Thank you for giving me the opportunity to interview for the position of admissions clerk in emergency. As I pointed out, I have taken a two-year secretarial course at Norton Business School. During that two-year period I worked as a nurse's aide in Norton General Hospital and did some volunteer clerical jobs at the church. I am very interested in the job at St. Luke's and I hope I am being considered for the position. Again, thank you for your time and interest during the interview.

Sincerely,

Pat Smith

Write a thank you letter of your own.

Be a Good Interviewer

After studying diligently and learning how to get and keep a job, you may be surprised at how quickly you work your way to the driver's seat. You may one day be acting the part of the interviewer, simply because you did your homework and your job well. When you reach this position, remind yourself of your days as interviewee. Put yourself in the place of the applicant—use empathy.

Most of the rules you used as an applicant apply as an interviewer. Extend your hand when the applicant arrives and offer a seat. Arrange the seating so as not to intimidate the applicant; do not let your desk separate the two of you. The best arrangement is a pattern of two chairs facing one another.

An interviewer must be clean and neat in appearance. Have a heart and put the applicant at ease, by beginning with some small talk to draw out the applicant's interests.

As the interviewer, you must take the lead. Learn as much as you can about the applicant prior to the interview. The resumé or application form gives you most of this information.

Show that you are interested in the applicant. Avoid awkward pauses or silences that might make the applicant uncomfortable. Keep the interview to twenty or thirty minutes. Do not exaggerate the benefits of the company or falsely raise the applicant's hopes. Allow the applicant time to ask questions, and at the end of the interview, inform the applicant when to expect notification of your decision.

Application Letter

In a letter of application you endeavor to sell yourself. A resumé differs from a letter, in that the resumé is a listing of what you have done and how long you have done it. It is a factual summary of your skills and interests. A letter is less structured than a resumé, and more enjoyable to read—if it has been written appropriately.

In a letter of application you present yourself, your skills, your job background, and your desire for an opportunity to prove yourself. If you consider this letter carefully, it will work to your advantage. You can have a very impressive, well written resumé and ruin it with a slip-shod, poorly written accompanying letter. Letters are more conversational than the factual listing that makes up your resumé. This letter must be professional looking, free of grammatical errors, and interesting.

Your letter is an advertisement for yourself—your skills, job experiences, schooling, and personality. Whenever you write anything, your personality shows through. Consider the following letter of application written by none other than the original Wet Noodle himself.

To Whomever:
I'm looking for a job and thought you might have one or no about one. I don't want to be no bother, but please call me either way. You can get me at 628-9913 before 2:00 p.m. and 628-4682 after 2:00 p.m. Thanks.

Wet Noodle

This person may have had an impressive resumé enclosed (although it is highly unlikely), but the accompanying letter would cause them both to find their way immediately into the wastebasket.

Write your letter with the following things in mind:

1. Your credentials
2. Your job ability
3. Your interest in the job
4. Your skills
5. Your capabilities

Show the confident, enthusiastic, positive side of yourself. Your letter must have power of persuasion, it should promote good will, it should show interest, and it should be friendly and informative. Let the opening of your letter make the reader want to read the body of the letter to find out more about you. Make it neat and an attention-getter. The end of the letter should respectfully request an interview. Avoid beginning sentences with the word, "I." Somewhere in your letter, refer to the fact that you have enclosed a resumé.

Examine the following sample letters and analyze each of them, paragraph by paragraph.

1622 Ridgewood Way
Kansas City, MO
April 2, 1984

Mrs. Barbara Heston
Babes In Arms
10 South Plum Way
Kansas City, MO 64117

Dear Mrs. Heston:

In answer to your ad in the *Tribune* seeking a person to fill your pre-school vacancy, I feel I can offer you many services. My number one qualification for pre-school employment is my love of young children. My patience is practically unending and I am prepared to give a great deal of tender loving care.

My enclosed resumé describes my tenure at the Day Care Center in St. Louis, Missouri. My teaching degree was earned at Kansas State University.

At your convenience, I would like to meet with you to discuss the position. You will discover someone who would like to be shared with children!

Sincerely,

Mary Walton

Enc: Resumé

In this letter, the writer opened in paragraph one with enthusiasm and she created excitement and interest. She stated her source of reference. In the next paragraph she referred to the enclosed resumé and briefly stated her qualifications. She ended by suggesting an interview and gave a very positive image of herself.

621 West 13th Street
Roanoke, VA
January 20, 1984

John Ross, Manager
Ross Appliances
2026 Center Road
Roanoke, VA 24018

Dear Mr. Ross:

A mutual friend, Peg Swanson, has informed me you are looking for a salesman to work on the floor and also do some traveling. This sounds like just the job I would like to have!

My enclosed resumé describes my two and one half years at Central Technical College in Roanoke studying repair of major appliances. It further states that I have had four years selling experience in the appliance department of Hodgons & Co.

My knowledge of appliances—how to sell them and how to repair them—could be just what you need in your appliance center.

When granted the opportunity for an interview, I will not disappoint you.

Sincerely,

Max Hamphaus

Enclosure: Resumé

Max starts his letter by stating how he became aware of a job vacancy. He immediately jumps in with an expressed interest. In paragraph two, he refers to the enclosed resumé and briefly states his qualifications. He closes by expressing a desire for an interview.

There are many ways to write a letter of application besides the formal conventional style. A less formal, rather unconventional letter might begin by eliminating an inside address and substituting an eye-catching one-liner or a headline. Here is an example:

1803 Center Road
Deer Park, WA 99006
November 10, 1984

The elderly can still be productive . . .

The elderly have a great deal to give and I have a great deal to give to them. In reading your monthly nursing home publication, I notice you need a director of activities. This is the opportunity I have been waiting for.

For six years I served as activity director in Golden Age Villa, a nursing home in San Diego, California. Business opportunities have recently brought my family to the Deer Park community. I have enclosed my credentials from Golden Age Villa.

My great admiration and affection for old people qualify me to work with them to create new and different activities in which they might participate.

The sooner we visit, the happier we will both be! My availability is practically unrestricted, and I can be reached at 386-0214 anytime.

Thank you.

Sincerely,

Sarah Lang

Enc: Credentials

The above letter is unconventional from beginning to end. However, it starts out by stimulating interest and ends the same way. Sarah would almost create enough curiosity for the recipient of the letter to want to interview her. She has no prepared resumé, but has enclosed her credentials. She certainly has a positive approach; she is confident and honest about her desire to work around the elderly.

Draft two letters, one using the formal, conventional style and the second one with a less formal, unconventional style. Be sure to keep in mind all the points you need to make. Create interest and organize your material well, paying careful attention to neatness and grammatical correctness.

Your letter should pack a wallop; that is, it should be attention-getting and entice the reader to read on and want to interview you. The letter of application represents you in your absence. It paves the way for the interview you seek. You cannot be too careful in organizing and thinking through the letter. After you have read and reread it, ask yourself these questions:

1. Did I state my objective?
2. Did I express my skills adequately?
3. Did I respond to the needs of the reader?
4. Did I create interest?
5. Did I instill a desire to grant me an interview?
6. Did I "reach out and touch someone" with my positive manner?

Write so that your letter has an impact on the reader. Make your letter personal to fit the needs of the position for which you are requesting an interview. The same resumé may be sent to various places without alteration, but the letter should be tailored to fit the specific job needs. Write a letter with some pizazz, some originality, and something of *you!*

Review these ten rules for your letter of application.

1. Use a specific name and/or title with the salutation.
2. Spell and punctuate correctly.
3. Come right to the point—avoid wordiness.
4. Be assertive, not aggressive or passive.
5. State your reason for writing.
6. Refer to your enclosed resumé.
7. Be positive.
8. Do not be repetitive.
9. Request an interview.
10. Write with impact.

Application Forms

Without fail, every type of business will request you to fill out an application form in addition to the letter of application and the resumé you have written. The length of the form is determined by whether or not the job is skilled or unskilled. Some businesses accept application forms almost anytime—whether or not they have vacancies. Other businesses accept forms only when a job is available. Most firms keep applications on file for a certain period of time (60 or 90 days), so you will need to know when to make out a new form to keep your file current.

Each business has its own policy as to when they require an application form. Sometimes it is required when you make a personal visit; sometimes you are sent an application form before a firm will talk with you. Preparing your resumé ahead of time simplifies and expedites filling out an application form.

Application forms are of all kinds. Some are professional in appearance—others are streamlined or xeroxed in a simple manner. Some ask general questions; others, specific questions. However, all types of businesses are after the same kind of information.

You will probably be asked your age, marital status, race, and handicaps, if any. By law you are permitted to refuse to answer these personal questions. Ladies, for heaven's sake—reveal your age, just this once! Your decision not to answer specific personal questions may be interpreted as lack of cooperation. You are expected to respond to the questions in some manner, so give the correct information without hesitation.

Basic information most employers want to know about you is:

1. Full name and address
2. Telephone number
3. Social security number
4. Marital status
5. Birthdate
6. Educational background
7. Previous work experience
8. References (usually three)

Your educational background should include schools attended, years attended, when graduated, and post-graduate work. Work experience should include the company name and address, name of your superior, the title you held, and how long you were employed.

You may also be requested to reveal:

1. Special skills you possess
2. Number of dependents
3. Exact type of job you want
4. Any limitations you may have
5. Health problems, if any
6. Hobbies and extracurricular interests
7. Someone to notify in case of emergency

When answering these questions, be honest. Be very frank about your health or medications you take. In the long run you are doing yourself a favor by your honesty. Be specific about the type of job you are applying for. "Just anything," as an answer will not "cut it"! Be sure to mention *all* the skills you have. One of those skills may be just the missing link to fill the employer's bill.

Below is a sample of what an application form usually looks like. This form, however, is abbreviated compared to some.

Name _____

Address _____

Telephone Number _____

Social Security Number _____

Birthdate _____

What are your long-term work-related goals? _____

_____

Are you interested in doing a good job in your work? Yes _____ No _____

If so, what motivates you to do so? _____

_____

Do you get along with people? Yes _____ No _____

If yes, explain _____

_____

What skills do you have that qualify you for this position?

_____

Where did you obtain these skills? _____

Complete the following information for all the schools you attended during the last 10 years:

Name _____

Address _____

Years Attended _____

Degree/Date _____

Complete the following information for all the places you have worked during the last five years:

Company Name _____

Address _____

Title _____

Dates of Employment _____

Name of Superior _____
List three persons and their addresses (other than relatives) who know your character, abilities, and work habits:

_____

_____

_____

An application form also tells more about you than just the written answers you have supplied. A written application shows how neat you are; it displays your handwriting and shows how you organize your thoughts and express yourself. It indicates whether or not you can think clearly and express your thoughts in a clear concise manner. It points out whether or not you are a positive person and have confidence in your abilities.

Resumé

If you were going on a safari you would study ahead and take the necessary weapons, equipment, and ammunition with you. After all, you are talking about your life! It would be ludicrous to take a pop-gun or sling shot, in hopes of bringing home some ivory from an oversized elephant. Would you consider a butterfly net to snag the king of beasts? You have built-in human instincts for survival, so you arm yourself appropriately and adequately before entering the jungle.

Apply this ridiculous example to the jungle that awaits you in the business world. That jungle is the *job world!* When seeking employment, arm yourself with the necessary equipment and ammunition—your positive attitude, your letter of application, and your resumé. The resumé has been referred to many times. At this point it is appropriate to discuss it in depth.

Preparing Your Resumé

A resumé can take the place of an application form, an interview, or a personal visit. This case is really the exception, not the rule. Some firms accept a resumé and nothing more, even when they have no job openings. "We are not taking applications at this time, but you are welcome to leave your resumé with us," is a foot-in-the-door opportunity! This kind of opportunity does not happen often, but be ready if it does. Always have on hand a well written, personalized, tailored-to-fit resumé. Be sure to make *plenty* of copies. In this case, copy money could be the best money you have ever spent.

You cannot expect to sit down and write a resumé quickly. You must think, plan, and study the many types of resumés. Know your options and remember how important it is to have a resumé that really represents you.

A resumé is a factual personal data sheet. Try to give it more than just facts. Impress the reader that you are worthy of a good job, have many accomplishments, are interesting, honest, and would be a valuable asset to the company. Let your personality show through. Dull and uninteresting do not fill the bill. Let your resumé answer these three questions in a clear, concise, and interesting manner:

1. Who are you?
2. What do you want?
3. What do you have to offer?

When making your resumé interesting, do not go off the deep end and use purple paper with a border of pink polka-dots. Indisputably this would attract attention—adverse attention! Colored paper is not advised—use good quality white bond paper and type neatly without errors.

Use an imaginative heading, not something dull and obvious like "Resumé of John Doe," or "Data Sheet." That type of heading is comparable to pointing at the sun, saying, "That's the sun," without describing its beauty or usefulness. A heading such as:

John Doe
Top-Management Qualifications
For Chain Store Grocers
or
Qualifications of John Doe
For Career in Electronics
or

MARY SMITH
Secretarial Credentials
For Legal Secretary

Consider framing your heading to set it off. Be creative, imaginative, and a little daring. Give your resumé your best shot. Make your reader want to read on!

Familiarize yourself with some simple, eye-catching techniques. Give more space to a credential that is important to the type of work you are applying for. Use less space for an item of lesser importance. Place the most important parts of the resumé at the top of the page. You may wish to repeat an especially valuable credential or ability. Present it in different ways and in different places throughout the resumé. Use capital letters to emphasize the importance of a word or group of words. You may underscore a word for further emphasis. Make this resumé represent *you* in your absence.

You are painting a picture of yourself; so make it a beauty! Brag about yourself—the resumé is the only appropriate place for boasting. Play down your weak points, or better yet, ignore them altogether. Build a strong bridge, square your shoulders, put on your best positive face, and dive headlong into the body of the resumé!

The chronological format is the most widely used style of resumé, so we present it first. Several reasons for the chronological resumé's wide use are the simplicity of writing and following this format and the fact most employers are accustomed to reading resumés written in this style. The chronological resumé has drawbacks, however. The biggest of these is the fact that you are more likely to dwell on your work experience rather than on your skills, abilities, and interests. The chronological resumé is difficult to make interesting, and the reader must often guess at your qualifications.

Most resumés begin with a heading that carries the following information:

- Name
- Address
- Telephone
- Marital Status
- Health
- Height
- Weight
- Age

In addition to the chronological resumé, two other kinds, the functional and the combination, are widely used. Look at all three and decide which will be most beneficial for you.

In any kind of resumé, write your given name (no nicknames). You may use your full name, or your first and last names with a middle initial. Give your current address in full—street address, apartment number, if any, city, state, and zip code. The telephone number should include the area code in parentheses. You are not bound by law to reveal your marital status, but it is best to be honest. Marital status rarely affects your chances for employment. If you are divorced, describe your marital status as single. Honesty is not only the *best* policy, it is the *only* policy when writing a resume. Use your birthdate—month, day and year, rather than your age, to prevent retyping when you add another candle to your cake.

Your objective should state your intentions clearly, honestly, crisply, and directly—what you would like to do for this employer.

Avoid using abbreviations—spell words out. Do not use such abbreviations as re (regarding), i.e. (that is), etc. (and so forth).

Be consistent with verb tense. If you begin using *had* or *have*, or *is* or *was*, stick with it. Be consistent!

You may or may not include references in your resume, but have names, addresses, and telephone numbers of four good references available. An alternative to including references is to write "References available on request." If you choose not to list them on your résumé sheet, have an additional page showing the reference listing. Contact people to get their permission before using their names as references. Common courtesy requires permission to use someone's name. Most people consent gladly to giving their names as references.

Chronological Resumé

A chronological resumé contains these categories of information:

1. Contact information (We are talking about *you.*)
2. Your objective
3. Work experience (Begin with your most recent job at the top of the list, and work your way to your first job.)
4. Education
5. Personal statement (This is optional.)

The order of presentation can be flexible. If your education is a better qualification than your work experience, put your education immediately following your objective. Avoid unnecessary detail and long-windedness or you will lose your reader quickly. If you have an outstanding qualification, or expertise in a specific area, state it clearly. Get in and get out; do not overemphasize and do not exaggerate.

Functional Resumé

A functional resumé differs from a chronological resumé in that no dates are listed for time employed at various work sites. One advantage of this format is that a period of unemployment does not show. A functional resumé lists your skills and abilities, rather than just your job experience. The information in this resumé differs only in this respect: Instead of listing work experience below your objective, list skills and achievements that are transferable and suitable for the job you are applying for.

Combination Resumé

A combination resumé simply combines the chronological and functional formats. This resumé is essentially the same as the first two, but under objectives you include both your transferable achievements and a list of your work history. Whatever format you choose, list the *most important* information first.

In addition to the essentials of a resumé that have already been discussed, include military experience, civic involvement, professional and/or social affiliations, special skills, and interests or hobbies.

Your military background should include the branch of service, your rank, assignments, and special achievements. (K. P. duty is *not* a special assignment— nor is it an achievement!)

Your civic or community involvement includes the organizations you belong to, the projects you worked on, the offices you held, and any skills or accomplishments you contributed. Professional or social affiliations include member-

K. P. DUTY

ships, offices held, and projects you worked on. Interests include hobbies or any special interests that might be directly related to your objective.

A personal statement could discuss job-related travel, your willingness to relocate, and your availability for starting work. Your references could be added here if you have not put them on a separate page. (One advantage to placing your references on a separate page is this: If your references change addresses, you avoid having to retype.)

Transferable Skills

Below is a list of skills that are applicable to specific types of work.

1. typing (a secretarial position)
2. sewing (a tailoring job)
3. welding (a job specializing in wrought-iron)
4. writing (an editorial position on the local newspaper)

Transferable skills, however, are those that are learned in one type of work and can be transferred to another. A list of traits and skills that are transferable to many different types of jobs are listed below. Study them and familiarize yourself with those you possess. Utilize them in your vocabulary when preparing your resumé.

self-confident	creative
imaginative	experienced
persuasive	unique
negotiable	outgoing
communicative	motivating
perceptive	reliable
easy-going	innovative
competent	personable
public speaking	friendly
designing	humorous
selling	supervising
objective	responsible
calm	improving
counseling	versatile
competent	pleasant
warm	willing
challenging	cooperative
analytical	

Some of your transferable skills might surprise you as you discover the advantages of having, utilizing, and adapting them to your employment search.

Sample Resumés

Following are examples of functional, chronological and combination resumés.

CHRONOLOGICAL RESUMÉ

ROBERT GREEN
1315 Coopermeadow Lane
Houston, Texas 77056
(915)111-1234

OBJECTIVE:	A professional sales position with potential to advance in management.
EDUCATION:	*B.S. in Marketing,* 1976
	Courses in marketing, selling, advertising, psychology, and written and oral communications.
SALES EXPERIENCE:	*ABC Clothing, Incorporated, 1212 Virginia Avenue, Sioux City, Iowa 51105:* Manager of casual wear department. Involved in sales, buying, inventory control, and handling customer complaints. Responsible for providing second highest sales year for this department since its beginning 35 years ago. Started in 1979 to present.
	XYZ Chronical, 355 South 37th Street, Austin, Texas 78759: Created and sold advertising for this daily newspaper. Selling an intangible provided a contrast in sales techniques. Employment period 1976 to 1979.
TECHNICAL EXPERIENCE:	Operated electronic cash registers. Created advertising brochures. Sold advertising and created advertising layouts. Created time management plan for casual wear department. Worked with high speed printers and word processing equipment.
PERSONAL:	*Birthdate:* August 22, 1955. *Health status:* excellent. Height: 6'2", weight: 177 lb. *Marital status:* married. Interested in people, human resource development and organiza-

tional development. Hobbies and activities include golf and dancing. Enjoy watching professional football.

REFERENCES: Available on request.

FUNCTIONAL RESUMÉ

ROBERT GREEN
1315 Coopermeadow Lane
Houston, Texas 77056
(915)111-1234

OBJECTIVE: A professional sales position with potential to advance in management.

EDUCATION: *B.S. in Marketing,* 1976

                   Courses in marketing, selling, advertising, psychology, and written and oral communications.

SALES/CUSTOMER   Involved in sales, buying, and inventory control. Handled
RELATIONS: customer complaints and dealt with personnel problems.

                   Created and sold advertising. Initiated new sales techniques for selling intangibles.

TECHNICAL   Operated electronic cash registers. Created advertising
EXPERIENCE: brochures. Sold advertising and created advertising layouts. Created time management plan and worked with high speed printers and word processing equipment.

PERSONAL: *Birthdate:* August 22, 1955. *Health Status:* excellent. Height: 6'2", weight: 177 lb. *Marital status:* married. Interested in people, human resource development and organizational development. Hobbies and activities include golf and dancing. Enjoy watching professional football.

REFERENCES: Available on request.

COMBINATION RESUMÉ

ROBERT GREEN
1315 Coopermeadow Lane
Houston, Texas 77056
(915)111-1234

OBJECTIVE:	A professional sales position with potential to advance in management.
SALES/ CUSTOMER RELATIONS:	Involved in sales, buying, and inventory control. Handled customer complaints. Created and sold advertising. Initiated new sales techniques for selling intangibles.
TECHNICAL EXPERIENCE:	Operated electronic cash registers. Created advertising brochures. Sold advertising and created advertising layouts. Created time management plan for casual wear department. Worked with high speed printers and word processing equipment.
EMPLOYMENT EXPERIENCE:	ABC Clothing Incorporated, Sioux City, Iowa XYZ Chronical, Austin, Texas
EDUCATION:	*B. S. in Marketing,* 1976
PERSONAL:	*Birthdate:* August 22, 1955. *Health status:* excellent. Height 6′2″, weight 177 lb. *Marital status:* married. Interested in people, human resource development and organizational development. Hobbies and activities include golf and dancing. Enjoy watching professional football.
REFERENCES:	Available on request.

Most people agree that a resumé should be kept to one page if possible. A second page is distracting and tends to lose the reader's attention. The sequence of your resumé will depend on which type of resumé you choose to write, but the most important information should come first. You will want your resumé to be neat and grammatically correct, use no abbreviations or slang, have good organization, catch the eye and contain all the necessary information. Your resumé is an advertisement of yourself. Be honest throughout and create a positive mood for your reader. Do not get lost in the crowd—join the crowd, or better yet—stand out in the crowd!

Practice

1. Prepare a letter of application for a managing position with a card and gift shop.
2. Prepare a chronological resumé that would be appropriate when applying for a position as salesperson with a sporting goods firm.

3. Write a request for an interview using a creative and imaginative approach. You may write about any job opening you wish.

4. Write a follow-up or thank-you letter in response to an interview.

5. List four things to remember in each of the three different categories below.

Grooming

1. _____

2. _____

3. _____

4. _____

Body Language

1. _____

2. _____

3. _____

4. _____

Speech

1. _____

2. _____

3. _____

4. _____

6. Name four things you should research about the firm you are applying to.

1. _____

2. _____

3. _____

4. _____

7. An interviewer has asked you a question that cannot be answered "yes" or "no." The question is, "Tell me about yourself." Describe briefly how you would answer this open-ended question.

8. How would you answer these open-ended stress questions?
   a. What salary do you require?
   b. Why do you want to work here?
   c. What are your greatest weaknesses?
   d. Tell me about your former employer.

Check Your Checklist

The following checklist should help you if you use it correctly before applying for a job or going to an interview. Be certain you *know* all the things on this checklist or you can find out quickly.

Checklist of Personal Information

_____ Your date of birth (exact)
_____ Your place of birth (city, state, county, and/or country)
_____ Your birth certificate
_____ Your social security number
_____ Your social security card
_____ Your military obligation status
_____ Father's age and birthdate
_____ Father's birthplace and nationality
_____ Mother's maiden name
_____ Mother's age and birthdate
_____ Mother's birthplace and nationality
_____ Names and ages of all children (if you are a parent)
_____ Telephone number(s)
_____ Names and locations of schools attended
_____ Dates of school attendance and grades attended
_____ Names and addresses of all colleges or trade schools attended
_____ All job-related training received
_____ Job titles of all paid jobs held
_____ Names of all past employers
_____ Names of any awards or honors received
_____ Memberships in organizations
_____ Offices held or committee memberships
_____ Names, addresses, and length of acquaintance of four good references

If your personal checklist is in good order, you are well prepared for almost any job interview or inquiry. Keep your list updated and always in a convenient place.

Some Interview Questions

These twelve questions may be asked on an interview. To the left of the question on the blank provided, write "U" for unacceptable or "A" for acceptable.

_____ 1. The names and addresses of the applicant's relatives (other than spouse and children)

_____ 2. The applicant's age

_____ 3. The person who suggested the applicant apply at this firm for a position

_____ 4. The name of applicant's bishop, pastor, or religious leader

_____ 5. Height or weight of applicant

_____ 6. The names of all clubs, societies, and lodges to which the applicant belongs

_____ 7. The maiden name of a married woman applicant

_____ 8. Whether an applicant regularly attends a place of worship

_____ 9. Questions relating to an arrest (arrests) of an applicant

_____ 10. Information about vocational, academic, or professional education of an applicant

_____ 11. Whether the applicant has ever worked for the company under another name

_____ 12. Color of eyes and hair

Other Questions

Listed below are 25 questions. Answer each of them honestly and precisely. Then discuss why you think an employer might ask these questions.

1. How would you rate your training for this job? Excellent? Fair?
2. What books have you read lately? What are your favorite magazines?
3. In what area do you need the most improvement?
4. Did you (do you) earn any of your own expense money while (if) you are in school?
5. Are you in good health?
6. What personal characteristics do you think are needed to succeed in your vocation?
7. What do you expect to be doing five or ten years from now?
8. Do you prefer to work with other people or do you work best alone?
9. What is your chosen field of work?

10. Are you willing to relocate?
11. Are you living with your parents?
12. May we write or call your last employer?
13. Have you ever taken drugs?
14. Give an example of a project you finished under pressure.
15. What is your school attendance record?
16. Do you belong to a civic organization?
17. Are you able to work all day Saturday and/or Sunday?
18. For what other jobs have you applied?
19. Have you ever stolen anything?
20. Do you take constructive criticism well?
21. Have you always done the best work you are capable of in school and/or on the job?
22. What does the word "cooperation" mean to you?
23. How could you be a contribution to our organization?
24. Why did you leave your previous job(s)?
25. What skills do you possess?

Fill in the sample application for employment. Be neat, spell correctly, and be honest.

PERSONAL INFORMATION

Date _____ Social Sec. # _____

Name _____
      Last   First   Middle

Present Address _____
      Street   City   State   Zip

Permanent Address _____
      Street   City   State   Zip

Phone No. _____
If related to anyone in our employ,
state name and department _____
Referred by:

EMPLOYMENT DESIRED

Position _____

Date you
can start _____

Are you employed now? _____

If so, may we inquire
of your present employer? _____

Have you ever applied to this company before? _____

Where? _____   When? _____

EDUCATION

	Name and Location	Yrs. Att.	Date Grad.	Sub. Studied
Grammar School				
High School				
College				
Trade, Business, or Correspondence School				

Subjects of special study or research work _____

What foreign languages do you speak fluently? _____

Read? _____   Write? _____

Activities other than religious
(Civic, Athletic, etc.) _____

Exclude organizations whose names or character indicate the race, creed, color, or national origin of its members.

This sample application form was just that—a sample. Other information might be requested, such as a list of all former employers, with dates of employment, names and addresses, salary, position held, and your reason for leaving. References might be requested at this time and they must be people you have known for at least a year. Their names, addresses, businesses and how long they have been your acquaintances will probably be asked.

Be sure to read carefully when filling in an application form. Follow the printed instructions explicitly. When applying for a job, you cannot be too careful, and following instructions is imperative. Whenever the form requests a signature, remember to *write* your name, not print it!

Summary

In summarizing this chapter, we remind you that this material presents only samples of how to write resumés and application letters, how to fill out application forms, and how to write letters of appreciation. It only suggests ways to get that all-important opportunity for an interview.

Use everything you have studied. Success in seeking a career depends upon good hygiene, impressive and powerful dress, assertiveness, goals and objectives, listening skills, attitudes, and more.

State your goals and objectives clearly in your resumé and cover letter. Keep your goals in mind at all times and update them each time you reach a plateau.

Applying for a job is like the dating game. Several people are always vying for the same opportunity. Put your ingenuity, your creativity and your imagination to use. Dare to be a little different, but at the same time follow the rules.

Your skills and abilities may fall short of what the job position requires. If this problem arises consistently—better yourself. Register for a night course, attend a seminar, practice your skills, go to the library and check out some reference materials. You must have the desire and the drive to sharpen or add to your skills.

Never lose sight of the fact that a job interview is nothing more than a task of selling yourself. You must convince the interviewer beyond doubt that you are the best choice for the position that is open. A potent resumé and letter of application, and a potent and powerful interview are almost guarantees of landing the job you want.

Go after the career you want and remember these words beginning with the letter "P" that can *Provide* the opportunity for success:

Pat
Plan
Power
Prove
Posture
Proceed
Position
Positive

Progress
Potential
Persuasive
Personality
Perspiration
Physical energy

Do not Procrastinate—go after that job before it is gone. Have a Positive attitude toward an interview. Assume that you have what it takes to obtain a successful Position. Once you obtain that Position, continue to assert your mental and Physical energy. Be Persuasive, let your Personality show, and use your Posture to advantage to indicate your confidence in your Potential. Your Power of Persuasion will Prove that you have a life Plan. Part of that Plan includes selling yourself as the best Person for the Position. After you have done all of these things well, Pat yourself on the back, wipe the Perspiration from your brow and Proceed to make Progress in your chosen career.

CHAPTER 19

Changing Careers

Go for It Again!

If you were looking for guarantees when you chose your first career, you soon found out that there were none. Perhaps you were not looking for happiness in your job, or hadn't considered happiness and work a compatible package.

Remember the "good old days" when an occupation or family business was passed on from generation to generation? Aptitude was not tested. Happiness was not associated with work nor was enjoyment of work given priority. Today job satisfaction is considered important in choosing a career, but you can bet there will still be plenty of opportunity to "earn your bread by the sweat of your brow."

When you talk with friends and acquaintances, you realize that some people are excited about what they do for a living. They speak in terms of a current challenging project or a past accomplishment. You may come away wondering why you have fallen into routine operation with no promise of anything better for tomorrow.

Thousands upon thousands of people day after day work their way through jobs that they hate. In some cases these people earn a great deal of money for their misery. In such cases, money may be a stronger motivator than happiness.

If you are unhappy in your job, but do not feel that enjoying your work is necessary and are motivated to do well for other reasons . . . fine. If, on the other hand, you want to derive some pleasure from your job, where you spend a great deal of your life, then begin a new career plan.

It is never too late to begin, provided you have not convinced yourself otherwise. Experts estimate that most people will change careers three to five times. Technological advances have brought about many career changes by creating new occupations. A new job opportunity may be more appealing than your original career choice. Technology makes some occupations obsolete. When this happens, a new career choice is mandatory.

Stagnation is another reason to change careers. You may feel unchallenged by the job itself, or your firm may offer no new challenges or opportunities for advancement. Whatever the reasons, you may find yourself returning several times to the career planning stage of your life.

Second careers are not uncommon, but people whose career plans permit adaptability, will be best able to deal with their futures.

Effort and planning are as important to career change as they were to your first choice. You have several things going for you that you did not have the first time around. Experience is on your side now. You have had more exposure and insight into occupations by working and talking with people, and these observations give you some knowledge of what other jobs involve. You have been through the career selection and preparation process before, so you know what you did right and what you could have done better.

When you consider a career change, treat it as your last change. This attitude encourages you to be certain and careful as you prepare.

Some people feel guilty about changing careers. They feel that they are "giving up" on their present occupation or retreating from a bad career choice. Perhaps this thought will ease those feelings: During World War II, a general who withdrew troops from a position they had been holding, explained the maneuver like this, "Retreat hell, we're just advancing in a different direction!"

Baby Boom

Changing careers is tougher because of the baby boom. This large pool of career seekers is well-trained and well-educated. They are coming out of community colleges and universities with backgrounds in the latest technologies and techniques. Because of this large, highly skilled work force, there is no such thing as a terminal education. Every person should be aware that learning is a lifelong proposition.

With this tough competition people need better career plans, so career planning is becoming a part of most curriculums.

If you are making a second or third career plan, you have the advantage of *experience*, but you have traded some other things for it. You have traded in a certain amount of youth, perhaps some energy, and a measure of health.

However, you have some first-hand knowledge from having made mistakes that you can now rectify. You know what traps not to fall into.

You can take one step in your career plan that the first-time-arounder cannot take: review. Remember when you made your first career plan? On your list of priorities it fell somewhere between where to buy your first beer, and where to take your date on Saturday night. Your emphasis on planning, problem solving, and decision making probably consisted principally of impulse. While not totally true, this statement may come closer to the truth than anyone cares to admit (including your authors).

Whatever you do, you make a decision for which *you* and *you* alone are responsible. Even the decision to do nothing is a decision; be sure you recognize it as such.

Everyone is unique—no one else is exactly like you. Yet as different as one person is from another, there are vast general similarities. At certain ages in your life you face predictable crises much like everyone else at that stage of life. The book *Passages*, written by Gail Sheehy, gives some insight into the different thoughts and concerns that typically affect our lives as we enter these different ages and stages.

Job Potential

If you are searching for a new career or a different setting for your current career, your present position probably does not provide you with the opportunity to realize the potential you see in yourself. You might be thinking, "I have a *job*. What I want is an *opportunity.*"

Perhaps the firm you are with has just promoted someone to the position you aspire to. You know you need that position to move upward in your career. You are not disappointed because you were passed over or because the individual who got the promotion was not qualified. You know that you were not quite ready to move up, but you realize that that position will probably not be open again for many years. When you are ready, there will be no place for you to go. You are at a dead end and the target you were aiming for has been removed. You realize that as your qualifications and experience grow, you will have to move to another firm. You find yourself trying to match your readiness for growth with the availability of an opportunity for growth.

At this point the "what ifs" enter the picture. Do you recognize these? "What if I change companies now—will I have the best chance for growth later? What if I wait until I'm ready—will other firms promote from within rather than hire a new person in the position I want?" There are more "what if" questions than there are answers. Try this one: What if you make a change and it does not work out? You are no worse off than you are now. This proposition assumes two things:

1. You cannot get where you want to be in your current situation.
2. You want to move up as part of your career plan.

Over and Over

Repeat, overlap, repeat some more. You are bound to have noticed how often one concept presented in this book is brought into other chapters. At times you are reminded to go back and refresh your memory and to apply something offered earlier to the present information you are receiving. At other times you have been told that a certain concept to be dealt with at length in a later chapter, will be used only in a limited sense as it applies to the current subject under consideration.

The reason for this back and forth reference is because throughout your life you employ your knowledge in many areas all at once to solve a current problem. Not every situation that presents itself will call for all of your knowledge, but like a smorgasbord, you are continuously selecting the right combination of tools to fix the situation at hand.

These paragraphs of explanation are inserted at this time simply because this situation is presenting itself again with the concept of risk. The general topic of risk and risk-taking will also be dealt with, but since life itself and certainly career/life planning involves risk, it needs to appear and be applied to the career concept.

Taking Risks

As you get older, your priorities and values shift. You become more conservative about taking risks. For one thing, the risks you were once willing to take alone, now involve other people. Your spouse and children also are committed to any risk you take right along with you. Choices were easier when you had only yourself to worry about. While concern and consideration for others are admirable attributes, taking a risk does not indicate a flaw in your character as long as you take responsibility for your actions. You take risks every day; you must take precautions and increase your chances of winning by gathering all the information you can before taking the risk. Know exactly what you are risking and what you are asking others to risk.

Sometimes the risks involved discourage people from changing careers. The saying, "better the devil you know, than a chance on the one you don't," means that you know the pitfalls and problems of your present situation. If you try something new, you find new problems and you have to learn to cope anew. Nothing is wrong with conservatism, but a great deal is wrong with giving up, with making the decision before getting the facts. To be happy about your choice, make an informed choice—whether you risk *change* or risk *staying* where you are (oh there is risk either way). Make your choice freely and accept it. Do not blame someone else.

No realistic goal is out of your reach, but you need to assess the risks. What has to be done is to begin to analyze where you are and how you got there. Then start with where you are and ask yourself "Where do I want to go?" and "How do I intend to get there?"

Begin to figure the odds by taking a look at the competition. For example, assume that your place of employment has a policy of promoting from within. As you size up your circumstances, you discover that there are three other people besides yourself who hold jobs that are promotable to the position you have been eyeing. Your chances of getting the position you want are one-in-four or 25 percent.

Next, look for factors that might give you an edge or work in your favor. Perhaps you have no competition because no one else wants the promotion. Approach other factors logically. Who among your competitors has been with the company longest? Which of you holds the position from which promotions are most frequently made? Whose ideas and suggestions are listened to and adopted when you are all at the same meeting? If your suggestions are implemented, does the top man know it was you who made them? Perhaps you have a supervisor who likes to take the credit. If such circumstances exist, you may not do well in this particular category when figuring your percentages.

Besides the logical approach, there are other, not-so-logical questions to consider. Who do your immediate supervisors put in charge in their absence? Which one of you plays golf with the boss or has more things in common, like similar family size or even a similar medical disorder? By the time you finish exploring all the possible factors you may decide you have a 50-50 chance for the promotion.

While you used this procedure to assess your risks, you have also completed the fact gathering for phase two. The risk examination reviewed your strong areas of performance and some of your weaknesses that hold you back. You now know where to concentrate your efforts to reduce the risk, and increase the likelihood of being selected for the promotion when the time comes.

You might take one of several approaches. You may choose to concentrate on your strong areas to make them even stronger, weaknesses to bring them up to strength, or to improve both your strong and weak areas. You may find that expending effort in certain areas would not benefit you. For example, if your immediate supervisor takes credit for your ideas, you need opportunities to become visible. You may have to accomplish this by a different route, perhaps by volunteering to hold an office in a civic or professional organization.

On Job Career Planning

Many supervisory and administrative personnel are now attending workshops, seminars, and conferences that center on human resource development. As a result, a lot of thinking and some action focus on career development for employees. Many employers are genuinely concerned about and committed to providing programs for employees. In-house training departments provide technical and management programs to enable employees to keep pace with changing technologies and to prepare for advancement. Some firms work with educational institutions to provide programs; others have established educational assistance programs that pay all or part of an employee's educational costs.

This concern of employers for employees has brought about another interesting development. In many cases, employees consult their supervisors when considering whether or not to take another job. Some supervisors are genuinely interested in the employee and give helpful and unbiased advice. They get right down to the bare essentials and honestly tell it like it is. If they evaluate the circumstances and find it in your best interest to leave their employ, they offer to back your decision with a good recommendation.

Other managers and supervisors may not be as frank. Therefore, be sure to take their advice for what it is—advice. Weigh it for yourself, and make your own decision. This recommendation does not suggest that you be distrustful, but realize that the person you are asking for advice is in a tough spot. Supervisors have a responsibility to the company that provides the paychecks that feed their families. That responsibility is to keep the company running smoothly and profitably. Losing you could interrupt that smooth operation. Replacing you, because you are good at what you do, may take considerable time and money. A new person must be brought to the point of knowledge and efficiency that you attained. Supervisors are conscience-bound to consider these things when advising you.

Some supervisors will recognize that you are unhappy, and that opportunities for advancement within the company are a long way off. These supervisors also realize that your discontent may grow until your efficiency falls off. In that case, both you and the company have been done a grave disservice.

Never Too Late

Much emphasis is placed on career-life planning in this day and age, and competition becomes more acute with each passing year. In spite of these things, many people still do not set work goals for themselves. How to plan their own careers is a mystery to them. In some cases they lack exposure to the how and why of career planning. More often, however, complacency and procrastination are the causes. Goal setting, plan formulating and following steps that guide their careers and lives are just too much work, and so the tasks are avoided.

If you recognize yourself as reluctant to do serious career/life planning, you are not unlike a great many others. Be assured that it is never too late to begin.

You may work at an occupation you like, but often there comes a time when a career change is desirable or feasible because of your own desires, or because you have demonstrated considerable ability. This type of career change is called *promotion.*

As you demonstrate that you are good at what you do, you encourage yourself to move up and put the idea of promotion in the mind of your supervisor. Just because you are good at what you do, however, does not guarantee that you will be good at something you have never done before. Advancement means new responsibilities and new tasks. The acts of a leader or manager are quite different from those of a good performer at a present job. The outstanding worker who becomes a manager is actually embarking on a second career.

If you have not planned your career, now is the time to begin. Get in touch with your chances to succeed if you wish to pursue and obtain that management position. If you have been a conscientious career planner, you were thorough from the beginning and have regularly updated the information you collected for your first plan. By carefully preparing basic plans and periodically updating them, you are always ready with a resumé and able to take an interview on short notice.

When charting a base plan, you ask and answer list after list of questions. The following is another list of questions to consider. This list is useful when changing careers or when facing advancement possibilities. Some of these items may already be included in your current plan; however, the list is included here in case some of the items are new to you.

Exploring for Career Changes and Advancement

1. Opportunities
   a. What opportunities are available to you if you decide to become a professional?
   b. What are your opportunities if you decide to climb the managerial ladder?
2. Management and professional career differences
   a. Managers are generalists, whereas professionals are more specialized. In which capacity are you more comfortable?

b. Are you good at delegating work and responsibility?

c. Are you comfortable with delegation or do you feel you must have your hand in everything, "so that it is done right"?

d. Do you enjoy dealing with people's problems and with problems between people?

e. Do you work well on schedules and can you adhere to deadlines?

3. What is a manager?

a. Have you talked with at least five managers (ten would be better) to find out what they do and how they feel?

b. What are your strengths that fit a management position?

c. What weaknesses might you have if you were to join management ranks?

d. Are your plus factors greater than your minus factors?

4. Career and Life

a. Are you willing to follow your decision through, even if it requires you to make changes?

b. Are you ready and willing to make lifestyle changes?

c. What kind of timetable do you need to realize your goal?

5. Plan

a. Can you follow up your decision with a plan to get where you have decided to go?

When working on your career/life plan, whether your first or your tenth, never fool yourself. This endeavor demands self-honesty. If you cannot be honest with yourself, you set yourself up for problems and disappointments.

Suppose you have done your homework and you decide that advancement is the route to follow. You can do several things immediately.

Set specific goals, both long and short range. Know exactly what position you are ultimately aiming for. Know what other positions you will need on the way, and the exact position that must be your first goal.

Get tough and picky with yourself. Make certain your current performance is the best work you are capable of doing. Eliminate errors. Do not do anything that is just good enough. Make your work the best and most thorough.

Work on those things that give you the experience and knowledge to reach your goal and to aid in handling the position once you have it.

Stay current with books, newspapers, periodicals, and trade journals. Spot trends so that you will be aware of what the future will bring for your company and its products and services.

Act as if you already had the position. Be confident—not cocky! When you look in the mirror, tell yourself you are looking at the Sales Manager of ABC Company. Act the way you believe the sales manager should act. You are practicing mentally, but you may find that outwardly you stand taller and straighter. This mental practice puts you in the frame of mind that produces self-confidence.

Crash Course

What follows is a crash course in how to get ahead in business. This method of presentation may help you remember five traits that are important to you because they will serve you in business and all aspects of life and because supervisors look for these traits in promotable people.

CRASH is a key word and stands for:

- C   Courage
- R   Realism
- A   Autonomy
- S   Stability
- H   Honesty

Courage—We defined courage as the ability to act and the willingness to take risks. To take action is to be assertive. To take action means to do something even if it is wrong. The only way to never make mistakes is to do nothing. Even then you may be at fault through neglect. Do not confuse the willingness to take a risk with gambling. While you must not be afraid to try something new, you should gather whatever information is available. Weigh the information so you know exactly what is at risk, and then make your decision. Do not play the long shot at every opportunity. Your good judgment gives you the gumption to take an unpopular stand and to stand straight and tall when admitting that something that failed was your idea. Your good judgment should keep you from foolish actions.

Realism—See things as they are. Tell it like it is. Unfortunately some people think a realistic person is negative and pessimistic, but this is not the case. A bad situation that is seen for what it is can be dealt with in a positive manner until it can be changed. If a bad situation is ignored, it will remain a bad situation, no matter how it is sugar-coated. The realist recognizes the bad situation for what it is, but is optimistic enough to believe that changes can be made, no matter how long it takes.

Autonomy—Think for yourself. Listen to others, especially to experienced people, but be careful to sort information from bias (an application for well developed listening skills). Some people are willing to accept the status quo because there is a certain amount of security in fighting change. It may be to everyone's advantage to upset the routine if you have found a better way to accomplish the job.

Stability—Be emotionally stable. Know your strengths and weaknesses and accept them. When you accept what you are, you can begin to change. Instability makes you unreliable. A person who gives in to the mood of the moment is difficult, if not impossible, to trust. Accept praise humbly and graciously. Accept criticism constructively. Face success and failure for what they are. Both can be built upon, and both are feedback from decisions you have made. Stability makes you trustworthy and dependable.

Honesty—First be honest with yourself. Be honest with your superiors and with the people you supervise. Some people try to tell others what they want to hear in the belief that there will be fewer problems. This practice usually leads to bigger problems later. For example, telling someone that you can do a task that you know cannot be accomplished in the time frame available causes bigger problems in the end. Establish a reputation for honesty and sincerity.

Family Factors

Spouse, children, parents, parents-in-law, sisters, brothers, uncles and aunts, cousins, and everyone else you call relatives, can bring pressure to bear on your career plan.

Those closest to you have the most to gain—and to lose—as you make career/life decisions. However, do not be surprised when you get advice—solicited or unsolicited—from everyone.

If you have a nine-to-five job that you enjoy and you can walk away from it each day at five o'clock without bringing some of it home, you may be accused of being lazy and having no ambition. If, on the other hand, you put in extra hours regularly and still bring home a briefcase full of work, or have meetings scheduled for weekends, you are open to accusations that you are unfeeling and neglectful of your family.

How do you balance the teeter-totter of career and family? The balancing point is different for each family. You have to work at discovering your own. Why the word "life" was added to career planning becomes less of a mystery.

All the skills you apply to your working/life situations are needed at home. Communication is number one.

Goals, commitments, and agreements at home must be communicated and updated constantly. The partnership of wife and husband may turn into the corporation of wife, husband, and children. As the offspring grow older, they too begin life plans and have needs that are affected by your career plan. Each has something to gain and something to lose whenever a career decision is made.

As if one career is not enough to cope with, consider that two careers exist in every family situation. The family unit itself is a career. A family needs capital. It has income, expenses, taxes, and all the rest of the elements that need managing.

When both wife and husband have careers in business and industry, plus the career of home and family, balancing the teeter-totter requires more skill.

Don't stop yet! As children grow older and continue to live at home, their careers also influence the overall situation.

Mutual understanding and respect, plus frequent communication are necessary to make these combinations successful. The skill of listening carefully is especially valuable.

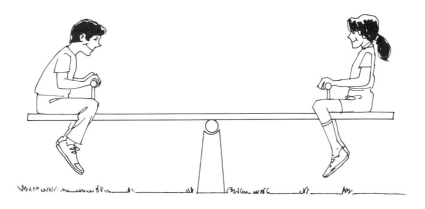

The attitude, priorities, and values of each individual must be communicated to and understood by the others. Agreement is not always necessary, but acceptance and compromise must be established. In this way, fewer surprises and confrontations are experienced.

If, for example, one spouse's goal is a mid-management position while the other intends to climb the promotion ladder to the top, whose career is sacrificed if relocation becomes necessary for either? In this situation, one spouse should not be disappointed in or critical of the one who does not want to go beyond mid-management. Perhaps the priorities and values of this person lie in pursuits other than the job. The other spouses's intention to spend whatever time and effort is necessary to reach the top should also be respected.

In the family setting the needs are the same. One may agree to do the dishes while the other does the cooking chores. Neither cares for cleaning the house or grocery shopping, so these jobs are split on a mutual dislike basis. Neither cares to do the weekly washing, so they decide to take turns or agree to use the local laundry. In any case, it takes communication and mutual decision-making.

Changing locations for career advancement can be a cataclysmic decision. Relocating to further the business career of one spouse could mean beginning all over again for the other. This situation brings into focus the term, *trade-off*.

"Trade-offs" are experienced every day. When you choose one thing you give up something else. When you choose a career to follow, you trade in all other possibilities for the one you select. However, to advance one person's career at the sacrifice of another's is a difficult choice. Much deliberation goes into such a choice so that it does not later become a matter for frustration and confrontation.

The advantage of multiple careers is money. The trade-off, obviously, is in less time spent together. Sacrifices must be explored and choices made. The decision becomes: Is the trade-off worth it? Both partners must agree to and accept the trade-off.

Final Thoughts

- Career/life planning is not a life and death matter. Thousands of people have never made such a plan and have survived.
- To plan properly you must establish goals.
- If you do not organize and put forth the effort to make a career/life plan, you are giving yourself an unnecessary handicap.
- A career plan is an organized process for making your career/life decisions.

- Your career plan answers two questions: What do I want? and How will I get it?
- A good career plan is a Marketing Tool.
- You must know your product—you. You must know your buyer—your potential employer. To accomplish this, gather all the information you can about both.
- The skills you have that you enjoy using are a key to what career you should follow.
- Use selling techniques (features and benefits) to evaluate yourself and your career options.
- Self-assessment includes six broad categories: skills, interests, knowledge, past experiences, traits and motives.
- As many reasons exist for *choosing* a career as there are careers, and maybe twice as many reasons for changing careers.
- Every career has advantages and disadvantages. Find the career that has the most advantages for you.
- Use these checklists to consider a career change.

Why Change?

1. If you are tired of the same old routine
2. If you are bored with your work
3. If your personal wants and needs have changed
4. If your family circumstances have changed
5. If your career is not going anywhere without a change
6. If retirement policy forces you out
7. If your health does not permit you to continue in your present employment situation
8. If working conditions have changed
9. If you are asked to compromise your beliefs and principles
10. If your job is being eliminated
11. If new technology offers you new possibilities and options
12. If you are fired

If You're Happy . . .

You may feel content in your chosen career and have no desire to change. Perhaps you are satisfied with what you are doing, your job pays you what you need to meet your commitments and gives you pleasure beyond that. Maybe you are so comfortable and content with your job that you never think of climbing the ladder or seeking a promotion. Don't think you must seek a better position if you do not want one.

Never let others pressure you to make a decision to please them, and in the end make yourself miserable and discontented. There is no shame in deciding that you are doing what you want with your life and that you do not wish to change.

Consider for example, a man named LeRoy. We call him LeRoy, because he brings to mind LeRoy Brown who was the "baddest man in the whole darn town." Only this LeRoy was just the opposite—the "goodest man in the whole darn town." At least he was the "goodest" *produce man* in the whole darn town. LeRoy started out as a carry-out boy in a large grocery chain when he was in high school. He advanced to checker and from there became produce manager because he wanted to work with the produce to make it more eye-appealing. He proved to be a veritable magician, making the fruits and vegetables look their freshest and most attractive best. LeRoy was very content with his job, and took great pride in his produce section. After a few years as a productive employee, he was approached by the company to become assistant manager in another store in another town. LeRoy took no time at all to refuse the promotion. He explained that he had never been happier in his life; he felt a real sense of accomplishment each day; he was able to leave his job at night and never worry about it at home. He was satisfied with the salary he was making; his family was content; he had good benefits and no desire to work up to the position of manager, which was the ultimate goal of his cohorts. Within the next four years, he was approached three more times, and each time he refused, giving the same reasons.

They finally let LeRoy alone to perform his miracles in his produce section, where he retired with full benefits, and a sense of well-being for all the years he had spent as a contented and happy employee. This example might seem off-the-wall, but it points out that *you* and only *you* can make the ultimate decision to seek career advancement or not. Everyone has different ambitions and desires, so do what you know is right for you! Whatever your career/life decisions are, you must ask yourself the following questions.

Planning for New Career Selection

1. Why do I want to leave my present employment?
2. What do I want in a new career?
3. What are my priorities?
4. What are my values?

5. What do I like best about my current career?
6. What do I like least about my current career?
7. What trade-offs do I make if I change?
8. What careers appeal to me? Why?
9. What careers hold the least interest for me? Why?
10. What are my personal strengths?
11. What are my personal weaknesses?
12. What are my professional and technical strengths?
13. What are my professional and technical weaknesses?
14. What education and skills do I lack and need to acquire?
15. What are my salary requirements now?
16. What salary increases are attainable to meet my future goals?
17. How will my career and my personal life fit together?
18. Where does my family stand and how are they affected?

- You will get what you want only when you know what you want and who you are!

Summary Questions

1. Explain the concept of risk.

2. What career risks have you taken in the past?

3. Explain why communications at home are so important to a career plan.

4. The questions you were asked as you read this chapter were placed so that you would work through them as they appeared. If you didn't answer them, do so now.

5. The exercise at the end of chapter 17 is applicable for those readers considering a career change. If you haven't completed the exercise already, do so now.

CHAPTER 20

Behavior

Behave Yourself!

No person is an island unto himself, but there are days when you wish you could be. However, since you must interact with other people, you should know something about why you act as you do, why other people act as they do, and why and how you react to each other.

The *concept* of behavior is actually simple; people are complex. Because behaviors manifest themselves in people, the understanding of behavior is complex also.

The intention of this study is to give you the basics so that you begin to understand and apply the modifications of behavior. You want to be able to apply these principles to yourself, and to understand them in others.

What Is Behavior?

The word *behave* is no stranger to anyone. All of us have heard it. The youngster following Mom and Dad shopping hears, "Behave yourself!" These words, spoken sharply, mean, "Put whatever you are holding back on the shelf, shut your mouth, and stay close!—Behave yourself!"

How did you behave yourself? You returned what you were holding to the shelf, quit asking Mom or Dad to buy it for you, and stayed close to them. That was behaving. Suppose you hadn't replaced the item, kept quiet, and stayed close. Disobedience, too, is behavior. You behaved either well or badly, in your parents' point of view. When you did not comply with your parents' wishes, you were probably asked, "Why won't you behave yourself?" Actually, you *did* behave, but not in a manner acceptable to your parents at that time. You could have replied, "I did behave, Mom, just not the way you wished," and been categorized a smart-mouthed kid and told not to talk back.

Behavior is not being good or bad, but the specific act you did or did not do to be rated good or bad. *Behavior is an action.*

You might be described as fast if you reach the finish line in a race before anyone else, draw your gun more quickly than an opponent, or finish your homework before anyone else in the class. Fast is a label used to describe some kind of performance.

If you are described as cool, you might be the first to turn on the air conditioner, or maybe you do not sweat much. "Cool" could mean that you do not holler, "Help, I'm dying," if you hit your thumb with a hammer, or that you do not panic in a crisis, but think things out before you act, and proceed in an organized manner. It could also mean that the way you dress gains approval from your peers. In each case, an observable action is the basis for the label. How you act or react is your behavior.

Behavioral Terminology

Certain terms are used in this chapter to describe certain behaviors. The following list is a short glossary to help you understand these terms.

Behavior Modification Terminology:

Behavior:	A specific action that is observable and measurable.
Consequence:	The result that follows a behavior.
Contingency:	The relationship between behavior and consequences. The consequence is contingent (depends) on the behavior.
Reinforcing behavior:	Assuring by means of consequences that a particular behavior will continue.
Positive Reinforcement:	Receiving something desirable as a result of a certain behavior.
Negative Reinforcement:	Avoiding something undesirable by behaving in a certain way.
Punishment:	Receiving something undesirable as the result of a behavior.
Extinction:	Cessation of a behavior that has been ignored.

Behavior Modification Terminology: (continued)

Punishing the Punisher:	Retaliating against the punisher through direct or indirect acts, or acts directed at other people.

Describing Behavior

A behavior is a particular act that someone does. To describe behavior you must refer to *specific* actions. When discussing students, you say that John or Mary is a good student. This statement is too general to describe behavior accurately. To describe behavior specifically you might use these statements:

- John receives high grades.
- Mary does not talk in class.
- John does not use crib notes.
- Mary does not throw erasers.
- John always has his homework done.
- Mary contributes to class discussions.

These statements describe specific behaviors or actions that result in the description, "good student."

General comments that label people might include:

- Larry is sloppy.
- Ann is not organized.
- Joe is conscientious.
- Andy is very friendly.
- Rose is stuck up.

Such remarks do not describe the behavior that leads to the labels. A more specific description of the behavior is needed.

Let us take Larrry as our example. It was said, "Larry is sloppy." To describe behavior, the statement must be more specific. Which of Larry's actions connote sloppiness?

- Larry never combs his hair.
- His shoes are not polished.
- He does not trim his beard.

- Larry always wears wrinkled clothes.
- Larry's shirt is torn or missing a button.
- He crosses out mistakes when writing, rather than erasing them.
- His fingernails are dirty and ragged.

You can probably think of a dozen more behaviors that describe sloppiness.

How Behavior Is Learned

1. Behavior is learned through interaction with other people.
2. We learn behaviors to get along with others.
3. The effect your behavior has on others teaches you what is acceptable behavior.

You interact with others all your life. You tend to repeat those behaviors that are acceptable, or those that result in pleasant consequences. As children you learned that a polite please, accompanying a request, was more likely to get you a cookie or a glass of milk, than a demand for the favor. You have carried that lesson about behavior into adulthood. A polite request for a meeting with the boss is received more favorably than a demand. The polite request recognizes the worth of the other person and calls for an action. The demand forces a reaction.

Learned behavior, therefore, is the result of interaction between two or more individuals. As a student, you may have needed help to understand a certain concept in one of your classes. If you asked politely for help from the instructor or a classmate, you probably received the explanation. The next time you need help in that class, you go to that same person and again ask politely for help. If you have demanded help in a tone of voice that states "It is my right to get help and you had better give it to me," your experience probably would not have been rewarding in terms of help or personal interaction. People resent being told they must do something, but are flattered to be asked for assistance.

Most behavior is learned in a give-and-take fashion. We learn what is acceptable and what is not acceptable by interacting with each other. If you constantly interrupt someone while they are trying to talk, they will eventually state flatly, "Stop interrupting me! You can talk when I am finished." You have learned that it is unacceptable to interrupt while another person is talking. In a theater or movie, if you talk to the person next to you, people will turn and stare and let you know that your behavior is unacceptable. You learn to be quiet in the theater.

When you describe a person's behavior, remember to be specific in giving examples of things the person says and does. The following paragraphs discuss three unpleasant types of persons using behavioral descriptions.

1. *The Egotist*—The person uses the word "I" excessively. Egotistical people want to talk about themselves, what they own, or what they have accomplished. They discuss only what they are doing or have done. You begin to think they are suffering from "I" strain, because *you* certainly are! These people seem to think they can push themselves forward by patting themselves on the back. Other outward signs that identify the egotist include: a wallet-load of pictures of themselves with the golf trophy, the new car, and an assortment of other accomplishments that can be photographed. They use any means to draw attention to themselves such as dominating the conversation. When they no longer control the attention of a group they move on to another group where they again can be the main attraction.

2. *The Grouch*—Someone who looks for the negative side of everything. This person lets you know when you have made a mistake and keeps reminding you of it. These people gripe and complain, find fault, and dwell on wrongs. The grouch rarely displays a smile. The grouch has usually thought out how to attack you and then after unloading on you, leaves before you have a chance to explain or defend yourself. Such people would find faults with paradise. These people will stop to think twice, to be sure to find something nasty to say.

3. *Fair-Weather Friends*—These people are always absent when you need help, but appear suddenly when they need help. When something you do together goes wrong, they disappear to let you take the blame alone. They use other people. These people are willing to tell others how much they have done for you but somehow forget that the majority of the help has come from you. You might say these people would roll out the carpet for you one day, and pull it out from under you the next. They are undependable, except for one thing—you can depend on *them* to depend on *you!*

Consequences of Behavior

1. A consequence is the result of a behavior.
2. Every behavior leads to a consequence.
3. The consequence could be that nothing happens.

The story of The Boy Who Cried Wolf is an example of behavior leading to a consequence. The first three times the consequence was that people ran to help him. The fourth time the little boy cried wolf, no one answered. The consequence was that the villagers did nothing.

This story, carried to its end shows that one behavior can lead to several consequences. The villagers reacted one way to the false alarms sent out by the boy. The consequences to the boy were that

1. the villagers refused to respond the fourth time he called for help
2. the wolf actually was there the fourth time and ate the sheep.

This story illustrates that:

1. One behavior may have several consequences.
2. More than one behavior may lead to the same consequence.
3. The consequence of a behavior can be another behavior.

In most situations a person chooses how to behave. A person waiting for a bus can smile, relax, and enjoy a moment of rest in a hectic day, or pace impatiently and be grouchy and upset about the delay. If the clerk in a store is busy, the waiting customer can become impatient and ill-tempered and snap at the clerk, or be pleasant about the necessary delay. Which customer will get the better service next time? Your actions (behavior) affect the other person, the outcome of the transaction, and possibly your future dealings in that store.

Reinforcing Behavior

Listed below are five principles of behavioral reinforcement:

1. Consequences reinforce behavior.
2. Desirable consequences reinforce behavior and tend to cause the behavior to be repeated.
3. Avoidance of undesirable consequences reinforces behavior and tends to cause the behavior to be repeated.
4. Behavior that is positively reinforced is repeated because something desirable is the consequence. A positive reinforcement is anything said or done that causes another person to repeat or continue a behavior. Examples of consequences used as reinforcers could be a special privilege, verbal praise, or a monetary gift.
5. Behavior that is negatively reinforced is repeated because avoidance of something undesirable is the consequence. A negative reinforcer is anything said

or done that causes another person to repeat or continue a behavior. In the case of the negative reinforcer the thing to be avoided may be losing a special privilege, being chewed out, being refused a raise, or anything the person dislikes.

To understand how these principles apply, think about these reasons why you answer a ringing telephone:

1. To talk to a friend. (*positive*)
2. To avoid listening to it ring. (*negative*)
3. To hear the voice of the one you love. (*positive*)
4. To avoid missing an important call. (*negative*)

A behavior that receives positive or negative reinforcement will tend to be repeated.

Punishment

Punishment is *receiving* something disliked or unwanted. This differs from negative reinforcement because negative reinforcement is *avoiding* something unwanted or disliked.

Punished behavior usually is not repeated. When a person does a job well, that person gets praise. Praise is something desirable and wanted, and that behavior is positively reinforced by praise. When an individual performs a task in a slipshod manner and receives a chewing out, the consequence is undesirable. The behavior is punished by the reprimand. Performing well to avoid a reprimand is negative reinforcement.

Punishment carries with it two side effects:

1. punishing the punisher
2. avoiding the punisher

Not many teenagers get through the teen years without blowing the family curfew or committing some similar infraction. The result is usually a punishment, possibly a campus—better known as "being grounded." The punishers are easily identified in this situation as Dad and Mom, but consider carefully who really gets punished. Answer these questions and decide for yourself.

1. Who didn't get to go out on the weekend?
2. Who else stayed home on the weekend to make sure the punishment was carried out?

3. Who stayed in and listened to the stereo, turned up just a bit louder than normal?
4. Who had to listen to the stereo, turned up a bit louder than normal?
5. Who slams the bedroom door all weekend?
6. Who gets irritated by the slamming of a door all weekend?

By now you should get the idea.

Most of the time, the person punishing the punisher is not even aware of doing it. Some examples of how an employee might punish the punisher (supervisor) are listed below:

1. Not filling the supervisor in on all the facts before he goes into a meeting with the boss.
2. Slowing your work pace.
3. Not catching all the errors in your paperwork as you used to.
4. Meeting deadlines at the last possible moment instead of being slightly ahead of schedule.
5. Starting a job a little late and stopping just before it is finished.
6. Getting to work a little late or leaving a little early.
7. Writing "nuisance" notes on memos.
8. Asking for more details than you really need.
9. Holding to the exact instructions given, instead of performing what you understood the instructions to mean.

Although the examples just scratch the surface, undoubtedly you can think of others. Think of examples that are not job-related but from home, school, or elsewhere.

The other alternative is avoiding the punisher. Why avoid the punisher? Simple! Who likes to be around a punisher? You might get punished some more. Standing around waiting for more punishment is silly—right?

Brief Recap

- Positive reinforcement—desirable consequences
- Punishment—undesirable consequences
- Negative reinforcement—Avoiding undesirable consequences

The most effective means of influencing the behavior of others is through positive reinforcement. Accentuate the positive, eliminate the negative. If this sounds familiar, it is. You encountered this philosophy in dealing with attitudes and a positive outlook. Look for the good things people do and be quick to acknowledge appreciation for jobs well done.

In too many instances a job well done is expected as the norm and is not recognized or reinforced at all; do something wrong, and a reprimand is drawn swiftly. If you are the recipient of this kind of behavior, take care not to operate this way yourself. If you are quick to punish, be equally quick to praise.

Extinction

A behavior is extinguished when its consequence is getting nothing you like, and avoiding nothing you dislike. A job well done that is ignored, is discontinued or extinguished because nothing is to be gained or lost by discontinuing the good performance. For this reason, you should accentuate the positive and compliment a job well done. Do not simply accept a good job as the norm and respond to a bad job with punishment.

Immediacy and Shaping

The concept of immediacy means that a behavior should be reinforced as soon as possible after it occurs. The sooner reinforcement is given, the more relevant it is to the act performed. The campus or grounding that was handed out to the teenager, should be imposed immediately or as soon as possible after the breaking of the rule. This does not mean a week later, after the incident has been forgotten.

Shaping is a method of changing behavior a little at a time. A bad behavior, like a bad habit, is difficult to change cold turkey! A gradual change is less difficult.

Shaping changes the frequency with which a behavior is repeated. Desirable behavior can be shaped to be repeated more often; undesirable behavior, less often.

Shaping is systematic, gradual, and regular change of behavior. The basics of behavior are simple. Because you work with people, the applications are complex. You now have a basic vocabulary for working with behavior, and an awareness of how and why you, and those around you, behave the way you do socially and on the job. A more in-depth study of behavior is interesting. This sample of the subject can help you decide whether or not to pursue additional information. What you learn about behavior can be used:

- To your advantage
- To manipulate others
- To avoid problems
- To be considerate
- To add to your skills
- To gain knowledge

Remember that it is easier to change your own behavior than someone else's!

Self-test—Review

1. When a behavior is positively reinforced will it be repeated?
2. When a behavior is negatively reinforced, will it be repeated?
3. What is meant by punishment?
4. Can a behavior lead to more than one consequence?
5. What are the side effects of punishment?

6. Does every behavior lead to a consequence?

7. When should behavior be reinforced?

8. Which example is the best description of behavior?
   a. June is a good worker.
   b. Jim shows he has had some experience.
   c. Betty works well with others.
   d. Jack shows interest by asking a lot of questions.

9. What effect does punishment have on behavior?

CHAPTER 21

Time Management

Black or white, Jew, Catholic, Protestant or atheist—no one is given one more day a year, or one more hour per day, or one more second per minute than anyone else.

Time Management, as a seminar topic or title of a book attracts large audiences. Films, articles, books, seminars, and the rest of the offerings draw people like the appearance of a movie star on Main Street.

The specific reasons for this interest are as numerous as the people involved. The common element among these people is a need to get in touch with themselves regarding the effective use of the elusive commodity called time.

People who start out to manage time discover that time cannot be managed at all. Rather people need to manage themselves. Time is merely a gauge to measure how well they are accomplishing their goals according to their priorities.

Time is an elusive resource. The here and now have come and gone before you can even say, "here and now."

Although everyone has a different life span, no individual can lay claim to one more second per minute than any other individual.

In order to get an idea of how you use time, contemplate this question: If you were granted one extra hour today, how would you use it? Some people can answer this immediately. Others must give the question considerable thought.

The important thing is that you make a definite decision about what you will do. Making the decision is more important than the decision's content.

Whether you decide to use that hour for study, for watching T.V., or for getting an extra hour of sleep does not matter. The hour should not come and go without your awareness of what you did to make it count in your priority plan.

Your choice of activity for making use of that extra hour, and your normal use of time depend on a number of things:

1. A reason or motive for taking advantage of the time you have
2. A desire to change your habits so that your accomplishments are not stifled by poor time-use priorities
3. Conscious decisions about how to use your time
4. An awareness of how you use your time
5. A knowledge of what factors influence your decisions about your use of time.
6. A desire to control yourself to get what you want from the time you have.

If you lack motivation for controlling your use of time, it may be that you have never considered how much potential you have. Time is the only thing that prevents you from accomplishing whatever you want.

Time Management and Your Potential

This chapter advocates strict self-management with regard to time. The next chapter encourages you to release your potential. At times it seems that these subjects are in conflict. To realize your dreams, you must reconcile these two concepts and discipline yourself to work on them.

Remember what you learned about the functions of the left and right brain. You must begin to use the whole-brain approach in order to have the courage to let yourself go. Couple this approach with your ability to work out a plan so you can get in touch with those dreams and bring them to realization.

Time management requires that you be disciplined as you approach the techniques of getting things done. Potential tells you to cast off restraints that hold you back from taking risks. The two can work together if you let them.

Payoffs

You may ask, "What is in this for me?" There are several possibilities. If they matter to you, you will immediately see what is in it for you. If they do not matter to you, then there is no problem and no reason for complaint or need to change. These payoffs of effective time management include increased productivity, satisfaction, improved personal relationships, reduced anxiety and tension, and as a result, better health.

Increased productivity—You can appreciate this payoff if you prioritize those things that hold value for you. You can always find time to do what you really want to do, whether it is doing nothing or becoming a millionaire. You may be accused of tunnel vision, but if you focus on what is vitally important to you, you will find it a simple matter to plan and allocate your time. Enormous increases in productivity can be realized as you do the things that count for you.

Satisfaction—Satisfaction comes from accomplishment. Knowing what you want to accomplish and getting those things done leads to satisfaction. The feeling of satisfaction gives you goose-pimples when you realize that you control your life. Control over yourself gives you power to attain self-established goals within your allotted time frames. You can enrich your personal life and your working life.

Improved personal relationships—The quantity of your time spent in personal relationships may decrease. Although quantity of time decreases, the quality of the time spent can increase. As you identify your priorities you control your time expenditures to satisfy yourself by attaining the goals that you value. If one of your priorities is family and friends, you will be able to spend more time with them and feel less guilt, knowing you are fulfilling one of your admitted priorities.

Reduced anxiety and tensions—If you classify yourself as a worry wart, feel guilt for what you have been doing, or fear that what you want to do is wrong, then you must take a close look at what you believe you want and need. You must decide if these feelings are self-imposed, or if you fear criticism from others. Constantly dealing with such feelings reduces your efficiency in making decisions. If you make decisions while you are working through these emotions, your decisions are less reliable and take longer to make. You may be your own worst enemy. Find out if you really know what is of value to you. Chances are, the guilt you feel is caused by doing what you think others expect, rather than making *your own goals your priority*. List your priorities according to what you want to accomplish. Establish a plan making time an important resource. Manage your plan. Accomplish what *you* want with your time.

Better health—Poor control of yourself and your priorities allows tension and worry to take over. The physical consequences that can appear include mental and physical fatigue. Eating habits can be affected as well. Awareness of time and your priorities for expending it, permits you to recognize your needs. You must recognize the necessity for the wise use of your time to keep yourself mentally and physically healthy.

Early Out

Whether or not you want to be effective with your life plan is entirely up to you, but desire is necessary to effectively manage yourself and your time. Without a deep-down desire to accomplish specific goals, it really does not matter how you use your time.

If you do not have definite goals and a burning desire to reach them, you should admit this to yourself. You do yourself more harm than good by worrying about not accomplishing things that do not matter that much to you. Spending your time fretting and feeling guilty will sooner or later present you with health problems.

Accept yourself. Learn to live with your current practices, if they satisfy you, and stop worrying about them. You have the decision to make. The concepts presented in any study of time management are merely suggestions for those who want to use them. The choice to put the information into practice or not is yours. If you choose not to use these ideas, then for heaven's sake, don't feel guilty.

Efficiency and Effectiveness

To be effective you must be efficient. However, you can be efficient without being effective. If you have ever asked yourself, "Why am I so busy, but get nothing done?" then you need to differentiate between efficiency and effectiveness.

Efficiency pertains to how well you perform a task. For example, you can streamline certain jobs by cutting performance time, using fewer materials, or performing the task with fewer people. Any one of these could boost efficiency. Effectiveness, on the other hand, pertains to how well goals and objectives are pursued and reached.

When you put the two together, you have a winning combination. Efficiency in tasks that lead to your goals, makes your performance effective. Performing well on tasks that are of little value to you gives you only a feeling of spinning your wheels. You exert effort and go nowhere so you become weary and frustrated, expending energy without accomplishing anything you value.

To be effective, you must identify those things that hold value for you. Then separate the vital tasks from the many tasks that are presented each day. Prioritize your areas of concentration; know what comes first to accomplish your goals.

Time Flies

Time flies when you are having fun. When you are doing something you enjoy or when you are with someone you love, time passes all too quickly. Savor this element. Even though this time does not produce income or further your career, the time is still valuable. The value could be in memories that make you happy. (*Happy* is good for your *health.*) Getting away from the practical in order to relax and renew is necessary. The *intention* to spend time on enjoyment is also important.

Look at time flying from another angle. How unfortunate it is if you ask yourself at the end of a day, "Where in the world did the day go?" and you have no answer. You can reconstruct the events of your day, step by step, but you find that you received no value for the activities experienced. When this happens, it is time to make a plan so as not to lose valuable time.

Team of Who?

As if you can't find enough ways to waste time on your own, many other people are eager to help you waste your time. Many of the demands on your time are exerted by others. (As you read this chapter, you may want to review your knowledge of assertiveness so you can tell others to bug off, in a *nice*, but *definite* way. Why should you do what everyone else wants, when you have priorities of your own?) As you become acquainted with time management, you realize that others value their time, but that these same people regard your time as theirs also, since you always seem to be available for a favor. If you have ever felt used, you know why—because you are! They may ask you to do things because you never seem to have anything important of your own.

You will be fortunate if you find yourself a teammate for your personal *team of two*—someone who regards you as a valuable person and who will help you realize your value as an individual and as a member of this team-of-two. You help each other to keep the team motivated and reinforce one another by practicing such principles as rewarding those who respect your time and not rewarding those who fail to show respect. Another important rule is to respect the time and priorities of others.

Where Does Time Go?

That question requires you to do some work. Keep a log of your activities for one week (two weeks would be better). This log will give you a good idea of where you are with your time expenditures in relation to your accomplishments. However, since you, your priorities, and the world around you change constantly, you must review how you use your time and how you want to use it. Keep such a log for five to ten days every six months, if you want to be sure you have not relapsed into careless habits. A simple chart like the one below will do the job.

DAILY ACTIVITY SHEET

Planned Time	Unplanned Time	Activity
8:00–12:00		Work
12:00–1:00		Lunch
1:00–5:00		Work
5:00–6:00		Dinner
	6:00–7:30	Neighbors came by. Talked about nothing in particular.
	7:30–7:45	Phone call
6:00–7:00		Planned to update my career plan (didn't get to it)
7:00–7:30		Wanted to talk to spouse about buying a new car (didn't get to it)

(Weekends are even more revealing.)

Always work backward from the long range plan to the short range plan. You end up with annual time plans, monthly plans, weekly plans, and daily plans. The accomplishment of daily time plans gives you the feeling that you are getting somewhere and this feeling keeps you going. This method can be compared to the difference between drinking a glass of water in one gulp or in several swallows. You accomplish the goal of draining the glass either way, but taking smaller swallows reduces the chance of choking and gives you more satisfaction.

To answer the questions, "What do I have to do today?" and "What will get me closer to my goal?" make lists, assign time frames to important tasks, and prioritize your daily activities.

Although the chart is broad based and oversimplified it gives you a tool to create a form of your own. It reflects how you spend those hours of the day that you have the most personal control over. The large chunks of the day devoted to work were only identified. You may wish to be much more critical and exacting with these time periods. The objective of keeping tabs on yourself is to find out how well you manage the part of your life you can control.

If you are in business for yourself, or are in a management position where you are responsible for setting most of your daily work schedule, your work hours are more critical in your daily plan. If this is the case, you must closely scrutinize those time periods in light of your business goals. Every principle contained in this chapter applies to managing your time—either personal or business time. (The chapter is not really about time at all, but about managing yourself to make the best use of your time.) As concepts and examples are used, some pertain to business and some to personal time. You should be able to use them interchangeably.

A management job has been described as a series of interruptions interrupted by interruptions. Unfortunately this description *is* accurate, and it can be applied to life also. Therefore, you must keep a log of daily activities to get in touch with where your time is spent. To work smarter rather than harder, you must use time the best way possible.

When you find out who controls your time, your first reaction may be anger. Be careful not to blame someone else, because ultimately the responsibility is yours. If you foolishly permit others to control your time, they do so because you let them.

The neighbors may control your time at home or the boss, the system, subordinates, or outsiders may control your time at work. If you make an activity sheet for your at-work time, include a category for each of those time users to find out who controls your time.

Plans

When you read about goal setting, you were introduced to the concept of planning. As important as planning was at that point, it cannot be overemphasized. Picture your life plan and your plans for time use as if you were a building a house of bricks. Each brick in the bottom five rows would have *The Plan* on it.

You may have wonderful and lofty goals, but unless you have a plan for accomplishing them and do something to attain them, nothing happens.

Planning is vital because it lays out the tasks to be performed to attain goals. Long-range plans are similar to goal setting itself. No time span is better than another. You can have a five-year plan, a three-year plan, or a one-year plan, depending on your goals, how you see the difficulty in reaching these goals, and how long you expect it to take to reach them. If you have a five-year plan you will need annual plans to keep you on track.

You may set up several forms before you find the method that works best for you. The first step is to find a good method for handling your time, the second is to *use it*. You may find it valuable to visit your local stationery shop, and examine the variety of daily planner schedules. They are designed to appeal to the masses, but one may fit your situation. If you do not find an exact fit, keep looking until you do. By looking at these planners, you get some good, basic ideas for creating your own.

Planning Tricks

Everyone has a prime time. Some people are morning people; some are more alert and productive in the afternoon; others get going only after the sun goes down. Take advantage of your most productive time to tackle the toughest jobs. When you are confronted with a choice of several tasks of equal importance, do the one you dislike the most first. After finishing the job you do not like, reward yourself with the jobs you do like.

Just as you broke your long-range plans into smaller, more manageable units, until you had a daily plan, break large, time-consuming tasks into more easily scheduled sub-tasks. This practice makes scheduling easier, and helps you fight procrastination. Motivating yourself to begin a long complex task may be almost as difficult as performing the task itself.

Put first things first. Prioritize the tasks you have to accomplish in their order of importance so that when interruptions come, you feel you have accomplished something.

Be your own best friend and most critical disciplinarian. Follow the priorities you set and do not let yourself deviate without a top-priority reason.

Pitfalls

As you walk through the jungle of life you need to be alert. Many traps await you. The most dangerous are the ones you set for yourself. The procrastination trap can destroy everything you are working for. Indecision accompanies procrastination. Together they are a formidable force and will stop you if you permit them to.

One of the allies of procrastination is fear. Fear of mistakes or failure can exert powerful emotional road blocks. The only way to fight back is to face fear head-on. Everyone makes mistakes. Not doing anything should throw fear in you more than doing something wrong. At least you can learn from a mistake. Failure, just like success, is only a feedback mechanism. Both help you know what to do next. It is what you do with experience that counts.

When you find yourself procrastinating because you fear making a mistake, ask yourself these questions:

1. Will my decision be any better by putting it off?
2. Will I be better off if I do nothing?
3. What is at risk or what will a mistake cost?

Most of the time, the worst that can happen is that you end up back where you started. In the selling field, salespeople are taught to make calls because they have nothing to lose and everything to gain. The principle is this: Before you make a sales call, you have no sale. If you make the call and get a No, you are back only to where you started. You have eliminated one "no" prospect. Now you can get on with business. The law of averages will help you sooner or later. However, if you learn from the mistakes (in this case the no's), you will improve because of your experiences and beat the law of averages.

Another way to fight your fears is to exaggerate them. Exaggerate them to the point of being ridiculous. Blow them out of all proportion until you know that the most terrible thing that could happen could not possibly happen. Anything less becomes something you can handle.

Things are never so bad that they could not get worse. That makes it appropriate to compound the problem just a bit. Suppose you are faced with fear of mistakes and failure and the task before you is an unpleasant one. This situation reinforces your inclination to procrastinate. The best and perhaps the only good way to cope with the situation is to make the project a high priority. Get at it—the sooner the better! Get it out of the way and move on to something else.

In the beginning, you may have to force yourself to do this kind of priority planning. It gets easier with practice, and with a success or two behind you, you begin to realize your self-worth.

When you feel comfortable with priority planning and find that it works, you see why you must adhere to a plan. You accomplish things you had only wished to do before. Be careful to allow enough time to accomplish a task. If you do not allow enough time in the beginning, you form a habit of giving yourself extensions. This habit is tough to break and gives you a defeated feeling. Instead, try to beat your time frames and you will feel better.

Another discipline you need is the ability to say no. To say no is difficult; no one likes to be thought of as a hard-nose. Everyone wants and needs to be liked. You do not want your family, close friends, bosses, or anyone else to think you are uncooperative. Some people know this fact and use it to manipulate others right out of their priorities.

When you say yes to everyone and everything, you feel used. Do not blame others, however; if you permit it, it is your own fault. You had probably wanted to be needed, not just available. Not being able to say no makes you a dumping ground for every job no one else wants.

In the chapter on assertiveness, you learned the basics of how and why you need to be in charge of yourself. Time management reinforces those concepts and provides you with additional reasons to assert yourself to be in charge of your career and your life.

When to Say No

When should you say yes and when should you say no? Ultimately, you have to decide this question for yourself. Identify your priorities and know what is important to you. Have definite ideas about what you will permit to interrupt your plans and what you will not. You may find these guidelines helpful:

Approval and acceptance—It is a wonderful feeling to know that others approve of you and that you are accepted by your work team or social group, but beware of the dangers. If you are gaining approval and acceptance at the expense of other goals that are more important to you, it isn't worth it. You may need to answer the difficult question, "Are you afraid that if you say no even once you might lose acceptance?" If you find that this is the case, take a long, hard look at your value to others and to yourself.

Avoiding hurt feelings—Whose feelings are you afraid of hurting? Are you afraid that if you say no, other people will think you do not like them? Do you have so little faith in their ability to understand that you have other obligations? The obligations may be to yourself, but who should have first claim on your time? Are you afraid that if you say no, and the other person simply accepts your refusal without begging for your help you will feel less important? Do not be disappointed. You are respected for your honesty. You are getting respect—accept it!

Capability—Perhaps you want to be considered a capable person. You want to say yes to prove you can do the job. If others think you are capable, their opinion will not change because you had to say no. If, on the other hand, you are thought of as always available, it is better to change that opinion. You are of more value to others when you value yourself.

Who do you say no to? Often your answer is based on who you like and who you do not like. This reasoning is human, but not always the best criteria. The people you should say no to often fall into one of the following categories.

Value violaters—These people presume that you will automatically relegate your values to a lesser place in favor of theirs. Feel no guilt in saying no when you are shown no respect.

Priority preemptors—You are expected to set your priorities aside and get involved as these people accomplish their goals. If you find yourself caught in situations like this, think about what your priorities really are. Are your priorities less important than theirs? To them, yes, but certainly they should not be less important to you.

Double dipper—Do you allow others to delegate part of their work to you so they can accomplish twice as much? They may enlist your assistance so that they can finish on time, leaving you to work after hours to finish your tasks. These people look twice as good as you—and you helped! Delegation is a legitimate technique when properly used in business and in personal matters. Proper use is when both the delegator, and the people who have work and responsibility delegated to them, benefit equally. When work is delegated to you and there is nothing in it for you except making someone else look better, you should consider saying no.

The thoughtless—Some people do things without thinking. By saying yes to these people you encourage their bad habit. The sooner they are forced to be thoughtful and considerate, the sooner they will be of more value to themselves. You do them a grave disservice by rescuing them. Not thinking may be an acceptable excuse for young children, but responsible adults must think things through before imposing.

Not Easy

Even with all the reasons why you should say no, do you still find it difficult? If you can employ the following technique you may not have to use the two-letter word.

If you are exceptionally good at prioritizing you may never have to say no. If you and the person who asks for your time put the request in its proper priority slot, you will never need to say no.

For example, assume you have four priorities on your agenda for this week:

1. Prepare a sales report for the annual meeting the following Monday.
2. Examine the budget for first-round submission.
3. Talk with two employees who have been absent without request.
4. Attend a one-day seminar.

You have your priorities identified and a timetable in place to accomplish your tasks. You have organized your week by careful planning. At this point, another employee requests that you help take inventory. This is not your job, and that employee can do the job without help, but the task would go faster with your assistance. You could say, "No, there is no chance I'll have any free time," or you could say, "I am tied up for this week but I could help you next Tuesday." The other person must then decide to wait for your help or go ahead alone and get the job done. The fact that the inventory is due *before* next Tuesday (as you know) may help the employee decide.

A personal example might be:

You planned your weekend to include:

1. Mowing the lawn
2. Washing and waxing the car
3. Grocery shopping
4. An evening out with friends
5. Finishing the book you started two weeks ago
6. Writing some letters you have owed for some time.

You get a call from your neighbors asking you to help them clean their basement so they can remodel it into a recreation room. You do not mind helping, but, you already have a plan for the weekend. You could say no or you could say, "I'm already scheduled for several jobs, but I could help you for two hours." (If you say this, be sure you have two hours available that you do not mind giving up.) You might also tell the neighbors that if they wait a week, you will gladly plan to give them a full day's help. Did you catch that big four-letter word, *plan?*

Although these are refusals, they carry counter proposals. You are saying, "You are important to me, but I am important to me also." Put outside requests in your priority line-up.

Your priority list for other people and their jobs need not be on a first-come, first-served basis. You may prefer to help some people more than others. It is *your* priority list. You should not feel guilty for setting it up to your preference. You are the boss when it comes to who you want to be with and what you want to do with your personal time.

Never put off saying no. If you know from the time you are asked that you do not want to do something, don't procrastinate by looking for an easy way to say so. The sooner you say no, the sooner other people can begin to look for help elsewhere. If you wait too long, they may not be able to get help. Respect other people's priorities and plans too. You benefit by not carrying the burden of worrying how to get out of the situation. The longer you wait, the longer your mind is preoccupied with that thought, and you prevent yourself from thinking about important things. No law says you must justify your refusal. Sometimes an explanation sounds more like an excuse anyway.

Focus on Yourself

Pause, reflect, and focus on your behavior regarding your use of time. Five questions are presented here to help you. Give more than one-word answers; take time to reflect. Talk your answers over with yourself. Find out where you are, where you want to be, and what you intend to do about your situation.

1. Do I consistently allow others to waste my time?
2. Do I consistently cause others to waste their time?
3. Do I habitually waste time in the same ways?
4. Do I spend too much time on unplanned and unimportant activities?
5. Do I fail to focus on important activities and prioritize?

Help!

Your own resolve is your greatest asset in deciding to be a better time manager. Effective time management does not just happen; you must reflect, plan, and work hard. Although much of your success depends on you, help is available.

Consider the possibility of forming a team of two—maybe several such teams. These teams will be your most reliable help.

Your first team is the one you can depend on, no matter what. You and your other team member share all aspects of life, from personal ambitions and problems to work-related aspirations, situations and problems.

A good team does not just happen. You must work to establish common ground, mutual understanding, caring, and sharing with another person. These six criteria are basic to establishing this kind of relationship:

1. Effective communication
2. Shared objective setting, shared planning, and shared problem-solving
3. Trust and confidence in each other
4. Thorough understanding of your mutual objectives
5. Steadfast commitment to your ideas and desires to improve
6. Honest performance appraisals

(Wouldn't make bad wedding vows, would they?)

You need a team member who gives you support, not criticism, when your resolve slips. Everyone can use dependable help from a concerned and caring partner. (Does this give you another way to sharpen those listening skills?)

Business Teams

While you need one team member for all occasions, you need specific team members for short-team projects.

A number of teams can be created where you work. You will explore many of these if you treat yourself to a full-blown time management course. This book will acquaint you with what they are, and isolate several examples. These teams might include you and your boss, peers, secretary, customers, subordinates, superiors, or vendors. Perhaps you can think of others.

Boss/Secretary Teams

The boss-secretary relationship as a working team serves as the first example. Like every relationship this one begins with communication. The boss-secretary team requires a blend of mutual benefits and mutual support. Mutual respect—not just the respect given by virtue of position—is a necessary ingredient.

Most secretaries contribute more to the success of a business than anyone admits. No one knows more about the day-to-day operation of the office than the secretary. The smooth operation of the office is the secretary's responsibility and the secretary needs the authority and backing to do the job. Some bosses have a five- to ten-minute meeting with the secretary each morning. In this way the secretary does not guess at what should be done first. The boss does not expect one item of work to be accomplished, while the secretary thinks something else is more important. Priorities change from day to day, sometimes from hour to hour. Immediate communication is mandatory for the team to work together. The boss is in a position to support the secretary if another office wants to borrow some secretarial help for a short-term project. If the help would prevent meeting deadlines, the answer must be no.

The management of the office is a partnership. Each partner knows who is responsible for which task and the total job is a cooperative effort. Routine jobs can be called routine only because a good secretary organizes them to make them look that way.

The secretary role is vital. Therefore, confidence in the secretary's abilities and decisions must be recognized and expressed. A secretary's suggestions should be sought and listened to with attention. With this kind of team, the secretary knows more about the office operation than the boss, and why not? The boss is then free to concentrate on the administrative tasks that are a manager's major concern.

With this kind of teamwork, nothing goes unnoticed and there are few, if any surprises. The flow of information is constant and thorough. Each person concentrates on the important aspects of the assigned tasks. Each complements the other.

Each member of the secretary-boss team performs a valuable time saving service for the other, called screening. Each runs interference for the other, to cut the amount of wasted time. The boss saves time when the secretary sorts mail so that important items are handled first and junk mail is trash-canned before reaching the boss's desk. Routine matters, always handled by the secretary, are not brought to the boss. Telephone calls and drop-in visitors are handled in the same way. This screening is effective only if communication takes place, so that the secretary knows exactly what the boss identifies as priorities.

This process is not one-way. When the secretary has a long report to type or a time-consuming, priority job, the boss can screen for the secretary to keep interruptions to a minimum. The boss should be prepared to handle requests from other departments for the secretary's help when the secretary is involved in a project.

No law says that the boss cannot answer the secretary's phone or handle a request, if the boss is working on a job of lesser priority than the secretary's current project.

Peer Teams

The second concerns a peer relationship. Consider a relationship between two secretaries. They share an outer office and each is responsible to a different executive; however, both share common duties like helping walk-in customers at the counter. Assume that neither executive has more authority in the company than the other. The teamwork relationship is the focal point. Each secretary has specific individual duties, plus shared duties. The need for cooperation should be obvious to you.

If both secretaries have important rush jobs, they should agree to alternate serving walk-in customers. If one has a lighter load, that secretary should volunteer to take all walk-in customers to help the one on a tight schedule to finish sooner. The secretary who benefits now from this arrangement, should reciprocate when the situation is reversed. A team can handle many such situations, so that everything progresses smoothly and everyone saves time. However, if communication does not flow freely and the team does not work together, the cost can be counted in terms of lost time, lost efficiency, lost business image, lost jobs, and lost business.

Consider the same situation where one secretary has an important rush job while the other has a light load. Assume that the one with the less pressing task ignores the walk-in customer, until the other secretary stops and serves the prospect. This behavior is repeated several times during the course of the morning. Before long the team-of-two become one-on-one adversaries. Recall from the chapter, "Transactional Analysis," the games people play. This situation is the perfect setting for such games to begin. The "I'll get you, you . . ." game would probably be one for the secretary who received no help.

One-way cooperation lasts only for a short period until one secretary complains to the boss. The boss is expected to choose sides and get in the game. This, of course, adds to the boss' work load. The job becomes watching the outer office, high school hall-monitor style, to catch the violator in the act. Then the boss and the secretary can holler, "Gotcha!" in unison.

Everything will probably be as it should be when the boss is watching. Soon, in an attempt to expedite a solution, one executive is talking to the other executive about the situation. The second executive whose judgment in hiring employees may be in question, is bound to have some bias in favor of the secretary who is criticized. Each of these four people may spend more time watching each other than they spend tending to business. Customers feel the tension in the office and avoid this uncomfortable setting, resulting in lost business.

Teams are important. Be sure you hold up your end, regardless of how your teammates play. Be cautious to not initiate game playing.

Eliminating Waste

Kinds of waste range from the innocent gum wrapper that is part of the daily garbage, to the industrial waste that enrages environmentalists.

Of no less concern is the flagrant waste of time, the most vital resource available to any human being.

The ways you waste time and allow others to help you waste it are a major concern. Before you can control this waste, you must identify the environment you are most vulnerable to.

Start with this partial list of common time wasters, then extend the list to cover your particular time wasters.

1. Lack of priorities
2. Lack of objectives
3. Lack of time frame planning
4. Lack of organization
5. Inability to say no
6. Poor communication skills
7. Visitors
8. Telephone

9. Procrastination

10. Socializing

This list is short and broad-based; extend it by considering your own circumstances. Get down to particulars. For example in the visitors category, list your biggest time wasters by name: Joe, Jim, or John. Then figure a way to do something about it.

In the book, *New Time Management Methods—For You and Your Staff,* R. Alec Mackenzie lists 153 time wasters. So you see, you have plenty of room to cut waste. Mackenzie concentrates on time management in business. When you consider the use of personal time, you discover that people are even more creative in finding ways to "piddle" away time.

Once you have completed your list of time wasters, follow up with a plan to reduce and eliminate them.

You have read about how to correct the difficulty of not being able to say no. One more example is appropriate here.

How can you eliminate unnecessary telephone interruptions? The following suggestions may help:

1. Have someone filter your calls. (*Screening* was the term used in discussing the boss/secretary team.) You can apply this technique at home as well as at work.

2. If you do not have the information the caller seeks, do not volunteer to get the information. Refer callers to someone from whom they can get answers directly, rather than do their work for them.

3. Do not accept calls during time set aside for a specific priority task of your own. Ask if you can call back later, when you have the time to talk.

4. Consolidate your calls. Set up a time frame for making several calls or callbacks rather than spreading them at random throughout the day.

5. If you have several topics to talk about, make a list so you remember to say everything, rather than call the same person several times.

These few suggestions might make your telephone a friend, rather than a time waster. Be innovative as you put together ways and means for combating time wasters.

Frustration

Nothing is more frustrating than becoming time management conscious while those around you are oblivious to how they waste your time. You feel frustrated when you find yourself in one of these situations.

Suppose you make an appointment—or try to—with a tradesman. You need a plumber, so you call one. You may be told that the plumber is booked up and will not be available for three days. At least you know you have a definite day to plan around. Next you try to find out what time of day to expect the plumber. The answer is usually, "Sometime in the morning," so you ask, "What time, exactly?" and are told, "Early, we will put your name first on our list for Thursday." Unable to get a more exact time, you tell your boss you need to stay home for a while on Thursday morning to let the plumber into your house, but you should be to work by 10 o'clock at the latest. Thursday morning comes—10 o'clock comes—still no plumber, so you call. The answer you get is, "There was an emergency call early this morning, but the plumber should be there soon. You were first on the list this morning and the plumber is in the neighborhood, so it shouldn't be long now." You wait. Noon arrives, and you call again. Now you hear, "It was unfortunate, but the problem was much larger than anyone thought. However, the job is done now and you will be the first stop after lunch." You call your boss and wait it out. (You have come so far; you do not want to start all over another day.) The plumber finally arrives at 1:30. All goes well, but now it is 2:30, and you have lost nearly a whole day at your job. If you are paid by the hour, you should bill the plumbing company for your time. They spent it for you!

This story by no means intends to single out plumbers, or to say all plumbers do this. Delays happen with carpenters, painters, merchants, and deliveries of appliances or furniture. You have to wait in a doctor's office, where they never intended to get you in at your appointed time anyway! Counting figures on wallpaper while waiting may excite some people, but people who value their time are not impressed with those who have no regard for it.

Another frustrating situation occurs when you have made an appointment with someone like the boss, an employee, or a friend at lunch. You are on time, but the other person is not. Then when these people arrive, they take phone calls or allow walk-in visitors to take time away from your appointment. At such times you wonder why you do not physically explode.

Time is money is a slogan that appears in many offices as a reminder of how important correct use of time can be. Actually, time is *better* than money. Without time, how and when could anyone acquire money? You could not accumulate knowledge or possessions without the time in which to do it. Emotions cannot exist without the time to experience them. Love and happiness are meaningless without time to enjoy them.

If you lose your money or your possessions, you can replace them as long as you have time. Since time is so valuable—your most valuable resource—be very possessive and selective in spending it.

Priorities

Because time is so important, you must be concerned with how you spend it. This fact brings up the subject of priorities.

You may or may not be consciously in touch with your priorities, but you have them, as does everyone. Whenever you do anything by choice, you devote that time to your priorities. You have freely selected that activity.

You fool yourself if you say that you have a certain priority, but spend your discretionary time doing tasks not even remotely related to that priority.

For example, perhaps one of your priorities is to write a book and have it published, but anytime you have thirty minutes to yourself you spend it in front of the T.V. set. Be conscious of what your actions tell you about your priorities.

What are your priorities? The following list may help you focus on what is important to you:

Wealth	Love
Power	Fame
Status	Knowledge
Popularity	Travel
Being Needed	Health
Pleasure	Success
Family	Leadership
Recognition	Another person

The list is open-ended. Discover your priorities and focus on them in considering how to spend your time. Then narrow your priorities to specific tasks that need to be accomplished to reach your ultimate goals.

Quitting Time

As you finish this chapter on time management, remember that there is much more to be learned about the subject.

Consider people's preoccupation with the word time. How many *times* do you use it in your speech every day without even stopping to think about it? Read through the following list and listen very closely to yourself and others for the next few days. You will be surprised and have fun adding to the list.

Time out
Time in
Halftime
Bedtime
Time to get up
Time for work
It's high time
I have time
I don't have time
Lunchtime
Dinnertime
Time lock
Waste of time
Time on my hands
Time flies
Time to think
Need more time
It's about time
On time
In time
Time of your life
Troubled times
Time for the meeting
Breaktime
Vacation time
Time after time
Time table
In the nick of time
Killing time
Time trials
Planning time
Feeding time
That time of year
Fun times
Time to get going
Coffee time
Story time
Time off
Time to relax
Time for school
Time for breakfast
Your time is up

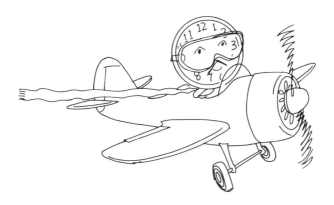

Time is money
Full time
Part-time
Twilight time
Party time
Time and time again
Departure time
Arrival time
Daylight Saving Time
Up time
Down time
Lost time
Do you have the time
This time
That time
Next time
Time frame
Time to get started
Take your time
First time
Second time
Third time
(etc.)
Told you a thousand times
Daytime
Nighttime
Prime time
Time to quit
Time slot
Time tested
Timed test
Time's running out

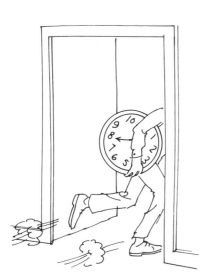

What time is it?
    Time to move on—
        Thank you for your time . . .

Summary Questions

1. Explain how fear contributes to procrastination.
2. How can exaggerating fear aid in overcoming it?
3. Why is it so difficult to say no?
4. How can prioritizing eliminate the need to say no?
5. Describe screening.
6. List six time-wasters.
7. What are your priorities?
8. Use this basic planning sheet for one week.

Time	Sunday	Monday	Tuesday	Wednesday	Thursday	Friday	Saturday
7:00 a.m.							
7:30							
8:00							
8:30							
9:00							
9:30							
10:00							
10:30							
11:00							
11:30							
12:00 p.m.							
12:30							
1:00							
1:30							
2:00							
2:30							
3:00							
3:30							
4:00							
4:30							
5:00							
5:30							
6:00							
6:30							
7:00							
7:30							
8:00							
8:30							
9:00							
9:30							
10:00							
10:30							
11:00							
11:30							
12:00 midnight							

9. List activities that have little value for you.

    a.

    b.

    c.

    d.

    e.

    f.

    g.

10. List some worthwhile activities you might substitute.

    a.

    b.

    c.

    d.

    e.

    f.

    g.

CHAPTER 22

Potential

How Much of You Are You Hiding from You?

People do what they do according to what they believe reality is. Take gum chewing for example. You have been advised that chewing gum during an interview is unacceptable. It is rude to talk with something in your mouth and the chewing action is distracting. The interviewer may think you are impolite and lack respect and manners. Therefore, you would not chew gum in an interview.

Now think about the individual whose father chewed gum while taking care of his customers, whose mother chewed gum in church, and who was told that chewing gum is better than smoking. This person will chew gum in an interview without a second thought.

The act of gum chewing is not immoral or illegal; it is just that one person's perception of it is substantially different from another's.

Recall what you read about behavior, transactional analysis, and other concepts about why you are the way you are. People, things, and surroundings have all contributed to make you the way you are and have furnished you with your concept of reality.

When you were growing up, you heard many times, "You can't do that," or "You can't do this." You probably had already done what you were being told you could not do. The consequences of doing those things were such that you were probably better off not doing them. The point is that you formed the opinion that you were *unable* to do a great many things, when in fact, you can do almost anything you want if you are willing to take the risk and reap the rewards or suffer the consequences of your actions.

For example, perhaps you were told, "You can't stick your finger in a light socket." You most certainly can! Why anyone would want to is difficult to understand, but the ability to perform the act is not beyond your capability.

What so often happens is that people become conditioned to the word "can't," rather than to the circumstance that brings about the use of the word. Examining the consequences of an action and choosing whether to perform or not perform it is what should happen.

After hearing *can't*, over a period of time, you take over for yourself. Have you ever told yourself things like this: "I can't do these math problems. I can't understand the section in this book on behavior. I can't play golf." Nearly everyone does this about something. What you mean and should tell yourself is, "I choose not to." Perhaps math is a difficult subject, but given the time, a better explanation of how to do the problems, and the desire to stick with it, and you can do it.

Tell yourself that there is nothing you cannot do. A great many things you may not want to do, but you must remove the imaginary limitations you place on yourself. Recondition yourself.

Of or Ov

In a short self-test people are asked to count the *f*'s in a single sentence. There are a total of six *f*'s in the sentence. People rarely find all six on the first count, because three of the words containing *f* are the word, *of*. The word is pronounced as though it should be spelled "*ov*." Conditioning causes us to miss the obvious.

Good News and Bad News

The bad news is that it is difficult to break old habits. People spend years becoming conditioned to one set of beliefs. They become so conditioned that they screen out evidence that does not agree with their beliefs. These blind spots, as in the case of "of" and "ov," are second nature and it takes a great deal of concentration to examine all the evidence and make changes.

The good news is that your past need not determine your future. When you realize that your *can'ts* are choices you make and not actual fact, you realize that you *can* do most anything. *You* choose what you want to become. What you can be, and what you will be, depend on you and the price you are willing to pay.

Human beings choose for themselves; other objects have choices made for them by human beings. For example, consider a tree in its present state. It appears tall and stately, strong and firm, a beautiful tribute to nature. Ask yourself what it might become. What you are considering is the potential for that tree. It might become part of a house, furniture, firewood, or any one of a thousand wood products. It could be used in the construction of a church. What it is, it is. What it can become, is its potential.

Your potential lies in whatever you can become. Unlike the tree, you have to see for yourself what your possibilities are; you must not wait for someone else to come along and make those changes in you. Do it yourself.

First of all you must want to change and you must believe in yourself. Then take the appropriate actions to realize the change. Be alert to the fact that you have built blind spots. Be aware of the evidence that supports and refutes your beliefs. Otherwise, you are like a poor judge who only listens to one side of a case before passing sentence.

Not only do individuals build blind spots around their particular beliefs, but there are universal or nearly universal blind spots. For example, consider the belief that the earth is flat. This fact was accepted until Christopher Columbus proved differently. The four-minute mile was an impossibility until Roger Bannister proved that the mile could be run in four minutes or less. Blind spots, universal or personal, limit potential and creativity.

How Blind Spots Are Built

When you build a blind spot you go through a process like the one described here.

Think about what happens when you buy a home. You look around until you feel you have found the house that best fits your needs. You believe your choice is wise, so you sign the contract, make the purchase, and move in. Now you begin to have doubts and you ask yourself, "Did I really do the smart thing?" You look for evidence that will support your decision so you can feel good about yourself. If you concentrate on finding supporting evidence, you will find it, or if you want to look for evidence to the contrary you will find that. In this case you want and need to feel good, so lo and behold, you discover that one of your neighbors is someone you have known and respected for some time. This fact gives you reinforcement for your decision. You think, "If that person chose to live in this neighborhood, I must have made a wise decision too."

Probably you knew the person before, but not very well. You probably did not hold that person in as high esteem as you do now that you need to confirm your confidence in your house-buying decision.

Then you get a call from a realtor who did not know you had made a purchase. This realtor tells you about a house that is available that meets your specifications. The realtor tells you the price and you are horrified because it is $15,000 less than you paid for the house you purchased. You will not allow yourself to think that this would have been a better deal than the one you made. You listen for those things, no matter how small, that are not what you wanted and disregard the positive features that might make you feel you made a wrong decision.

The tendency to look for people whose opinion supports your own and to avoid people and circumstances that differ is normal. Once you have a strong belief or make a commitment, you establish blind spots so that evidence to the contrary will not upset you. Your beliefs then alter what you see, as in the case of "ov" instead of "of."

How people perceive the world has more to do with beliefs than with intelligence. How you perceive the world and yourself causes you to place limitations on what you believe your potential is. You set up blind spots that support your beliefs and the beliefs become real because you believe they are real.

Rules

What makes you think of yourself in a certain way? Who makes your rules? What makes you think you must not or cannot do certain things?

For some people, the golden rule is, "The person who has the gold makes the rules." These people may not be all wrong. Your rules are made by your parents, friends, peers, the boss, the company's policies and procedures manual, and your heroes, whose example you want to emulate. You make up a few rules of your own. This book suggests a good many rules about how you should dress and what you should do to be successful. Look at this material as input only. Weigh the concepts and *think* for yourself. The ideas that fit what you already believe are easy to accept. Others that do not coincide with your beliefs might be the ones you need to review.

Rules tell you what you can do and they set limitations. Rules can be good or bad. Examine each rule you live by and analyze it so you know exactly what life style you have chosen.

Earlier you read about the rule that you should not stick your finger in a light socket. This would seem like a pretty good rule to cling to. Unless, of course you want to "light up your life," from the inside out!

Suppose you have a rule that every Sunday the whole family must sit down for dinner together. This rule may have been good when the children were young. Sunday dinner was a family sharing time, a time for closeness, a time to enjoy each other's company. Circumstances change and rules need re-examining.

Now the children are adults, but a rule is a rule—right? It does not matter that the cook of the house would prefer eating out once-in-a-while, rather than cooking every Sunday. One member of the family would rather be on the golf course, another was invited somewhere else, and others have different interests and priorities. What was a setting for togetherness, love, and sharing has become a circumstance for resentment because a rule is a rule, and rules cannot be broken—or can they?

Once a rule, always a rule is an overwhelming and limiting rule to live by. You may be unaware of the limitations you place on yourself. In that case, you fail to take advantage of your resources and abilities because you do not recognize that they exist.

Self-esteem

One of the most important aspects of listening is listening to yourself. You send yourself messages all the time. Listen carefully, because once-in-a-while you lie to yourself. The lie seems like the truth because of those blind spots you developed to conceal the truth. Listen carefully and then reason with yourself, especially at times when you are telling yourself you cannot do something. Reason out why you prefer not to risk trying, but get past the idea that you are not able.

Humility is a virtue, but be careful that while being humble, you do not get a low opinion of yourself. *Believe in yourself.* How can you expect anyone else to think more of you than you do? You must be good before you have anything to be humble about.

Your self-image influences what you permit yourself to do. What do you expect from yourself? The expression, "I feel like a fish out of water," usually means that someone is in a situation that he or she has never been in before. It is a feeling that accompanies being in unfamiliar surroundings or with new people—in an unknown area. Fear of the unknown is a real fear.

When faced with the unknown, people reach for some familiar anchor—one familiar face, for example. As you stretch to discover and realize your potential, you begin to believe you *can* do what you want, but when you reach, you extend yourself into unfamiliar territory. When you discover yourself in unfamiliar territory, when you realize you are taking a risk, when you feel fear, you are liable to scramble back to familiar safe territory where you felt comfortable. You need to prepare yourself for the places you are going before you get there so that you will not be as uncomfortable.

One way you prepare yourself is by creating mental pictures of yourself in the places you intend to go. If you believe you are worthy of a better position or a higher income, why not picture in your mind what you will look like and what you will be doing when you get that position or earn that additional money?

Is this daydreaming? Daydreaming is probably as good a label as any. Do your daydreaming at night just before you go to sleep. You are making yourself comfortable in a situation before you physically get there. When you arrive, you will not be a stranger. It is like seeing a picture of someone you have never met just before you meet them. You can then pick that person out of a crowd without prior personal contact.

Goals/Potential/You're OK

When you set goals you say that you have the potential to reach those goals. Perhaps you need to stretch—mentally, physically, or emotionally—to reach for those goals. Perhaps you have given up some goals because of discomfort you experienced.

Setting goals is a gutsy commitment. If you have a goal, you are saying you are dissatisfied with where you are and you are going after something better. You are going after something worth taking a risk for and something worth the time and trouble to reach. When you suffer setbacks, you do not feel good. When you reach some of those short-term goals on your way to your major goal, you feel great.

Remember that "You're OK." Most of the things you want and dream of having are OK. Rich people are OK. Ambitious people are OK. People committed to doing a good job, working hard, and wanting more than they have are OK. People with potential are OK. People who want to fail are OK. They may be difficult to understand, but they are OK. Believe you are OK, or you will not be. Choose to be OK, want to be OK, and you will be.

Risk

The term *risk* has appeared repeatedly, since risk is an integral part of growth and the realization of potential. Risk is necessary when you decide to reach beyond where you are. When you risk, you move into unknown areas. When you were a child you took risk after risk, because you did not know fear or self-doubt. When you began to walk, you fell, but you got up and tried again and again. Everything you ever want involves a risk. Everything you get involves a trade-off. You give up something to get something you want more. You risk to find true love; you risk to get a job; you risk when you take a new job, change companies, or buy a new car. You risk when you make an investment.

When you risk, you give up an old way of seeing yourself and pick up your option for change. Not taking a risk can be the biggest risk of all. You never move from where you are unless you initiate an action to keep growing. If you do not take your life in a chosen direction, it will go in whatever direction the rest of the world pushes you.

The situation can be as personal as love or as public as seeking a job. If you are not willing to take a risk, someone else will. By the time you decide to try—the job belongs to someone else. In love, one of the twosome issues an ultimatum of marriage after a long engagement, so that both can get on with their lives.

Risks bring about fear of the unknown. Expect to experience some fear; this is normal and natural. Be careful that your fear is natural and not guilt.

Guilt is a powerful force that can deter you from taking a risk. The ability to have deep feelings for others is a marvelous trait unless you use it as an excuse. Once again, take the time for self-communication, self-listening, and self-analysis. Consider the following thoughts as you have this talk with yourself.

1. Can you really help others if you cannot help yourself?
2. Can you give to others if you cannot give to yourself?
3. Are you selfish if you give to yourself?
4. Will you be disappointed if your self-denial is not appreciated?
5. Do you use self-denial to put others in your debt?
6. Do you help someone else if you fail to realize your potential?
7. Does your unhappiness make others happy?
8. If your unhappiness makes others happy, are they worth your sacrifice?
9. Do you have the consent of the people you make sacrifices for? Would they do the same for you?
10. Is your self-denial appreciated or simply expected?
11. Have you conditioned others to simply expect your self-denial?
12. Will you be hurt and resentful, if you are told, "You didn't have to give that up for me. I thought you did it because you wanted to."
13. What is it you really want? This is a choice, remember?
14. Whose destiny are you trying to shape? Yours? Others'?
15. Do you choose your risks?
16. Be honest with yourself. How can you be honest with anyone else if you cannot be honest with yourself?

Fear

Recognize your fears, and face them. Fear makes you cautious; it makes you stop and think so you do not become reckless. Some people who like to live dangerously boast, "I don't know the meaning of the word *fear*." The best advice for them is to buy a dictionary and look it up. Fear is real and shared. Respect it as a caution sign; without it people are liable to self-destruct.

Risk-taking begins with goals and plans and results in growth. Life, after all, is a journey—not a destination. You are going somewhere; you might as well choose your destination.

A commitment on your part to toss away thoughts, attitudes, or habits that inhibit growth is important. A commitment is more important than motivation that comes from promised raises or recognition or a kick in the pants from the boss. You must decide—are things just going to happen or are you going to make them happen?

The Winner

If you think you are beaten, you are;
if you think you dare not, you don't;
if you'd like to win, but you think you can't,
it's almost a cinch you won't.

If you think you'll lose, you've lost,
for out in the world you find
success begins with a person's will . . .
it's all in the state of mind.

If you think you're outclassed, you are;
you've got to think high to rise;
you've got to be sure of yourself before
you can ever win the prize.

Full many a race is lost
before ever a step is run;
and many a coward fails
before ever the work's begun.

Think big and your deeds will grow;
think small and you'll fall behind;
think that you can and you will . . .
it's all in the state of mind.

Life's battles don't always go
to the stronger or faster woman or man;
but soon or late the one who wins
is the person who thinks he or she can.

—Author Unknown

Summary Questions

1. Be honest with yourself and write down five things you think of as things "you *can't* do."

   a.

   b.

   c.

   d.

   e.

2. Now go back over the list and explain why you can't do those things.

   a.

   b.

   c.

   d.

   e.

3. Go through the list once more and explain how you could do these things if you really wanted to, or why you don't want to do them.

   a.

   b.

   c.

   d.

   e.

4. Explain what blind spots you have created that limit your potential.

5. Name two or three rules you live by.

   a.

   b.

   c.

   Who made those rules?

6. List two or three instances in which you took a risk and it paid off.

7. Explain risk.

CHAPTER 23

Personal Finance

Money, the Root of All—

Few items are more personal than an individual's bank account. The subject of personal finance is included here by request.

Money worries are forced on everyone, since this medium of exchange is what feeds, clothes, and puts a roof over everyone's head. Money keeps you alive so that you can set and realize other goals.

Personal finance begins as a simple concept and becomes complex. The explanation begins with income and expenses. If you know what your income is and you know what your expenses are, then be sure they are equal and you will never have to worry.

The simplicity ends there. If income exceeds expenses then you must decide what to do with the extra money. If you chose to spend the difference there are as many choices as there are products and services on the market. You could choose to save the difference. If expenses exceed income, you must trim expenses or increase income to break even. In this situation also, you have a world of choices.

One chapter in this book cannot cover all the options available in the world of personal finance. However, you can get a glimpse of the many areas to become involved in as you earn, spend, and try to save money.

Careful money management is a must. You can set yourself back many years by poor financial decisions, or you can improve your economic well being with sensible money management. A good plan for your personal finances gives you one less worry as you pursue other interests and goals. If one of your goals is the accumulation of wealth, you must satisfy the basic money needs before you can concentrate on the investment prospects available.

Plan

Once again the concepts of goal setting and planning are important. Without a financial plan, the chances of achieving your goals—financial or otherwise—are remote. To meet your financial goals, your plans revolve around the two items of income and expense.

The core of a financial plan is a budget. In this visual mechanism you list your sources of income and how you allocate that income. In crude terms, a budget is where you get your money and where you spend it. Usually your salary is the primary, if not the only source of income. The outgoing flow of money is multi-faceted.

Career

Because income is usually derived from one principle source—your job—we emphasize the importance of your career choice and planning. Career selection has a great deal to do with the economic and personal satisfaction you experience in life. The career decision should not be left to chance or made without considerable time and effort. Changing occupations becomes more difficult and involves more risk once you have committed yourself to family responsibilities and the other demands of life.

Budget

Budgets come in all sizes and shapes. However, since the budget is central to financial planning, it will be the hub of the information presented here. You may or may not adopt the budget format used here. Yet, it serves its purpose if it helps you think about how to tackle your particular budget problems.

Pay periods vary from weekly, to biweekly, to monthly; base your budget on your pay period. People who work on a commission basis must base their budgets around their particular irregular circumstances.

Because bills are typically issued monthly, the references here are based on a monthly pay period.

To have a good budget, try to identify every item that claims some of your income. First, be as specific as you can. List all bills due each month, such as the gas, electric, water, sanitation, and telephone bills. You may later group these under the heading of utilities. Listing the items individually at the outset assures that you have not overlooked any item.

As you identify each item, categorize it, as an immediate (short-term) expense, an eventual (long-term) expense, or a part of your savings program. This practice enables you to develop a strategy for your money allocation.

SAMPLE BUDGET ITEM

Identification

I

Immediate Expenses (Short-term)

food	gas	garbage	entertainment
clothing	electricity	gasoline	presents
rent	water	oil changes	savings
insurance	telephone	general repairs	miscellaneous

Eventual Expenses (Long-term)

II

washer	refrigerator	furniture	home
dryer	T.V.	lawn equipment	weddings of children
stove	car	travel	miscellaneous

III

retirement	wealth accumulation		
investment	college for children		miscellaneous

The above layout provides a base for further discussion on budgeting. A few items deserve additional explanation at the outset.

The term *rent* could also apply to house payments. The term *entertainment* refers to movies, dinner out, or other occasional change-of-pace treats you give yourself.

Presents is a broad category that includes birthdays, weddings, Christmas and other occasions. *General repairs* applies to anything from replacing the muffler in your car to reupholstering the davenport.

Miscellaneous appears in every category because something unexpected always comes along. This category helps prevent a financial shock. When you have a miscellaneous expense regularly, add its name to your list.

The Shuffle

All of the budgeted items seem to fit neatly into three categories, but before long you will be tempted to shift one or several items from one category to another. You may move more of them until you have reshuffled the whole plan. This shuffling is not unreasonable, since no one budget fits everyone.

An item you make payments on should appear in category number one. If you make car payments monthly, the car expense is immediate and should be in the first group. This method of categorizing applies to other items on your list as well.

Assume that you own your car outright, but in five years you intend to buy a new one. You allocate $100 each month toward that new car. At the end of five years or 60 months, you will have put aside $6,000. If you used the services of a financial institution you received interest on the money in savings during the time period. You made this long-term expense a part of your savings program and provided yourself with options. Option one is to take the $6,000 to buy the car and leave the interest as part of your investment plan. Option two is to use the accumulated interest to buy your car sooner. The same strategy can be applied to any large, long-term-expense item.

Any of the items listed in the second category could appear in the first group. Only if you own the item can you begin to build funds for replacement. You can use the long-term-expense items as short term savings items and get double duty from your dollars, only if you are not making payments.

If you save for these items so that you can replace them through outright purchase, you save not only the interest you pay, but you earn interest on the money you put aside until you make the purchase. In this way you save twice.

If you are making payments on a car, a washer and dryer, the furniture, and so on, it takes time to reverse the process. One way to change your budget structure is to make the regular payments for items you have paid off, but now make those payments to yourself in a savings account. When it comes time to replace the item you will be ready with the cash.

Another option is this: When you finish paying for an item, apply the amount you regularly paid for it to the payment for some other item. In this way, you accelerate the pace at which you get your payments out of the way. Then you can plow the payment monies into a savings account for replacement items.

Savings As an Expense

Savings, even long-term savings, should be viewed as an expense. Systematic saving is a habit that must be cultivated early. Time is what makes money grow. Although retirement may seem a long way off when you are in your twenties, it is the savings plus the interest, and the interest on the interest, that provide the dollars for your sixties.

Think of your savings program in this way: Your savings account is another monthly bill that *you owe to yourself.* You pay the grocer, the utilities department, the clothing store, the automobile dealer, and a dozen other people—why not pay yourself? You are as important as anyone else. Aren't you worth at least a part of your income? You should be the first one you pay. After all, you are worth it; you worked for it!

Elusive Income

Although the income factor seems easy to figure, it has its elusive side. The most familiar claims against your income are taxes and social security. Like most people, you probably receive a check from your employer, with those deductions made from the check before you see it. You may have authorized the payroll department to make other deductions, like union dues, allowance for savings bonds, contributions toward a retirement plan, or charitable contributions. Your check could be reduced by 20 to 30 percent before you receive it. What you receive is the amount you have to work with in your budget.

Records

Businesses keep records and you need records to keep track of your personal business. When you pay for an item you get a receipt. Keep it! Your receipt is your record of where your money went, and your proof that you paid for and own the item.

If you make payments, the people you make the payments to know what you paid and what you still owe—you should too.

If you pay your bills from a checking account, the institution you deal with keeps a record of your deposits and withdrawals. The same thing is true of your savings account. Proper use of both is of great assistance. Abuse of either can be devastating, to your financial well-being and to your reputation as well. Double check every entry to substantiate your financial position. Even with sophisticated accounting systems, financial institutions occasionally make mistakes. Keeping accurate records is in your own interest.

Your checking account provides you with a set of records proving you paid your bills. Cancelled checks are receipts in themselves. This account shows you where you spent your money; periodically review it to determine where you were frugal, and where you were extravagant.

The overdraft is the most embarrassing and damaging misuse of the checking account. Writing a check for more than the amount you have in your account can happen to anyone, but it does not happen repeatedly to anyone who cares about good financial management and a good reputation.

If you write checks for more than you have in your account, the financial institution serving you has two choices. First, it can refuse to honor that check.

The check is returned to the person or establishment you gave it to with a note that you have insufficient funds. Your check bounced. The person or business wastes little time before contacting you to let you know your check was no good, implying, perhaps, that you are not either! Unless you make an immediate and honest effort to make the check good, you will never again be able to pay that person or establishment with a check. The word gets around the business community to watch out for you and your "no good" financial situation.

The second option the financial institution has, is to honor the check, even though your account is short of funds. This institution then looks for you to make up the difference. What they have done, in effect, is make you a loan, and they too, want to get their money back. For this service, which saved your reputation, they charge you a penalty. If you are overdrawn, you can probably ill afford the penalty dollars. You pay this price for not keeping good records.

Credit

The abilities to get credit and obtain a loan are wonderful things. Both are privileges, and both are something you earn. You are extended credit or granted a loan because you have demonstrated by past actions that you are financially responsible.

Your creditors expect you to honor the indebtedness, and assume that you will pay faithfully for the privilege of enjoying items immediately that you have not saved for. Not only are you expected to pay regularly, but you are charged for the privilege of using other people's money. The charge is that interest you could be saving and receiving, had you decided to postpone the purchase until you have the money.

Loans and credit let you enjoy a home, a car, appliances, furniture, and a great many other items sooner than if you had to save first.

While you make payments, you enjoy your purchases and build your reputation by proving you are a good financial risk. Your credit continues to be available when you need it. Missed payments, however, cause embarrassment, reputation damage, and fear. Fear enters the picture when you find yourself unable to meet your commitments and fall behind. Bill collectors and collection agencies threaten you with legal repercussions. Overestimation and overextension of your earning potential and loss of income due to unemployment can bring about such a situation. A well-thought-out long-term financial plan, a sound budget, and faithful recordkeeping help prevent these financial problems.

A substantial income is no reason to neglect keeping a close eye on your financial activity. People with incomes of $30,000 to $50,000 often declare personal bankruptcy because they did not realize they had overextended themselves through use of easy credit.

You must understand the cost of credit, the amount of credit that can be handled at different income levels, and the options available when credit is abused, to make informed decisions about being a cash or credit buyer.

Calamities

Although the farsighted planner expects the unexpected, accumulating finances for devastating setbacks is often impossible. These setbacks might include the loss of a home by fire, or the loss of a loved one and accompanying loss of income. Not only can these and other calamities exert financial stress, but they are also accompanied by emotional stress. When emotions are high, business logic and business decisions take second place. Financial decisions do not seem as important and are not made as astutely as under normal circumstances.

The typical way to avoid loss in these types of tragic circumstances is with insurance. The purpose of insurance is to provide funds to alleviate financial burdens in times of personal, emotional, and financial crises.

The most familiar types of insurance are life insurance, health or hospitalization insurance, property insurance, automobile insurance, and liability insurance. While the huge amount of money needed in a crisis may not fit your budget, insurance premiums can.

A smorgasbord of insurance options is available to provide the protection you want and need. Shop for insurance just as you would shop for anything else. Shop for the company you want to represent you, for an agent of that company that you can trust and feel comfortable working with, and for the combination of policies and coverages that matches your needs and circumstances.

Savings

You must include savings in your plans early if you ever expect to have investment choices. One philosophy that may give you the incentive to get started is that every time you buy an item, you make a choice. Be aware of the distinction between items you want and items you need. You need food, clothing, and a roof over your head. You may want a six pack of beer or your favorite soft drink or the latest fashion in clothing even though you do not actually need it. You choose between having what you want and having the money. When you have the money, the choice to keep it is often easier because you know that as long as you keep the cash you can have what you want whenever you want it. This feeling puts you in control of your financial destiny. When you are short of cash everything seems more desirable because it is out of reach. If this philosophy works for you—good! If not, find one that motivates you to save.

When you have saved regularly and money begins to accumulate, you begin to look for more lucrative investments. You want to build your reserves rapidly with something providing higher interest rates. As with insurance—choose the company, the representative, and the investments that fit you. The safety of the money you have saved should be your first consideration with early investing. The more money you have, the greater the risks you can take with part of it. The higher the risk, the higher the return, but also the higher the possibility of losing your original investment.

Summary

Sound financial planning involves much more than the meager exposure you have had in this chapter. If you pursue no other concept, pursue this one. For better or worse, money is a primary influence in your life. Manage your finances and manage your time well so that you can be in control.

Activity

1. Build your budget. Work with your instructor through a financial institution to set up this exercise.
2. Get a book of checks or a simulated book of checks and practice filling them out. Do the necessary record keeping and a reconciliation.

Suggested Sources for Additional Reading

A Man's Guide to Business and Social Success
Barry James
Milady Publishing Co.

Are You Listening?
Ralph G. Nichols and Leonard A. Stevens
McGraw-Hill Publishing Co.

A Secretary's Guide to Beauty—Charm—Poise
Ruth Tolman
Milady Publishing Co.

Assertiveness at Work
Linda MacNeilage and Kathleen Adams
Spectrum Publishing Co.

Behavioral Insight for Supervision
Ralph W. Reber
Prentice-Hall Publishing Co.

Body Language and Social Order
Albert E. Scheflen and Alice Scheflen
Spectrum (Prentice-Hall)

The Career Game
Charles Guy Moore, Ph.D.
Ballantine Publishing

Charm and Poise for Getting Ahead
Ruth Tolman
Milady Publishing Co.

Creativity: Its Dimensions and Development
Blanche Edwards
Training by Design, Inc.

Frogs into Princes
Richard Bandler and John Grinder
Real People Press

Games People Play
Eric Berne, M.D.
Grove Press, Inc., N. Y.

Getting a Better Job
David Gootnick
McGraw-Hill Publishing Co.

Getting Your Act Together
George L. Morrisey
John Wiley and Sons, Inc.

High Impact Resumes and Letters
Ronald L. Krannich and William J. Banis
Progressive Concepts, Inc.

How to Get Whatever You Want out of Life
Dr. Joyce Brothers
Simon and Schuster Publishing

How to Organize Your Work and Your Life
Robert Maskowitz
Doubleday and Co. Publishing Co.

I'm OK—You're OK
Thomas A. Harris, M. D.
Harper and Row Publishing

Listening—The Forgotten Skill
Madelyn Burley–Allen
John Wiley and Sons, Inc.

Mastering Assertiveness Skills
Elaina Zuker
AMACOM (American Management Association)

Megatrends
John Naisbitt
Warner Books

Passages
Gail Sheehy
E. P. Dutton and Co. Publishing

Performance Appraisal
Richard F. Olson
John Wiley and Sons, Inc.

Planning for Organizational Success
Robert Kaufman and Bruce Stone
John Wiley and Sons, Inc. Publishing Co.

The Power Look
Egon von Furstenberg with Camille Duhe
Holt, Reinhart, and Winston Publishing Co.

Practical Magic
Steve Lankton, ACSW
Mila Publications

Priorities
Dorri Jacobs, Ed. D.
Franklin Watts Publishing Co.

The Professional Listener
James VanLase
Training by Design Inc.

Professional Selling—A Practical Approach
R. J. Kranz and M. K. Kranz
Kent Publishing Company

Realize Your Potential
Robert J. McKain, Jr.
AMACON, (American Management Association)

Risking
David Viscott, M.D.
Simon and Schuster Publishing Co.

Seven Steps to Employment
Ted R. Morford and Shelley M. Mauer
EAI Publishing Co.

Success
Michael Korda
Random House Publishing

Supervisory Management
Monthly publication of
American Management Associations

T.A. Games
Adelaide Bry
Perennial Library Publishing Co.

The Third Wave
Alvin Toffler
William Morrow and Co., Inc. (A Bantam Book)

The Time Trap
R. Alec MacKenzie
AMACOM

Trade-Offs
David Hon
Learning Concepts

Unmasking the Face
Paul Ekman and Wallace V. Friesen
Spectrum (Prentice-Hall) Publishing Co.

The Winning Image
James Gray, Jr.
AMACOM Publishing Co.

The Woman's Dress for Success Book
John T. Molloy
Follett Publishing Co.

You Are What You Wear
Silliam Thourlby
Sheed Andrews and McMeel, Inc.

Answers to Selected Questions

CHAPTER 5

1. balanced diet
2. rest, water, squinting
3. soft, supple
4. pores
5. crow's feet
6. rinsing
7. moisturizer
8. water
9. normal, dry, oily, combination, problem
10. blackheads
11. T-zone
12. dermatologist
13. massage, tension
14. subtle
15. cell renewal
16. younger

CHAPTER 6

1. oily, dry, normal
2. fine, coarse, average
3. dandruff

4. flatters, softens, accentuate good features, diminish shortcomings
5. heart, diamond, round, square, triangle, oval
6. hair roots
7. massage
8. two
9. rinsing
10. tone
11. professional
12. trimmed and cleaned

CHAPTER 7

1. a. stomach in
   b. buttocks tucked
   c. shoulders back
   d. head erect
2. a. wish to appear shorter
   b. discouragement
   c. fatigue
   d. lack of confidence
3. a. normal breathing
   b. look and feel better
   c. proper functioning of organs
   d. lessen backaches

4. a. too thin
    b. too heavy
    c. bowed
    d. knock-knees
5. a. twiddle thumbs
    b. pick imaginary lint
    c. clench the hands
    d. jingle coins in pockets
6. a. feet close together
    b. knees together
    c. soles of both shoes on floor
    d. ankles crossed—not knees

CHAPTER 8

1. polite or courteous
2. respect
3. calm
4. your fingers
5. first impression
6. sincere
7. goodbye
8. introduce
9. stand
10. shake hands
11. sensitive
12. harmony
13. church, interview, closed vehicle, elevator (private home without permission), a store, or anywhere there is no ashtray evident
14. left, right
15. left
16. farthest
17. fingers
18. side

CHAPTER 10

1. false
2. true
3. false
4. true
5. false
6. false
7. false

8. true
9. true
10. true

CHAPTER 16

1. In infancy
2. 40%
3. 25%
4. employees, friends, housework, birthdays, personal desires, employers, car repairs, homework, death in family, buying home—anything fitting
5. Any answer referring to listening with concentration and receiving a complete communication
6. None needed.

CHAPTER 18
("Some Interview Questions")

1. U
2. U
3. A
4. U
5. U
6. U
7. U
8. U
9. U
10. A
11. A
12. U

CHAPTER 19

1. yes
2. yes
3. a consequence that is disliked or unwanted
4. false
5. a. Punisher is punished.
   b. Punisher is avoided.
6. True
7. Immediately after, or as soon as possible after
8. d
9. The behavior tends to stop.

Index